Violent Murders

VIOLENT MURDERS

John Dunning

Introduction by
Colin Wilson

MULBERRY EDITIONS

First published in Great Britain as *Truly Murderous*
by Harwood-Smart 1977
Hamlyn Paperbacks edition 1979
Arrow edition 1986
This edition published 1992 by Cresset Press for
Mulberry Editions

ISBN 1–873123–08–6

Printed and bound in Great Britain

CONTENTS

Foreword by John Dunning ix
Introduction by Colin Wilson xi
1 The Reek of Death 1
2 The Fatal Orgy 25
3 Repeat Performance 39
4 The Future Belongs to Youth 57
5 Frozen Stiff 72
6 Mad Dog! 86
7 A Family Affair 98
8 Travels with a Killer 113
9 Rough Justice 128
10 The Passionate Paramours of Portsmouth 143
11 To Love is to Kill 158
12 The Insatiable Wife 176
13 Ladykiller 192
14 Hatchet Work 206
15 Ghoulish Practices 220

To My Mother, Mrs Crystal Belder

FOREWORD
by
John Dunning

If the reader of a book of factual crime reports has the right to expect an accurate and literal presentation of the facts, so then does the writer of these accounts have the obligation to present them in this manner. Crime, and particularly murder, is by its nature secretive and more subject to deduction than to precise determination. Very often no one living knows exactly what took place, and equally often those who know are inclined to distort and conceal the true nature of events.

In this book I have made every effort to present a factual picture of the crimes concerned, but there are certain deliberate changes and omissions. I do not use the real names and titles of police officers because some Criminal Investigations Departments prefer that their investigators remain anonymous. Likewise, the names and descriptions of witnesses and other innocent persons are usually changed in order to prevent public identification and possible embarrassment.

Conversations and thoughts are, of course, reconstructed – and in such a manner as to render them intelligible to the English-speaking reader. Without wishing to offend those who believe in the homogeneity of the human race, the reactions and remarks of a French or German-speaking person confronted with a given situation are not identical to those of an English-speaking person.

The names, ages and descriptions of the victims and their murderers are as accurate as I can make them, as are the details of the events and the dates on which they took place.

If the presentation seems dramatic, it is because murder *is* dramatic. It is the ultimate experience. Once you have been murdered there is little else that can happen to you, other than in a metaphysical sense. The reader, snug in his armchair, may shudder as the knife enters the entrails, but the shudder is vicarious. Reading about murder is nothing at all like the experience itself.

During the past ten years I have written the accounts of some six hundred crimes, most of them murders, but the familiarity with horrifying events which this has inevitably brought has not dulled my awareness of the grim realities – I am always acutely conscious that murder is sordid, brutal and painful beyond belief.

INTRODUCTION
by
Colin Wilson

In the year 1910 there appeared in San Francisco a bulky volume entitled *Celebrated Criminal Cases of America* by Thomas S. Duke, a captain in the San Francisco police force. It was an epoch-making volume, for it was the first attempt at a comprehensive collection of the crimes of one particular period – in this case, the past eighty years; it was, if you like, a criminal history of America in the 19th century. And, as such, it still remains a work of singular fascination. For many years now, together with the more famous *Newgate Calendar*, it has been one of my favourite bedside books. And not solely because of its 'morbid' interest. It is the history of an epoch, and it gives you a better insight into the true nature of America in the 19th century than any number of history books about great statesmen and generals.

For we must face this fact: history, by its very nature, tells lies. History books deal with 'important events', the rise and fall of kings and nations. You could read all about the age of Shakespeare in the great historians; yet if some time machine could transport you back to London in the time of Queen Elizabeth, you would realize instantly that you didn't know the first thing about it. When Shakespeare got up in the morning, his mind was focussed on dozens of minor details, not on great events. What kind of a bed did he sleep in? What did an Elizabethan chamberpot look like? Did he use soap to wash his hands? Did he even bother to wash his hands when he got up? What did he eat for breakfast? Did he drink tea? How often did he wash his socks? How did he comb his hair? How did he trim his beard? (Did they have scissors then?) Unless we know the answer to hundreds of similar questions, we cannot even begin to formulate an accurate picture of the Elizabethan age.

But then, as you read Thomas Duke on American crime, you realize there is another kind of history which also gets left out of most of the history books. Of course, we know a little more about America in the 19th century than England in the 16th – to begin with, it is closer to our own age. It was visited by various English writers – like Charles Dickens, Fanny Trollope and Oscar Wilde – who left their impressions. It was a rough, turbulent and violent country, the land that paid scant attention to the genius of the author of *Moby Dick*, and that allowed Edgar Allan Poe to die as a result of some obscure bar room brawl. If you want to get a clear idea of what it was actually like to be Edgar Allan Poe, then you would do better to read Thomas Duke than even the most eminent historian. You can learn about the Vigilance Committees that were set up to do battle with squatters, about the Chinese Tongs that sprang up in the gold fields, about Alfred Packer, the cannibal who ate five fellow prospectors, about marauding Indians who murdered settlers, about the assassination of the Mormon leader Joseph Smith, about various bomb outrages committed by anarchists, as well as about such *causes célèbres* as the murder of Dr Parkman by Professor Webster, or of the architect Stanford White by Harry Thaw. This was the America that Poe and Melville really lived in, and saw around them every day. In some ways – perhaps in most – it was a better and more innocent America than the one that exists today. One of its stories describes 'The Murder of Norah Fuller by a Degenerate'. Norah was a fifteen-year-old San Francisco girl who was lured to a house by means of an advertisement, and there strangled, raped and mutilated. The murderer, a man named Charles Hadley, was never caught. A modern writer would simply call the chapter 'The Rape of Norah Fuller' and leave it at that. Duke obviously finds it a little difficult to understand such a crime; he is more at home chronicling various robberies, assassinations and poisonings. In his world, human beings needed a real *motive* for committing a crime, usually cash. And his reactions are always there, implicitly in the writing. The chapter on the Bender family, who killed travellers in their tavern, is entitled: 'The Hideous Murders Committed at Bender's Tavern in Kansas'. There is 'The Diabolical Plot Concocted by Dr Hyde of Kansas City', and 'Tom Blanck, the Desperado Killed near Seattle'. We are in a violent world, yet a world in which crime is never taken for granted. The underlying assumption seems to be that most of the population are law abiding, even virtuous, and that a few evildoers have backed out of their obligations to society.

In America, Duke's book was the beginning of a flood of anthologies of 'true crime stories'. In England, it had started rather earlier. The Elizabethans were fond of pamphlets describing the crimes and trials of notorious characters, and around the year 1700, various compilations of such cases began to appear under the title of *The Newgate Calendar* (although the most famous and comprehensive edition of that work appeared in 1774). This continued to appear, under various incarnations (such as *Chronicles of Crime*) until the late 19th century. In 1873, Luke Owen Pike produced a two volume *History of Crime in England*. In 1898, Major Arthur Griffiths published his popular two volume work *Mysteries of the Police and Crime*. But I suspect that it was the Crippen case of 1910 that suddenly aroused the interest of the British public in true tales of gore and mayhem. (This word – meaning committing violence upon the person – seems to be derived from the same source as maim.) Crippen – who dismembered his wife's body – was effectively condemned on the medical evidence given by Bernard Spilsbury. The case made Spilsbury's reputation; from then on, any case in which he gave evidence was newsworthy. And many of his later cases involved gruesome dismemberments – Voisin, Patrick Mahon, Norman Thorne. The reading public developed an appetite for horrors. It is also worth bearing in mind that a new reading public had come into being since the late 19th century; workmen were learning to read, and enterprising publishers deliberately catered for them with works of popular education. This was essentially the public of 'groundlings' for whom the Elizabethan playwrights produced 'shockers' like *The Spanish Tragedy* and *Arden of Feversham.* A few of them read Ruskin and Darwin; but the majority wanted their ha'penny newspapers with tales of violence and of scandal in high life. Since 1870, the 'best seller' among Victorian tabloids had been the *Illustrated Police News*, which specialized in sensational sketches of hangings, floggings and decapitations. After the turn of the century, there was suddenly a market for books with titles like *Cavalcade of Justice* or *The Fifty Most Amazing Crimes of the Last Hundred Years*. (It was a copy of this latter that was largely responsible for my own early interest in crime.) In America, Munsey invented the 'pulp magazine', and reached a new audience with its tales of incredible adventure. And then, some time in the 1920s (I have been unable to track down the date) an American magazine publisher hit on the idea of a magazine form of the old *Illustrated Police News*, with photographs taking the place of the drawings. 'True detective' magazines caught on quickly, and as the post-1918 crime rate soared, material was even more plentiful than in the Victorian era. 'Troodicks' (as John Dunning likes to call them) have never looked back.

And – perhaps unfortunately – there is no reason why they should. With the 20th century, we have entered a new age of murder. This is apparent even to the most casual student of crime. The Crippen murder is basically an 'old-fashioned' type of crime; it might have been dramatized by an Elizabethan playwright. It is essentially a drama of good against evil, of a fairly decent human being, under strain or temptation, giving way to 'diabolic' impulses – like Macbeth. The same element seems to enter all 'classic' murder cases – the Red Barn murder, Lizzie Borden, Professor Webster, Constance Kent. The Victorians found it necessary to apply the same explanation to the strange crimes of Jack the Ripper, who killed and disembowelled five prostitutes in 1888; the favourite theory was that he was some sort of religious maniac – perhaps also a surgeon – driven mad by brooding on sin. (It is perfectly clear to us that he was an ordinary sadist, probably with a morbid obsession about wombs.)

In 1918, New Orleans had its own series of 'Ripper' murders; an individual who became known as the 'Mad Axe Man' broke into houses at night, and attacked sleepers with a hatchet; in a few cases he also cut their throats. He was never caught; but, like the Ripper crimes, this series of murders suddenly ceased. There seemed to be no connection between the axeman's crimes – except that many of the victims were Italian grocers – and robbery was not the motive. The Axe Man crimes simply fail to fit the pattern of murder as it had been known up till then. He wasn't even a 'degenerate' – at least, there were apparently no sexual attacks on the victims. The new age of murder had begun.

And nowadays, we look back on the older type of crime with a certain nostalgia. The American Modern Library series, which specializes in reprints of 'classics', has included Edmund Pearson's *Studies in Murder*, with its long study of the Borden case. The Viking Portable Library – which has produced portable volumes of Shakespeare, Nietzsche and James Joyce – has also published a Portable Murder Book, consisting mainly of such classic mysteries as the murder of Julia Wallace and the crime of Constance Kent. We read such things as we read the Sherlock Holmes stories – as period pieces. We may deplore the violence, but we still read with a kind of fascinated detachment. But imagine an updated Murder Book that includes the Moors Murder case, the Manson murders, the mass homosexual killings by Dean Corll in Houston, and such recent cases as John Frazier, Ed Kemper and Herb Mullin. Could anyone – no matter how blasé – read such cases with detachment? They really belong in textbooks of pathology – like Magnus Hirschfeld's *Sexual Anomalies and Perversions*. We try *not* to think about what the Moors murderers did to their child victims, what Dean Corll did to teenage boys once he had tied them to his 'torture board'. This new type of murder seems to be motiveless because it is fundamentally 'psychological'.

What has caused this change in the pattern of murder? Where America is concerned, the answer is fairly obvious.

As Duke's compilation makes clear, America has always been a country with plenty of violence. But in the 19th century it was also a country with plenty of freedom – at least, in the purely physical sense. Life was hard for the underprivileged, but there were still inviting wide open spaces out west. By the 1920s, most of this feeling of freedom had vanished. Living standards were higher – industrialization had seen to that – but cities were bigger, and people felt trapped in them. A modern American is no longer in much danger of seeing his wife and children starve to death. But the children feel themselves regimented and controlled from the moment they are old enough to cross the street. The famous – the people who have 'made it' – exist up there in a kind of Olympus; you are 'down here', together with hundreds of millions of others, and nobody will ever see your name in a newspaper or see your face on TV. You are an immeasurably small fragment of an anonymous mass . . . But since a high proportion of that anonymous mass is at least as intelligent as the TV stars and politicians, they feel resentment at this unfair scheme of things. Everybody wants to be Somebody – or at least feel that the opportunity is there. Among the young, the natural reaction is to 'drop out'. The more idealistic talk about human rights and preservation of the environment. Others dream of violent revolution and destruction of the 'pigs' (i.e. the middle aged and successful). Others drift into the underworld of drugs. A youth like John Frazier becomes increasingly paranoid and finally murders the whole family of a successful Japanese optician – simply because he is obviously well-to-do. The 'Symbionese Liberation Army' kidnap an heiress and order her father to donate $2 million-worth of food to the poor, then brain-wash her into helping them commit robberies. A follower of Charles Manson writes letters to businessmen threatening them with death if they pollute the environment, then attempts to shoot the American President as a protest . . .

In other countries too, the pattern of crime is changing, although less drastically than in America. West Germany – the most prosperous country in Europe – has a flourishing

Urban Guerrilla movement, which robs, murders and kidnaps the 'capitalist oppressors'. In Italy, kidnapping becomes almost a national sport. In England, Ian Brady and Myra Hindley, the 'Moors Murderers', kidnap and murder children simply as an expression of Brady's contempt of society and his admiration for the philosophy of De Sade. In general, 'philosophy' – or a muddled idealism – seems to play an increasingly large part in crime. But while Urban Guerrillas and homicidal 'drop outs' continue to make the headlines, organized crime continues to spread and flourish – without publicity – in almost every country in the world.

For many years now, I have felt that these 'patterns of crime' deserved closer study. Criminologists are inclined to confine themselves to statistical analyses and studies of the criminal's behaviour in prison. But the most interesting criminals are often 'loners', and few of them are professionals. With the aid of Patricia Pitman, I compiled *An Encyclopedia of Murder* in 1961, and followed it with two further books on the changing patterns of crime in western society. In 1973 I drew up an outline scheme of a twenty-volume 'encyclopedia' of crime; this appeared under the title *Crimes and Punishment*, and although it makes many concessions to the taste of 'troodick' readers, it is still probably the most comprehensive general work on crime that has ever appeared.

There is one important respect in which I feel that *Crimes and Punishment* falls below the original conception. I had hoped to make it a work on *world* crime, with volumes on European crime, Australian crime, crime behind the Iron Curtain, crime in the Far East – even crime in Iceland and Greenland, if such a thing exists there. And the problem here was simply lack of information. Few nations in the world seem to have the interest in criminal history that characterizes the English and Americans. The French take a lively interest in *crime passionel*, but it was left to an Englishman, Rayner Heppenstall, to produce a comprehensive study – in four volumes – of French crime from the age of Vidocq down to modern times. When I wrote *An Encyclopedia of Murder*, information on German cases was kindly provided by a German editor, Frank Lynder, who sent me accounts of Denke, Seefeld, Grossmann, Pommerencke, Matushka and others. The editor of *Crimes and Punishment* – Angus Hall – established links with various police forces in many countries of the world, which was certainly useful. But what was really needed was a whole series of Frank Lynders – or perhaps of Edmund Pearsons: that is, of people who regarded crime with the eye of the novelist rather than of the policeman. A country's criminal history is basically a history of its most interesting cases, and these can only be chosen with an eye to psychological subtlety and dramatic effect. It would be marvellously convenient – a criminologist's daydream – if there was a Scandinavian version, a Japanese version, a Russian version, of *The Fifty Most Amazing Crimes of the Last Hundred Years*. But apparently there is not. In my own crime library of a thousand or so volumes, less than a dozen are devoted to crimes of other countries – apart from England and America – and many of these are anthologies with titles like *My Strangest Crime* by Police Chiefs of the World.

Oddly enough, it was this volume that led to my acquaintance with the author of the present volume, John Dunning. One of the cases contained in *My Strangest Crime* is written by Kriminal Hauptkommissar Mattias Eynck, and describes the curious series of murders allegedly committed between 1953 and 1956 by a psychopath named Werner Boost. According to his confederate – who confessed – Boost used to hold up courting couples in cars, and force them to take a drug that stupefied them. He then robbed the men and raped the women. One young couple were killed – the girl was given an injection of cyanide – and then their car was pushed into a haystack, which was set alight; another couple were knocked unconscious, then their car was driven into a deep pool, where they drowned. Boost was caught in 1956 when creeping up on another courting couple, and finally sentenced to life imprisonment.

In the early 1970s, an English 'troodick' magazine published an account of the case which differed in certain details from the account given by Hauptkommissar Eynck – most notably in the dates, which were all about ten years later. I had had occasion to find fault with 'true detective' magazines on a number of previous occasions, but their editors had never taken the trouble to reply to my letters. But on this occasion, the editor replied fairly promptly, saying that he had taken the matter up with the author, who would be writing to me himself. I checked up on the author's name – to which I had so far paid little attention – and realized that it was already fairly familiar to me. John Dunning specialized in articles on German crime, and his contributions were usually the most amusing and best-written in the magazine.

In due course, a letter *did* arrive from John Dunning – who lives in Luxembourg – explaining the discrepancies. It seems that he derives much of his material from an agency, which is, in turn, supplied by needy journalists. It had occurred to one of these suppliers that there is a readier market for recent cases than for those of older vintage. His solution was simply to update the older cases. Whether this stratagem actually improved his sales seems to me doubtful; editors of 'troodick' magazines are notoriously lax about dates. (They still have a nasty habit of leaving out all dates until the last line of a story, when they conclude: 'On June 7, 1954, so and so paid for his crimes in the electric chair at San Quentin . . .'.) At all events, it embarrassed Mr Dunning, who wrote to me on November 30, 1972, a letter that commenced breezily: 'View halloo and/or demi-yoicks! The fell scoundrel responsible for the outrage in the Boost bash has been run to earth and subjected to the merciless punishment he so richly deserved . . .'. Whereupon Mr Dunning proceeded to have the last laugh. It seemed that even Hauptkommissar Eynck was not free of sin in this matter of inaccuracy, and had allowed a number of mistakes to creep into his account of the case – which I had reproduced in my account in the *Encyclopedia of Murder*; he seems to have mixed up dates, given cases in the wrong order, and got several names wrong. Mr Dunning added the information that Boost was acquitted of all murders except that of a Dr Servé, for which he was sentenced to life imprisonment.

We continued to correspond, I continued to read his

contributions to *True Detective* avidly, and I suggested one day that his articles ought to be published in book form. The idea horrified him. To begin with, he said, he had some hundreds – possibly thousands – of articles. Secondly, they had been written at speed, for publication in a variety of 'troodick' magazines, and were not good enough for hard-cover publication. I was able to reassure him on this last point. Many journalists seem to have an inferiority complex about the writers of books, falsely assuming that it is an altogether more difficult and dangerous art. Writers of books know better; and writers who produce books *and* journalism – like G. K. Chesterton, H. G. Wells, Bernard Shaw, Arnold Bennett – probably know best of all. Shaw and Chesterton had themselves described in their passports as journalists. It *is* possible to write too casually and journalistically; it is also possible to write stodgily and pedantically, and this is the commoner – and more irritating – fault. I recall a journalist named Philip Guedalla, a contemporary of Wells and Chesterton, who produced some excellent volumes of occasional pieces; a few months ago I came across a book by him on the Second Empire, and prepared myself for a treat. It was unbelievably disappointing. Evidently he had decided that a writer of history should be on his best behaviour, and the result is dull and turgid.

But it is not simply because he writes well that I wanted John Dunning to venture into hard covers. German crime is one of those subjects on which it is frustratingly difficult to find information. Which is a pity since, from the criminologist's point of view, Germany is one of the most interesting countries in the world.

The German temperament is, in a way, peculiarly conducive to crime – far more so than the English or French temperament. The English are too easygoing to make good criminals; their 'genius for compromise' is against them. The typical English murder takes place in a domestic setting, and the motives are usually fairly trivial; a woman poisons her drunken husband with weed-killer; the husband strangles his nagging wife, then buries her in the back garden. The French allow their emotions to lead them into crime; a man murders his wife to marry his mistress, or plots with his mistress to murder her husband. But the German temperament is realistic and pedantic and grimly logical; as a result it can also be idealistic, exalted and romantic. Bach's Passions are typically German; so are Goethe's dramas, Wagner's operas and Thomas Mann's novels. But the German who sees murder as the solution of his problems approaches it with the same realism and thoroughness. Fritz Haarmann, the butcher of Hanover, not only killed young men for sexual purposes, but made a profit on the corpses by selling them as meat. Karl Denke, a landlord of Münsterberg, murdered tramps and journeymen and pickled their bodies in brine, apparently as a precaution against the famine that followed post-1918 inflation. Georg Grossmann, a pedlar, murdered innumerable women with whom he spent the night, and sold the bodies for meat. Peter Kürten, the Düsseldorf 'monster', easily surpassed Jack the Ripper; he killed men, women, children and animals, and was a necrophile as well as a sadist.

I have lost the documentation on one of my favourite German cases: a man who murdered his wife and children with extraordinary ingenuity. The family was found dead in a locked room, all hanged; apparently the mother had killed her children, then committed suicide. But the police inspector who examined the husband found in his room a novel with an ingenious method of murder. The fictional killer drilled a tiny hole through the door, inserted a long hair from a horse's tail, and used it to draw the bolt when the door was closed. After the murder, he bolted the door – from the outside – snapped off the horse's hair, then sealed the hole on the outside with brown wax. The police inspector examined the door of the murder room, and found a hole that had been filled in with wax. The murderer's sole mistake was to keep the novel that had given him the idea. Again, the story is somehow typically German; an Englishman, a Frenchman, an Italian, would not have the patience to plan a murder with this fiendish thoroughness. It was the same kind of thoroughness that produced Hitler's attempt at a final solution of the Jewish problem.

It can be seen why German murder cases fascinate all students of crime. It can also be seen why I was so anxious to persuade John Dunning to start collecting some of his more interesting cases into volumes. Fortunately, my persistence prevailed, and the present volume is the result – the first, I hope, of many.

The selection of cases is John Dunning's own. Anyone who knows any of my own books on murder – for example, *Order of Assassins* – will immediately see that there is a basic difference of approach. I have always been interested in 'extremists' – men and women who kill because they feel a fundamental alienation from the rest of the human community: Jack the Ripper, Carl Panzram, Peter Kürten, William Heirens, Peter Manuel. These are all characters who might have been invented by Dostoevsky, or observed by him in his Siberian prison, described in *The House of the Dead*. John Dunning has the journalist's eye for the gruesome, for human oddity, and for sheer dramatic tension. There are no Kürtens or Panzrams in this book, but nearly every story in it could be turned into a film or a TV drama. His quirky sense of humour emerges in the actual material as much as in the writing. What could be odder than the activities of the alcoholic Fritz Honka, who absentmindedly murdered four of his mistresses, stuffed their bodies in the attic, then forgot all about them, so that he was as puzzled by the smell of decay as his neighbours were? What could be more unintentionally funny than the activities of ex-policeman Ernst Karl, sentenced for the murder of two hoodlums, who appointed himself executioner of a rape-murderer in prison, and assured the audience in court: 'Have no fear, good citizens of Austria. Whether in prison or out, you can depend on me to continue and even intensify my battle against the criminals and law-breakers in our midst . . .'

But what really seems to fascinate John Dunning are those cases in which life seems to imitate art – or at least, the structure of the thriller. The police search frantically for the daughter of a murdered woman, convinced that she has also been murdered; in fact, she is quietly staying with a neighbour. The police in a small German town are convinced that a corpse lies somewhere beneath five hundred square miles of moorland; the chances of finding the body are minimal, but a cunning ruse persuades the killer to confess. A killer accuses his Turkish mistress of the crime and she confesses; but the police are convinced she is innocent, and work feverishly to find the vital piece of evidence . . . The story of the man who is frozen to death in the woods ends with a car chase that might have come straight out of Kojak. In all these tales we observe Dunning's unerring eye for the dramatic.

It is the final story in the volume that strikes me as most typical of Dunning's style and method. It is a horrifying and nauseating account of sexual perversion that will turn all but the strongest stomachs. The vampire seems to have walked straight out of the pages of *Dracula*. As the gruesome details pile up, you find yourself unconsciously creating a picture of a maniac with pointed teeth and fingers like claws. The actual description of the murderer, the shy little deaf-mute with his steel-rimmed National Health glasses, comes as an almost comic anticlimax. Yet the story takes on overtones of a different kind of menace when the police discover that Kuno Hofman was inspired by his collection of books on black magic, vampirism and satanism. He may have been mentally retarded, but he was intelligent enough to read and be influenced by what he read. Like Ian Brady, the child killer who admired the works of the Marquis de Sade, or Edward Paisnel, the rapist who terrorized Jersey for a decade, who owned a library of works on satanism and believed himself to be a reincarnation of the sadistic Gilles de Rais. These alienated 'outsiders' are perhaps the most typical, if not the most common, of modern criminals.

Equally typical – although perhaps less significant – is the bewildered Hans Appell, who murdered his brother-in-law Dieter when he discovered that he *and* his brother had sexual orgies with their sister in the marital bed . . . In this story, as in the tale of the home-made spear, Dunning reveals an ironic interest in the problem of the *crime passionel* in a permissive society.

No, altogether I can see no reason why John Dunning

should be modest about this book. He possesses qualities of intelligence, style and humour that raise him above the average; and he is entering a field in which there are dozens of hacks, but few outstanding talents. (My own short list would include William Bolitho, F. Tennyson Jesse, William Roughead, Alexander Woolcott, Edmund Pearson and Rayner Heppenstall.) And then, he has the additional advantage of having cornered an area of the market. There are many writers who have produced a whole shelf-full of books on assorted crime – Leonard Gribble and Edgar Lustgarten spring to mind – but they seldom venture across the channel; at least, beyond Paris. Mr Dunning probably knows the criminal history of Germany and Austria better than any man alive, and it is my fervent hope that he will now begin to make this systematically available to the English reader. (I would like to see a book on German mass murderers, from Haarmann and Grossmann to the recent autobahn killer.) If his own estimate is correct, he already possesses enough material for about fifty more volumes like this one. But even if he gives up after a dozen or so, he will have performed a real service for all those who – like myself – are fascinated by 'patterns of murder' in the 20th Century.

1

THE REEK OF DEATH

There was something very wrong with the old house at 74 Zeiss Street.

It stank.

Standing in her dark, narrow kitchen, Mrs Elsie Beier took a cautious breath. Yes, the smell was still there, but mingled now with something like pine needles. The contrast seemed to make it actually worse.

Hurriedly, she filled the kettle, stood it on the stove and retreated to the living room. There were traces of the smell in the air even here, but it was, at least, bearable.

'Either Heinz does something or I move,' muttered Mrs Beier in the flat, slurred German of her native Hamburg.

Heinz was the caretaker who looked after the building in return for the use of a small room at the back.

Of course, the place always had smelled. A building that old could be expected to smell, but that also helped to keep down the rent so that a widow on a small pension might be able to live there for twelve long years.

Mrs Beier had moved into 74 Zeiss Street in January of 1962 and now it was August of 1974. She had rather counted on spending the remainder of her days there, but she was beginning to fear that she would not have many days remaining if she was forced to live much longer amidst this stench. It was decidedly unhealthy.

She did not think that Heinz was going to do anything. It was nearly the end of August now and she had been complaining since the first week. Heinz had spoken to Fritz Honka, the night watchman who lived on the top floor above, and to Klaus Kienzle, the street sweeper who lived on the first floor below, about checking to see if their toilets were stopped up and Honka, at least, had apparently bought some deodorant tablets for she had seen him carrying them up the stairs. They were, no doubt, the source of the pine needle scent.

However, it was going to take more than deodorant tablets to kill that smell and, besides, it did not resemble any stopped toilet she had ever smelled. In fact, it did not resemble anything that she had ever smelled in her whole life.

On November 1, 1974, after almost daily complaints to anyone who would listen, Mrs Elsie Beier struck her colours and moved out. She moved completely across to the other side of Hamburg and although the rent was somewhat higher she paid it willingly. The stench in her kitchen was, by this time, beyond belief.

The apartment was promptly rented to forty-six-year-old John Fordal, a Norwegian seaman, who did not complain about the smell or even seem to notice it as he made a practice of passing his time ashore in such a profound state of alcoholic stupor that he could scarcely see or hear, let alone smell.

Seaman Fordal fitted well into 74 Zeiss Street. It was that sort of a building and Ottensen, better known to the local residents as Mottenberg or Moth Hill, was that sort of district.

Stretching along the fringe of St Pauli, the famous Hamburg entertainment quarter, with its great, main artery, the Reeperbahn, its thousands of prostitutes, its Eros Centre, its bars and strip joints and massage parlours and pimps and jack-rollers and the sailors of a hundred nations, Ottensen is neither glamorous nor respectable. It is a place where the old prostitutes, the crippled pimps, the alcoholic waiters and derelicts from all professions cling to a worthless life for lack of courage to end it.

It is not, of course, the bottom. The bottom is the great Bismarck monument at the Landungs Bridge where every night the grey alcohol-soaked hordes gather with their tattered blankets, stored during the day in the luggage lockers of the railway station, for another rest beneath the cold stars of North Germany.

Such a life is only possible to sustain under the numbing influence of substantial quantities of alcohol, and alcohol in St Pauli and Ottensen is more common than water.

Sex is also common, although not of very good quality, or perhaps it would be better to say of excellent quality due to the long experience of the practitioners, but aesthetically lacking because of the age and physical failings of those involved. It is, however, entered into with considerable enthusiasm by those still capable of it and it is cheap, a single beer or a packet of cigarettes sufficing for a night of intimacy, if not love.

The house at 74 Zeiss Street displayed almost all possible variations of the district's sex life with the family on the ground floor producing children in the orthodox manner and at intervals of nine months, Klaus Kienzle on the first floor being ready, willing, but totally unable and resigned to it, Seaman Fordal on the second floor often believing that he would like to, but then falling asleep so that his companion departed with everything movable in the apartment, and finally Fritz Honka, the dapper, thirty-nine-year-old night watchman with the little moustache, the cocked eye and the penchant for uniforms and peaked caps.

Divorced and the father of a grown son, Honka was, despite a staggering consumption of alcohol, apparently sexually active for he usually had one woman or another living with him in the attic apartment.

All of these women shared certain peculiarities. None of them was taller than five feet four inches, which happened to be Honka's height, and none of them had any teeth. Mr Honka, as he confided to his friends, had a great and perhaps not completely baseless fear of being bitten on the more sensitive parts of his anatomy.

Such women were, of course, not hard to find and Honka usually made his acquisitions in either the Golden Glove or the Elbschloss Keller, two terminal bars of the sort which employ a thumper.

The thumper is a person who goes from table to table at

intervals, beating the tops with a mallet to rouse the mostly unconscious customers sufficiently to order and pay for another drink. Not infrequently, no amount of thumping will arouse the customer and the police are then called to come and take the body away in the neat, white, metal trailer known officially as a corpse transporter.

Actually, the Hamburg Police have several corpse transporters as they have quite a number of corpses to transport. However, sometimes a sack is more suitable.

This was the case with the remains found on November 2, 1971 by, among others, two of the children of the Ernst Schmidt family living on the ground floor of 74 Zeiss Street. The scene of the discovery was the yard of an abandoned chocolate factory three blocks away and the object discovered was no more than an isolated human head. It had obviously been lying out in the yard for some time. Strangely, it had not decayed very much nor had it been seriously nibbled by rats of which Ottensen has a large contingent.

The police having been informed, a thorough search of the yard was carried out and two legs, two arms and two breasts were recovered. All of these were in remarkably good condition with the exception of the breasts which were little more than flaps of leathery skin with nipples.

Dr Ludwig Strauss, the cheerful, brisk medical expert attached to the Hamburg Department of Criminal Investigations, took these parts and placed them in a bath of glycerine and other chemicals where he swished them about gently at intervals for several months.

At the end of this time the head and the hands had regained so much of their shape that it was possible to make a photograph of the face and to take fingerprints from the fingers.

Although the photograph did not really do justice to the subject, the fingerprints permitted her identification as one Gertraude 'Susi' Braeuer, born near Dresden in 1929, a refugee from Communist East Germany in 1956 and since that date, aside from a few short intervals, a licensed prostitute.

Miss Braeuer's fingerprints had come into the police files

as a result of a charge of drunk-rolling in the Golden Glove on July 6, 1969, but she was currently wanted in connection with quite a different affair.

Late in 1969 Gertraude Braeuer had abandoned her profession and had gone to live with a thirty-four-year-old welldigger named Burkhard Stern. The couple had shared a garden house with Stern's eighty-year-old father in a suburb called Groot Osterfeld and plans were made for an early marriage.

Living next door was a two-hundred-pound porter named Winfried Schuldig, an ominous name as schuldig means guilty in German. On January 20, 1970 he invited Stern and his fiancée over for a drink.

It was presumably more than one drink for, according to Gertraude Braeuer's statement to the police, she had become drunk and had begun to engage in sexual intercourse with the host before the outraged eyes of her fiancé.

Stern had objected. There was a fight. In the morning, Stern was found lying in front of the door with his head smashed in. Schuldig pleaded self-defence. Braeuer, now sober, said that he had beaten Stern's brains out with a leg torn from the sofa.

While the case was awaiting trial, Gertraude stole the elder Stern's pension payment and disappeared. The police were unable to find any subsequent trace of her and Schuldig was acquitted, there being no witness to contradict his story of self-defence.

'Well, at least we know what happened to her,' said Inspector Frank Luders, the senior investigations officer of the Criminal Investigations Department. 'Better check out Schuldig. He had an obvious motive.'

'We checked him out at the time of the trial,' said his assistant, Detective-Sergeant Max Peters. 'There was no indication that he knew where Braeuer was any more than we did. It would help if Ludwig could give us a time of death.'

Dr Strauss was not, however, certain as to when Gertraude Braeuer had died.

'Near the end of nineteen seventy,' he said, 'but I could

be off by months. I could tell more if I had the torso. As it is, I can't even say how she was killed.'

Gertraude Braeuer's body remained missing. Had the police known where to look for it, the mystery of her murder would have been solved.

Eventually the sergeant was able to find witnesses who had seen the woman after September 7, 1970, the date of Winfried Schuldig's trial.

'Meaning,' said the sergeant, 'that Schuldig had no motive. His case was already dismissed before she was murdered.'

'Probably rough trade then,' said the inspector. 'You can send it to the Unsolved file.'

Rough trade is the prostitute's term for the perverts and psychopaths to whom so many fall victim.

Aside from the discovery of the head and limbs of Gertraude Braeuer, 1971 had been a comparatively quiet year for the residents of 74 Zeiss Street.

True, the police had been called in once, but that had been a minor incident such as might happen to any bachelor like Fritz Honka.

Fritz, or Fiete, the common nickname by which his friends called him, had been celebrating his thirty-fifth birthday on July 31st with the ruins of a prostitute named Erika Kynast whose fiftieth birthday fell on the same day. Miss Kynast was, of course, shorter than five feet four inches and had no more teeth than a chicken.

She was, however, remarkably agile and strong considering the amount of schnapps she had consumed and when Mr Honka's sexual advances became actually painful, she resisted.

Fritz Honka had responded by slinging her pantyhose around her neck and drawing them so tightly that her eyes nearly came out of her head. He had enormous hands, far larger than normal, and he was even stronger than she, although he had consumed as much or more schnapps.

Fortunately, Miss Kynast was able to get her fingers under the pantyhose in the last second so that she was not entirely deprived of breath and, taking advantage of Honka's preoccupation with his sexual needs, she kicked him solidly in the groin, fled naked down the stairs and shortly thereafter appeared at the local sub-station of the police, wearing the pantyhose around her neck and nothing else.

The police, who were used to such apparitions, went to 74 Zeiss Street and arrested Mr Honka who said that he was sorry, but that he had been carried away and that a woman who comes to a man's room and drinks the best part of two bottles of expensive schnapps should expect to do a little something in return for it.

He was charged with simple assault and released until such time as the hearing might take place. By Ottensen or St Pauli standards, it was not a serious matter.

During the remainder of the year, bachelor Honka made do with the casual acquaintances he picked up at the Golden Glove or the Elbschloss Keller. He was not a stingy man when it came to setting up the drinks which, of course, made him intensely popular in both places.

Although some of these friendships lasted for two or three nights, no suitable, permanent companion appeared until April of 1972 when forty-seven-year-old Irmgard Albrecht came to share the attic apartment at 74 Zeiss Street.

A widowed char woman, slightly taller than five feet and, of course, toothless, she was becoming tired of scrubbing floors and, moreover, found that it interfered with her drinking so that she was happy to take a vacation and enjoy the free food, shelter, drink and perhaps even the attentions of the gallant Mr Honka.

For, as she was later to state, Fritz Honka was a fiery, passionate lover, so jealous that whenever he went off to work or elsewhere he locked his beloved up in the living room so that she would not run off with some other man. It was also, perhaps, because he did not want her snooping about the apartment.

Mrs Albrecht found this flattering, but she was distressed by the fact that while locked in the living room she had no access to food or drink and, worse yet, none to the lavatory.

Fritz resolved these complaints by leaving her an ample

supply of food, a somewhat less generous amount of drink and a bucket.

Irmgard Albrecht was happy and content. The only criticism of her new home which she might have had was that it sometimes smelled.

When she mentioned this to Mr Honka, he replied that he too had noticed it and that he would get some cans of spray deodorant. He did as a matter of fact buy a whole case, but the spray was not strong enough to suppress the nauseating odour entirely. Miss Albrecht was not too disturbed. It was not the first stench to which she had been subjected in her life.

At this time Mrs Elsie Beier was still living downstairs and she had noticed nothing of any smell, nor would she for over a year and a half, but then her apartment was, of course, larger and lighter and had more windows than the attic rooms under the eaves.

This attic apartment was a stuffy, cramped and largely airless place. At the head of the narrow stairs coming up from the floor below was a short hall running parallel to the street outside and ending in a wall made of slats with a door in the middle. Behind the slats was storage space, theoretically for the use of all in the house, but in practice used for keeping coal briquettes and other junk belonging to Mr Honka. No one else in the house had anything to store there, but it was available to all.

To the right of the corridor next to the stairs was the kitchen with the lavatory beyond it and on the left was the entrance to the living room which had a door leading to the bedroom beyond the end of the corridor and adjoining the storage area.

Each of the rooms had one sloping wall formed by the roof and in this wall was set a small window. In the living room and bedroom, Mr Honka had decorated these sloping walls with magazine cuttings showing young ladies in poses varying from sweetly innocent to hard-core pornographic.

The remainder of the furniture had been assembled largely from the Sperrmüll, the junk which is placed out on the sidewalks once every few months for carting away by the garbage disposal service. As is often the case with Sperrmüll, much of it was solid and of good quality, although not stylish.

During the spring and summer of 1972, the smell in the attic apartment of Fritz Honka grew even stronger, although it was still not apparent on the floor below. Miss Albrecht was of the opinion that the smell was strongest in the hall and in the bedroom, which she found puzzling. It had not occurred to her that the wall between the bedroom and the storage space was little more than a sheet of cardboard over a wooden frame.

By August, with the temperatures under the roof soaring into the nineties, the smell was becoming almost too much for her sturdy nostrils and in an effort to cheer things up Mr Honka suggested a small party.

Miss Albrecht loved parties so she set off immediately and soon returned with a guest, a forty-five-year-old prostitute named Ruth Dufner, whom she had found in a very convivial state in the Golden Glove.

While Fritz Honka sat watching in a chair with a bottle of schnapps resting in his lap, the ladies removed their clothing, clambered onto the bed and began to engage in simulated lesbian activities.

At least, they were simulated as far as Miss Dufner went for, when Miss Albrecht requested that she assuage the passions she had aroused, she refused.

This display of prudery so outraged Mr Honka that he fell upon the party guest and beat and strangled her so violently with his huge hands that she, fearing for her life, tore free and ran out of the room, down the stairs and into the street as naked as Erika Kynast had been.

Unlike Erika, she did not run to the police station but took refuge in the doorway of a courtyard where she was the subject of some ribaldry on the part of the neighbourhood children until the police arrived, wrapped her in a blanket and took her away.

Fritz Honka was once again arrested and charged with assault. The desk sergeant suggested that if he had any more assaults in mind it might be well to commit them now so that he could be tried for all at the same time.

Honka made a few remarks about the ingratitude of party guests in this day and age and returned to his attic.

In May of 1973 Irmgard Albrecht severed her relationship with Fritz Honka and moved out of 74 Zeiss Street. There was no quarrel, not even a difference of opinion, but for some time Irmgard had not felt quite at ease. Something, she was not sure what, was troubling her. It was perhaps the smell, she thought.

Actually, the smell was not quite as strong as it had been, possibly because the weather was not as warm or possibly because there is simply a limit to the strength and endurance of any smell. Mr Honka was long since used to it.

Others, it seemed, found it less easy to accept and Fritz Honka's domestic arrangements were to remain troubled for the next two years when he would, once again, find a more permanent companion in the form of fifty-two-year-old Anni Wachtmeister, prostitute, under five feet four inches tall, toothless, etc.

It was also during this period and beginning with the first week in August 1974 that the Hamburg Police began to have problems with disappearing women.

Now disappearing women are not at all uncommon in Germany or any other Western European country. Many young girls leave their families to join communes or otherwise express their independence and not a few fall into the hands of the white-slave rings which furnish girls, and sometimes boys, to the brothels and harems of North Africa and the Middle East. Several thousand such girls disappear each year and, generally, they are never seen again.

They all, however, have a number of things in common. They are young. They are pretty. And they are stupid.

The woman who disappeared on or about August 3, 1974 was neither young nor pretty, although she was perhaps somewhat stupid. At least, her husband's account of her past life showed no evidence of any great intelligence.

Anna Hahn had been born in 1920 in Thüringen and had, consequently, been twenty-five years old when the American army marched in at the end of World War II. Not a woman to cling to lost causes, she had immediately acquired a friend and protector from the Americans and the title of Ami-Whore from her countrymen.

Some nine months later she presented her American friend with twin sons and, upon his return to the United States, agreed to his taking them with him. Anna herself could not go as she was still regarded as an enemy national and not qualified to espouse legally one of the conquerors.

It was, however, obvious that the twins would fare much better in the United States than as the sons of an Ami-Whore in Germany. Anna Hahn gave up her children and, a short time later, turned up in St Pauli where she acquired her first prostitute's licence, officially becoming a whore for all nationalities and not merely Amis.

From this point on, her career showed the typical decline from twenty-five dollar prostitute to ten dollar prostitute to five dollar prostitute and finally to all offers gratefully accepted. At the same time, her housing sank in quality from apartment, to studio, to furnished room and finally to the chilly airs of the Bismarck Monument.

This sad but fairly typical career of the St Pauli prostitute was all neatly recorded in the formal, official German of the Hamburg Vice Squad which, since they licence and inspect prostitutes, also keep track of them to a certain extent.

According to these records Anna Hahn was, by the end of 1968, at the end of her career and, presumably, not too far from the end of her life.

She was forty-nine years old and, whatever attractions she might once have had were no longer evident. She was suffering from a half dozen ailments and she was a confirmed alcoholic, never voluntarily doing anything other than falling down drunk. Her abode was the Bismarck Monument and a number of park benches. Her source of income was the performance of any sexual services desired at any place or time at any price and, generally, for a clientele too drunk to see clearly what they were getting.

It was obviously only a matter of time until disease, alcohol or mishap would put an end to her altogether.

Incredibly, none of this was necessary. Germany is a very social country and had Anna Hahn made application for assistance, she would have been placed in a comfortable home, well fed, her ailments treated and, if possible, taught a trade or profession less strenuous than that which she now pursued.

There was only one disadvantage. Not a drop of alcohol.

For Anna Hahn and for the thousands of others like her, this did not represent a choice. Better to die with your head on the table in the Golden Glove than to do without the only thing which made life bearable.

And, astonishingly enough, it was in the Golden Glove that the miracle took place.

Shortly before Christmas of 1970, Anna met in the Golden Glove a cook and waiter named Thomas Beuschel who also came from Thüringen in East Germany. For reasons best known to himself, Beuschel, who was only thirty-four years old, well-built and handsome, took Anna home with him where she gave him a demonstration of the arts which she had acquired in her long career and prepared him a duck in the Thüringen manner.

Beuschel must have been fond of duck for in April of 1971 they were married. Anna was fifty-one years old and a wreck, but she was saved.

Or was she?

Unfortunately, it is a matter of record that most prostitutes make at one time or another surprisingly good marriages and, just as surprisingly, often revert to their old habits.

Anna Beuschel was no exception. As Thomas Beuschel was to tell, rather sadly, the officer in charge of the Missing Persons Bureau, she had begun by costing him his job, to say nothing of her own.

Being a good waiter, Beuschel had quickly found employment with one of the better Hamburg restaurants and had arranged for his new wife to take over as ladies' room attendant.

Anna was, however, not very interested in ladies and no sooner had she got her hands on the tips than she converted them into the cheapest and most concentrated alcohol available.

Forgetting then that she was now a respectable married woman and that her prostitute's licence had actually expired, she decided to do a little advertising in the front entrance of the restaurant.

Anna believed in displaying the merchandize in the most crude and direct manner possible. Removing her underwear, she lay down on the floor and raised her skirts.

It was not a spectacle to stimulate any of the appetites of the amazed arriving diners and Beuschel and his wife were not only fired but thrown bodily off the premises.

After that, Thomas Beuschel did not make any further attempts to find work for his wife and did his waiting alone while Anna spent her days and most of her nights in the Golden Glove. Since her husband provided her with enough money to stay permanently drunk, this was probably one of the happiest periods of her life.

Inexplicable as Thomas Beuschel's attachment to his wife might be, there was no doubting his sincerity and he invariably dropped in at the Golden Glove when he came off work to see if she was there and conscious.

On the afternoon of August 3, 1974, she was there, but barely conscious.

'Go away!' she mumbled. 'Go away. Leave me alone.'

It was the last time he ever saw her alive.

The following day she was not there and, after a brief canvas of her second choice bars, he went to the police and reported her missing.

'Any idea of what might have happened to her, Mr Beuschel?' asked the Missing Persons duty officer who had just listened to a summary of Anna Beuschel's background. Her husband had found this necessary in order to explain why he had simply gone off and left his wife half-conscious in the Golden Glove.

Thomas Beuschel looked uneasy.

'The Elbe?' he murmured.

The Missing Persons officer thought that this was a very likely suggestion. The Elbe is the great river on the end of which Hamburg lies and quite a number of St Pauli prostitutes end up in its broad waters.

Generally, however, their bodies are fished out by the Water Police. The Elbe is a tidal river and things floating in it do not wash quickly out into the North Sea, but normally make several trips up and down as current alternates with tide.

However, the Water Police did not fish out Anna Beuschel nor did their colleagues on land find any trace of her. Eventually, the Missing Person report was forwarded to the Department of Criminal Investigations with a note that Mrs Beuschel had possibly been the victim of foul play.

'A strange conclusion,' remarked Inspector Luders, gazing morosely at the report. 'She had no money. She was old and unattractive. No one benefited from her death. Here, take this and see if you can turn up any kind of a lead.'

Two days later, the sergeant handed back the file.

'Not a thing,' he said. 'Missing Persons was thorough. There's no trace of the woman.'

On the same day that he suspended his investigation into the disappearance of Anna Beuschel, Mrs Elsie Beier was complaining bitterly to Heinz, the caretaker of 74 Zeiss Street.

'It's more than a body can stand!' she screeched. 'Just come in here and smell it for yourself!'

But Heinz would not. He did not like the smell any better than Mrs Beier did. It was a horrible smell, nauseating, foul, faintly and revoltingly sweetish.

It was an interesting point that, although both were old enough to remember the second world war, neither Heinz nor Mrs Beier had happened to be in one of the badly bombed cities where the corpses lay rotting in the ruins.

Anna Beuschel's case also came to the Unsolved files of the Criminal Police and, since her married name began with a 'b', found itself next to the Unsolved case of Gertraude Braeuer.

By one of those strange coincidences, so common in real life, but forbidden to fiction, the ladies themselves were filed in much the same manner.

On November 1, 1974 Mrs Beier gave up and moved out to be replaced by the less fastidious Mr Fordal, and on Christmas Eve of that same year a Miss Frieda 'Rita' Roblick disappeared after having been seen for the last time in the Golden Glove at approximately four in the afternoon.

The matter came rather quickly to the attention of the police as the fifty-seven-year-old Miss Roblick was, so to speak, an old customer of theirs. A confirmed alcoholic who had held a prostitute's licence in most of the larger cities in Germany, she was seldom able to resist the temptation to rob her clients before leaving them and had consequently acquired a police record of imposing thickness.

At the time of her disappearance she was actually on parole, and it was her parole officer who reported her missing.

The report on Frieda Roblick did not remain long in the Missing Persons office, but was sent to Inspector Luders with a sheet of paper noting the similarities between this and the Beuschel case only some four and a half months earlier.

Both women had been old, broken-down prostitutes. Both had been alcoholics. Both had been small women, only a little over five feet tall. Neither had had any teeth, a point important in cases requiring dental identification. And both had last been seen in the Golden Glove.

'Interesting,' said the inspector. 'I wonder if it means anything.'

The sergeant did not reply, but got up to go and look in the Unsolved file. After a few moments, he returned with another file in his hand.

'Except that she was somewhat younger,' he said, 'all those things also apply to the Braeuer case.'

The inspector took the file and leafed through it.

'She wasn't last seen in the Golden Glove,' he observed. 'Or, at least, we don't know that she was. Still . . .'

'Do you think it would be worth putting a stake-out in the Glove?' said the sergeant.

'Nobody from the force,' said the inspector. 'They'd end

up alcoholic. See if you can get one of the canaries who's already an alcoholic.'

A canary is a bird that sings. The German police usually have quite a number of such birds working for them on a part-time piece-work basis.

That same afternoon, a remarkably scruffy gentleman with a fine, red nose joined the revellers in the Golden Glove and began to alternate beer and spirits in the orthodox north German manner. Sometimes he put his head down on the table and appeared to lose consciousness, but this was a sham. There was probably not enough alcohol in all Hamburg to render the gentleman unconscious and, for this reason, he enjoyed the esteem of the police who were also paying for the drinks.

The gentleman with the red nose did not find out anything except that Frieda Roblick had mentioned to several persons shortly before her disappearance that she was onto 'something solid' and she would soon be enjoying greener pastures. It had been assumed by her listeners that she meant that she was about to take up residence with some man.

On January 10, 1975 the man with the red nose was still sitting in the Golden Glove listening and drinking, although not necessarily in that order of importance, when Ruth Schult disappeared.

Fifty-two years old, five feet three inches tall and with not a tooth to her name, Mrs Schult was a prominent fixture of the St Pauli scene. Beginning her career as a prostitute at an early age, she had in 1948 met and married a wealthy widower named Schult, but as a result of her immoderate consumption of alcoholic beverages and her commercial attitude toward chance acquaintances of the opposite or even same sex, had found herself divorced almost immediately thereafter.

She had then gone to practise her profession in Cologne, Dusseldorf and a number of other cities only to return to Hamburg and St Pauli as she became increasingly short of tooth and long of wind.

This being a fairly average career, it would not, in itself, have been enough to gain her fame.

What had done that was an anonymous telephone call to the Hamburg Police on the afternoon of March 9, 1974 in which it was reported that two naked men were raping a naked woman at the Bismarck Monument.

A police car had been dispatched and had found Ruth Schult and two male companions, all naked as described, but, far from being raped, she was cooperating enthusiastically and, it appeared, even directing the operation.

Hamburgers are not easily startled, but such an event in an open square and on a chilly March day had drawn something of a crowd including a number of newspapermen.

The following morning several newspapers carried headlines of 'Group-sex at Bismarck Monument!' and Ruth Schult's modest niche in history was assured.

Having served a short sentence for indecent exposure, she returned to her normal haunts, one of which was the Golden Glove.

It was, however, no one from the Golden Glove who reported her missing, but rather a waiter from a first class restaurant.

Not, of course, that Mrs Schult ate at first class restaurants or for that matter at any restaurants at all, but she was a woman of regular habits and invariably made her lunch of bread with a bit of sausage on a park bench facing the restaurant across the street.

Over the years, she had become a sort of fixture to the waiter gazing out the front windows of the restaurant and when on January 10, 1975 she did not appear, he was disquieted. He knew who the woman was and also that she was no longer young and he thought that she might be ill in her room, assuming that she had one at all.

He therefore reported the matter to the police who took rather more note of it than they might under normal circumstances. The fact was, Ruth Schult met all of the physical and moral qualifications for inclusion into the group of what was now beginning to become known as the Golden Glove Disappearances.

The investigations continued for a month and at the end of that time were dropped for lack of leads. There was little question remaining in the inspector's mind; Mrs Ruth Schult had joined the club.

All this bothered him a great deal. He was used to superannuated prostitutes who died of alcohol and disease or who flung themselves from high buildings or bridges or who even got themselves murdered, but not of old prostitutes who simply disappeared.

'The fact is,' he told the sergeant rather sharply as if he were holding him personally responsible, 'it is not at all easy to dispose of a human body in a city like Hamburg. If these cases are all connected, and I am beginning to feel certain that they are, then someone is going to great trouble and I cannot see why.'

'Logically,' said the sergeant, 'the knowledge of the identity of the victims would lead to the identity of the murderer. However, that is not the case here because we know the identity of the victims and it hasn't helped us a bit.'

'Of course, we don't actually know that they are dead,' said the inspector, scowling ferociously at the top of the desk and tapping with his pencil. 'With the exception of Braeuer.'

'They certainly weren't shipped to North Africa or the Middle East,' said the sergeant. 'The sheiks would have crucified the white-slavers.'

'But,' continued the inspector, ignoring the remark, 'they have probably been killed because it would be even harder to make a living woman like that disappear than a corpse.'

The sergeant did not make any further comment. For months now, he had been racking his brain over the case of the missing prostitutes and the only result had been a monumental confusion.

Were the cases connected? Was there a pattern? And if so what in Heaven's name had become of the four hundred pounds or more of human flesh, dead or alive, which was presumably somewhere in Hamburg?

Astonishingly, there is some reason to believe that by March 16, 1975, when short, toothless, fifty-two-year-old Anni Wachtmeister moved into the attic apartment at 74

Zeiss Street with her new friend, Fritz Honka, there was no one who could have answered the sergeant's questions.

Miss Wachtmeister did not remain long at 74 Zeiss Street, moving out again on June 12th with the double complaint, made to anyone at the Golden Glove who was prepared to listen, that Fritz was too rough a lover for her liking and, secondly, that the place stank like the plague.

Before moving out, she had complained about the smell to Mr Honka who said that he was aware of it and that he was already buying deodorants by the case, something which was perfectly true.

He had also said that he had no idea what was causing it and it was to appear later that this was also perfectly true.

Unlike Irmgard Albrecht, who had left in a warm glow of mutual understanding, Anni Wachtmeister left rather precipitously and without bothering to put on all her clothes. She had often spoken of going back to fetch them, but had not done so a month later when, on the morning of June 17, 1975, the bells in the fire stations of Altona and St Pauli began to ring.

The fire which had been reported at 74 Zeiss Street at three-thirty-seven in the morning had begun in the second floor apartment of Seaman John Fordal and had been caused by his leaving a burning candle next to the bed as he fell asleep.

The bedding had caught fire and so had a considerable part of the furnishings before Fordal awoke, thought incorrectly that he was trapped, crawled out of the window and along the cornice to the stairwell window which he kicked in, and descended calmly, if unsteadily, to the street.

He was sitting on the kerb dabbing with his shirt tail at a nasty cut on his shin, which he had acquired kicking in the window, when the fire department arrived.

The fire in Mr Fordal's apartment was extinguished quickly but it had by then transferred itself to the storey above and was raging in the roof, a large part of which was destroyed before it was finally brought under control at approximately six-thirty.

In the meantime the house had, of course, been evacuated

and the door to Fritz Honka's attic apartment smashed in as the firemen did not know that he was a night watchman and would therefore be working.

They had, naturally, found no one in the apartment and at shortly before seven Walter Aust, a thirty-one-year-old, broad-shouldered, black-haired fireman, was digging through the smouldering rubble of the storage space adjoining Honka's bedroom.

Fireman Aust was unhappy because in addition to the smell of smoke and burned rags there was an underlying odour of something so foul that his nose refused to accept it.

Prodding in the darkness beneath the eaves, he caught hold of a length of charred timber with his gloved hand and drew it out.

There was a gold-coloured sandal on the end of the timber which he now saw was not timber at all. What fireman Aust was holding in his hand was a woman's leg and foot.

'Mein Gott, Erwin!' shouted Aust. 'Somebody was trapped up here! It looks like a woman.'

Fire Captain Erwin Schuen hurried over from the head of the stairs, followed by Fireman Wilfried Harz.

'We went through the apartment . . .,' he began and then broke off in mid-sentence as Harz shone his flashlight onto the object.

The leg was little more than a bone covered by brown, dry, leathery skin. It looked like the leg of a mummy and it gave off a horrifying odour.

For a second, the three firemen looked at each other in bewilderment.

'That's been here for a long time,' said Schuen finally.

He crouched and began to pull aside the pile of old rags from the corner under the eaves and as Harz shone his flashlight onto what lay beneath, a body appeared, the skin as dried and mummified as the leg had been.

That it was that of a woman there could be no doubt. Apart from a wine-red pullover, the body was naked and, although the face was a hideous mask of gaping eye sockets and rotting, toothless jaws, it was unquestionably a woman's face.

'Call the police, Walter,' said Fire Captain Schuen. 'This is out of our province.'

The police were immediately summoned, but before they had had time to arrive, Firemen Schuen and Aust had suffered another nauseating experience. Digging into a pile of coal briquettes, they had come upon a blue, plastic sack which had burst as they were dragging it out.

The wave of stinking gas which had shot from the sack had sent them reeling to the head of the stairs and had terminated the operations of the fire department in the attic until the air was cleared.

A short time later, the first officers from the Criminal Investigations Department arrived and, having learned that anyone in the house had access to the storage space in the attic and that the fire had been started by John Fordal, immediately placed him under arrest on the supposition that he had started the fire to conceal the evidence of murder.

However, Inspector Luders and Sergeant Peters then arrived and ordered a thorough search of the entire floor. By the time that Fritz Honka came home from his night watchman's job at a quarter to eight, the police knew that there was not only one body, but four, and that only Fritz Honka could be responsible for their being where they were.

Honka seemed only mildly astonished to find the house full of firemen and police officers.

'My goodness!' he exclaimed, gazing at the ruins of his apartment. 'What's going on here anyway?'

'There was a fire,' said Inspector Luders and then with deliberately startling abruptness, 'Criminal Police. What do you know about these two women?'

He thrust the personal identity cards of Irmgard Albrecht and Anni Wachtmeister under the night watchman's nose. They had been found in Honka's apartment and it was assumed that they represented two of the victims.

Honka glanced at the cards. 'They used to live with me,' he said, 'but they left and never came back to pick up their cards. If you want to get hold of them, you could try the Glove.'

The inspector was taken aback. Honka was not acting

like a trapped murderer at all and yet he almost certainly was.

The woman whose body had been found in the storage area by the firemen had definitely been murdered, although he still did not know how. The body found under the pile of rags had consisted of only the torso and the lower parts of the legs.

The arms, the thighs and the breasts had been in the blue plastic sack where they had rotted to an almost liquid consistency. It seemed improbable that the body could even be identified.

As a matter of fact, only one of the four bodies found in the attic appeared to be subject to identification and that was the torso lacking arms, legs, head, breasts and vagina found behind a low door leading off Honka's kitchen to the space under the eaves. This was believed to be the remainder of Gertraude Braeuer's corpse, the head and limbs of which had been found in the abandoned chocolate factory yard in November of 1971.

Lying on top of the torso of Gertraude Braeuer was the body of another woman which had not been mutilated in any way, but which had dried out and cured to resemble a side of bacon. This was later identified as the corpse of Frieda Roblick.

On the other side of the house, behind a trap door which had since been wallpapered over, in the wall of the living room, the dismembered parts of the corpse of Anna Beuschel lay heaped together.

All of these bodies were eventually identified by the police, but it was only through the confession of Fritz Honka at eleven-thirty that same night that it was learned that the dismembered corpse in the storage area was that of Ruth Schult.

The Missing Ladies of the Golden Glove had been found and the sergeant's question as to what could be done with four hundred pounds of flesh was answered.

It could not, however, have been answered before because the only person who knew all the details was forgetful. Fritz Honka could not even remember how many women he had killed and carelessly shoved under the eaves of the attic, maintaining at first that it was only two and then three and finally four when the pictures of the victims were shown to him.

Nor, according to Dr Strauss, was he pretending. The women had been a bother to him, he had not known what to do with the bodies so he had simply shoved them out of sight and had forgotten about them.

Fritz Honka was telling the literal truth when he had said that he had no idea where the smell was coming from and he had not been alarmed by the presence of the police in his apartment because he did not remember that he was a murderer.

Abstinence from alcohol in the detention cells of the police headquarters, however, worked a considerable improvement in his memory and he was eventually able to recall most of the details of the murders, if not exactly to which woman they applied.

Mostly, he said, he had strangled the women because they had scoffed at his inability to have orthodox sexual relations. Honka, it seemed, preferred oral sex, although only with women who had no teeth, or, alternatively, anal sex. He also enjoyed necrophily, having on at least two occasions carried out sexual intercourse with the corpses of the women after he had strangled them.

Despite the mutilations of the breasts and sex organs of all the victims but one, Honka maintained that his purpose in cutting up the corpses was to dispose of them. However, with the exception of Gertraude Braeuer, he had always found the cutting up, carried out in the kitchen sink with the kitchen knife and a small hand saw, so exhausting that he had lacked the energy to remove the body from the building and had merely stuffed it into the most convenient corner under the eaves.

A strange murderer, Fritz Honka. With some women, he lived peacefully and even moderately happily for months on end. Others he strangled and stuffed into the corners around his apartment, forgetting that they were there and buying deodorants by the case to combat the stench of their rotting bodies.

Was there a motive for these crimes?

If so, it is almost certain that Fritz Honka does not know what it was.

The crimes, however, took place. They were acknowledged. And Fritz Honka was sentenced to life imprisonment in punishment for them.

2

THE FATAL ORGY

Early in June of 1972 Kurt Rheiners made a spear. The thirty-six-year-old plumber was an above average hand-worker and it was a good spear.

The shaft of the spear was of hard maple, slightly over an inch in diameter and five feet long. Fixed firmly at the end was the blade, a slender dagger of high-grade steel, ten inches long and sharpened to a razor edge on both sides. The point was as sharp as a needle.

Having made the spear, Kurt did not quite know what to do with it. A few hundred years earlier a spear such as this might have been extremely useful in Hannover, West Germany where Kurt lived, but there was not much to be done with it in 1972.

Nor could he, for that matter, have explained why he had made the spear in the first place, except that he was slightly at loose ends with Julia and the boy, Thomas, off on vacation in the Tirol.

He had thought that it might be something a little different, a taste of freedom after eleven years of marriage so to speak, when he had let Julia and Thomas go off on vacation alone, but it had not turned out exactly that way.

The fact was, he was bored. Julia was only two years younger than himself, but she was a good deal younger at heart, and Thomas, already ten, made the difference between an empty, lonely house and one full of noise and excitement.

Kurt Rheiners sighed, stood the finished spear in the corner of the living room and went down to the Ant Tavern where he told Willi Jacobi how much he was enjoying his freedom, drank a good deal more beer than was good for his health, stood a good many more rounds than was good for his pocket and finally went home depressed and wondering what was the matter with him.

The newspapers and magazines were full of the adventures enjoyed by husbands while their families were away on vacation, but in real life this sort of thing appeared to happen much less frequently.

Not, of course, that there were not plenty of lovely young girls and, if the magazines could be believed, they should be approachable if not downright eager.

The trouble was, not many of them seemed to come into the Ant and Kurt felt himself a little too old to hang out in the discotheques where the noise hurt his ears and the lighting his eyes.

'Pity that Norbert doesn't bring that Petra Schumacher in with him a little more often,' murmured Kurt, drifting into beery sleep. 'I just wonder . . .?'

Actually, he had no need to wonder. Petra Schumacher was eighteen years old, pretty, and a modern German girl in every respect which meant that she was well versed in sexual matters – and not only from a purely theoretical standpoint.

She was, in the informal manner popular among younger Germans, engaged to Kurt's friend, Norbert Splett, the apprentice pastry cook.

Norbert was almost Kurt's best friend and probably would have been except for the considerable difference in ages, Norbert being only twenty.

Nonetheless, Kurt and Norbert had known each other for years and the relationship was warm, if sometimes slightly puzzling to outsiders who, until they knew otherwise, tended to suspect an overt or covert homosexual attachment.

In actual fact, there was none. Norbert was a somewhat sensitive soul and had broken off his apprenticeship as a butcher because he could not stand slaughtering the calves. Sexually his interests were directed toward the person of Petra Schumacher.

Sometimes, when they had had a good deal of beer together, Norbert would tell Kurt about how it was with Petra and the other girls of his age group. According to these accounts, it was just the way the magazines said it was.

Casual, carefree sex with no taboos and in all its forms, no more significant and no more difficult to arrange than a game of tennis. But, of course, a great deal more exciting. Norbert's accounts tended to make Kurt drool slightly.

The fact remained, however, that he was thirty-six years old and of the preceding generation. Yearn as he might, he simply could not bring himself to make a direct proposal to any of the young girls with whom he came into casual contact.

There was, of course, the alternative of the contact advertisements. Many German newspapers and magazines carry pages of sex contact advertisements and some magazines carry nothing else. There, under code numbers, are offers for homosex, heterosex, voyeur sex, bi-sex, group-sex and omnisex. In the magazines devoted to such advertising, the offers are usually illustrated by photographs of the advertiser or advertiseress in the costume and, frequently, in the poses in which they propose to entertain anyone answering the advertisement.

Some of these advertisements are commercially orientated, such as those reading, 'Beautiful girl (see photo). 18 years. Experienced. Wishes to be indulged by wealthy industrialist. Age not a consideration.'

The majority are, however, merely the Germans of the last generation trying to catch up with the sex revolution. Most of them are, like Kurt Rheiners, in their middle thirties.

Kurt had bought a good many such magazines and had studied them, making selections in various fields that sounded attractive, but he had never answered any. He simply did not have the nerve.

The thought of a total stranger or strangers turning up on his doorstep ready for a bout of group-sex or even perfectly ordinary one-to-one sex on the living room carpet was terrifying.

Kurt suspected that he would, under such circumstances, be disgracefully unable to perform and he was probably right. Germany's psychiatrists report that the most common complaint among younger men today is impotence brought on by an inability to match the standards set by the media.

Kurt Rheiners therefore did nothing and complained about it incessantly to the owner of the Ant. He did not mention his problems to Norbert Splett because he did not want Norbert to think of him as an old man or behind the times. He sometimes made up quite interesting stories of his experiences in connection with the contact advertisements which caused Norbert to think that it must be nice to be so active sexually at such an advanced age.

However, as time passed and the first two weeks of Julia's and Thomas's three week vacation were at an end, Kurt's complaints to Willi Jacobi began to take on a note of desperation and his consumption of beer and corn, the clear, potent, grain spirits so popular in North Germany, increased alarmingly.

Not, of course, that he got drunk. Like most Germans, Kurt had a hard head for alcohol and he and Norbert could, and frequently did, put away forty and more glasses of beer with, perhaps, half that number of shots of corn in a single evening without any very serious effect on the one or the other.

Petra Schumacher did not have a hard head for alcohol. Not because she was young. There are eighteen-year-old German girls who can drink a French vintner under the table. The reason that Petra Schumacher could not drink very much was simply that she seldom had anything much in her stomach.

The sad fact was that Petra had a slight tendency to overgenerous proportions and, although this rendered her extremely attractive to Kurt Rheiners and others of his generation, the modern trends were for something more gazelle-like.

On the evening of June 20, 1972 as Petra Schumacher entered the Ant Tavern with her fiancé, Norbert Splett, she had eaten during the preceding twelve hours precisely three very small potatoes and one small cup of yogurt. It was not the ideal condition in which to start a hard evening's drinking.

The time was more late afternoon than evening and, by midnight, the threesome of Kurt Rheiners, Norbert Splett and Petra Schumacher had disposed of a good many more than forty glasses of beer, to say nothing of the corn, and Petra was in a state where she was inclined to giggle wildly at anything or nothing and fling herself onto the nearest male neck available.

They left together and Willi Jacobi watched them go with approval and benevolence. Unless he was greatly mistaken, Kurt Rheiners was soon going to be relieved of an itch that had been bothering him for some time now.

Willi Jacobi would not see his friend and client, Kurt Rheiners, again, but another drinking partner named Hardy Bruggemann would, and under shocking circumstances.

The incident took place the following morning at approximately nine-thirty when Bruggemann dropped by the Rheiners' home to see how Kurt was getting on. Being an old friend, he did not hesitate when there was no answer to his knock, but simply opened the door and walked into the house.

Kurt Rheiners was in the living room, just in front of the door. He was completely naked and projecting from his back was the polished five-foot shaft of the spear which he had so carefully made. There was a wide trail of partially dried blood leading from the sofa to the body and a large pool surrounding it. The blade of the spear was driven completely into the body so that none of it could be seen at all.

Hardy Bruggemann was astounded and appalled. He did not know that Kurt Rheiners had made a spear and he did not recognize the shaft protruding from between his shoulder blades as a spear shaft.

To him it appeared that his friend had, in some inexplicable way, been impaled on a long, round piece of wood, presumably while lying naked on the sofa and had then dragged himself in the direction of the door before expiring.

How this could have happened he could not imagine.

However, as the surprise subsided slightly, his gaze took in other details of the room and he saw that Kurt was lying amidst a welter of clothing, food, utensils and playing cards. The impression was that there had been a very lively party of some kind.

All of this transpired in less than an instant even while Bruggemann was running forward to drop on his knees beside the body of his friend. He had hoped to find some trace of breathing or a heart beat, but there was none and the body was already quite cold.

Bruggemann got sorrowfully to his feet and, for the first time, the realization struck him that Kurt Rheiners must have been murdered. There had been a wild party and one of the guests had rammed a wooden pole into his back with such force that it had killed him.

Having more than a scanty idea of his friend's extramarital ambitions and having heard a number of his fictional stories concerning the contact advertising experiences, he immediately suspected the worst. Kurt had made a contact through the advertisements and it had turned out badly.

The thing to do now was to try and save as much of appearances as possible.

Picking up a pair of bloody trousers from the floor, he attempted to slip them over the dead man's legs, but found this much more difficult than he would have expected.

It was while he was struggling with the trousers that it occurred to him what he was going to have to do.

He was going to have to call the police.

Still holding the trousers in his hand, he went out to the hall and dialled the emergency number of the police from the small, printed card of emergency numbers taped to the wall over the telephone.

Up until this point, he had been acting in a state of shock, but there was now time to think while waiting for the police and, by the time that the first patrol car arrived, he was a very worried man indeed.

He had handled things in the living room, his fingerprints must be everywhere. It would be a wonder if he were not charged with murdering Kurt himself.

In fact, the two patrolmen from the car were much inclined to think just that. Both young and relatively inexperienced officers, they were nearly as dumbfounded as Bruggemann had been by the scene.

They did, however, recognize the spear for what it was and, after handcuffing the trembling Bruggemann to the radiator, one man went out to the patrol car to report while the other guarded the prisoner with drawn pistol.

This merely complicated matters still further for it was Sunday morning and the man on duty in the Criminal Investigations Department was a very junior detective third-class who could not leave the offices.

He had, of course, taken Hardy Bruggemann's original report as transferred to him from the communications centre, but he had not entirely believed it. Bruggemann in a state of shock had sounded not unlike a drunk.

Now, however, the patrolman from the patrol car was on the line and he not only maintained that there had been a homicide but that the victim had been speared to death.

It had been a very long time since anyone was speared to death in Hannover and the detective was not at all anxious to call out his superiors on a Sunday morning with such a report unless he was absolutely certain that it was true.

He, therefore, stalled in an agony of indecision and someone, presumably the dispatcher on the communications desk, called the emergency ambulance which rushed to the Rheiners' home carrying an intern with even less experience than the detective at police headquarters.

The intern, who had an exaggerated idea of the authority of the medical profession, insisted on taking the corpse to the hospital and was only restrained by threats of force from the patrolmen whose orders were to let no one approach the body.

This disagreement, however, finally produced constructive action as the intern calling police headquarters over the radio telephone in a great fury convinced the detective in the offices of the C.I.D. that, whatever the situation at the Rheiners' house, something was very radically wrong and would require the attention of the senior members of the department.

A half-hour later Detective-Sergeant Willi Froebes slid

out of his car and came loping up the front walk of the Rheiners' house looking very much like a Doberman pinscher and nearly as inclined to bite.

A dark, sleek, muscular man who did not suffer fools lightly, he disliked disorder of any kind and the scene at the Rheiners' house looked as if someone were shooting a low-budget, B-grade movie.

Hardy Bruggemann was still handcuffed to the radiator, the patrolmen and the intern were defying each other to the amusement of the hard-bitten ambulance driver and stretcher bearers, and a very considerable crowd had collected and was trying to peer through the windows of the house.

The sergeant straightened all this out as quickly and as ruthlessly as a sheepdog might have straightened out a herd of unruly sheep, sending the intern and his ambulance back to the hospital with burning ears and some valuable information on the penalties involved in interfering with a police officer in the performance of his duty, releasing the nearly hysterical Bruggemann from the radiator and sending the patrolmen into the crowd with instructions to collect any and all identity cards for future questioning.

He then turned his attention to the corpse.

'What do you know about this?' he asked Bruggemann.

'Nothing,' said Bruggemann. 'I just came to visit him and found him like this. I called the police.'

'You can go,' said the sergeant. 'Give me your identity card. You'll be called for questioning later.'

Hardy Bruggemann left gratefully and the sergeant went out to the patrol car, called headquarters and issued instructions that his superior, Inspector Karl Kreidemann, and the department's medical expert, Dr Manfred Hammerstein, be informed that a homicide had taken place.

He then lit a cigarette and settled down to wait. It being Sunday morning, Hammerstein, he knew, would be at the golf links. The inspector would, presumably, be at home, but he was not a man who was inclined to hurry, not even for a homicide.

Forty-five minutes later they arrived, the doctor still in his golfing clothes and shoes, and the inspector calm and unruffled as ever. He was a tall man with long, aristocratic features and greying, bushy sideburns who looked far too distinguished to be a police officer.

The doctor did not look distinguished at all, being very young and having a deceptively timid manner of peering through his huge, horn-rimmed spectacles. He was, however, a very competent practitioner of forensic medicine and he promptly set about an examination of the corpse of Kurt Rheiners. While he was doing this, the sergeant went through the dead man's clothing and eventually came up with his identity card.

The inspector did nothing, but, having looked over the scene, withdrew to the police car where he lit a long, thin, black cigar and waited for the reports.

Presently, the doctor came out and sat down beside him.

'The man was speared to death,' he said without preamble. 'An extremely well-made weapon of high grade steel, not primitive workmanship at all. The blade entered his back just below the right shoulder blade, passed at an angle through the heart and left lung and emerged through the skin of the chest. He died approximately nine minutes later.'

'Not instantly?' said the inspector, frowning. 'Was the spear hand-held or thrown?'

'Hand-held, definitely,' said the doctor. 'It could not have entered at the angle it did, if it were thrown. He was lying down at the time.'

'Perhaps a fight?' suggested the sergeant, who had come out to stand beside the car and listen. 'He was knocked down and then stabbed as he lay on the floor.'

'Well no, not really,' said the doctor. 'As a matter of fact, he was lying on top of someone and it wasn't on the floor but on the sofa. There was no fight. He was just lying there having intercourse . . .'

'What?' said the inspector and the sergeant simultaneously.

'Yes, that was what he was doing,' said the doctor apologetically as if he were in some way responsible for this behaviour. 'He had nearly reached his climax, too, and the shock of the spear thrust was enough to finish the matter. It must have been quite a shock for his partner as well. There's a possibility that the tip of the spear broke the skin of her chest or back, as the case may have been.'

'Are you quite sure of all this?' said the inspector, taking the cigar out of his mouth, looking at it reflectively and putting it back again.

'Yes,' said the doctor simply.

The sergeant looked exceedingly unbelieving, but said nothing.

'Time of death?' said the inspector.

'Between one-forty-two and one-fifty this morning,' said the doctor.

'All right, Willi,' said the inspector. 'Full lab squad out on the double. It will probably take half the day to locate them all. The body can be sent down to the morgue as soon as they're finished with it. I want the whole room gone over for prints. It looks to me as if there was some sort of a party there last night and there may even be witnesses to this. I'll be receiving reports at the office.'

The inspector thereupon drove back to police headquarters. The first report he received when he arrived was from the charge room.

'There is a man down here,' said the officer on duty, 'who says that he speared someone to death last night. I thought you might be interested.'

'Send him up,' said the inspector.

A few moments later a tearful Norbert Splett was ushered into the inspector's office.

'I killed him!' he sobbed. 'I killed my best friend! He was raping my fiancée!'

'A grave provocation, certainly,' said the inspector. 'Sit down and tell me about it.'

The portable tape-recorder was brought in and the suspect was warned of his rights, following which Splett made a full confession to the murder of Kurt Rheiners.

'We left the Ant a little before midnight,' he said. 'Kurt, Petra and I. Petra was pretty drunk, but Kurt and I were all right.

'Kurt wanted us to go to his house. He said that he had

something to drink there and that we could cook some sausages and have a good time.'

'Did you have any idea of what he meant by "a good time"?' asked the inspector.

Norbert Splett looked slightly uneasy. 'Well, drinking and eating and so on, I guess,' he said.

'Continue,' said the inspector.

'When we got to the house,' resumed Splett, 'Kurt got out some wine and champagne and a bottle of cognac. We made some sausages and opened a tin of pusta salade.

'Then Kurt suggested we play cards.'

'For money?' said the inspector.

Norbert squirmed. 'For our clothes,' he said. 'Every time anybody got the jack or the ace of hearts, they had to take off one article of clothing. It wasn't very long before all of us were naked.'

'And then?' said the inspector. 'You still had no idea of the kind of good time Mr Rheiners had in mind?'

'I didn't feel good,' said Norbert Splett defensively. 'I can't drink cognac on top of beer. I had to go to the bathroom and bring it up.

'When I came back into the living room, Petra was lying on the sofa and Kurt was lying on top of her between her legs. They were both naked and she was fighting him.

'I thought he was raping her and I picked up the spear that was standing in the corner and stuck it in his back. I didn't think it would go in so easily, but it went all the way.

'Kurt made an awful noise and fell off Petra. I got her up and helped her into her clothes and dressed myself. Then we left and went to my place and went to bed. I got up just now.'

'And you made no effort to help Mr Rheiners?' said the inspector. 'You could have called a doctor.'

'He was dead,' said Splett. 'I knew he was dead. The spear went all the way through him.'

Norbert Splett was charged and taken to the detention cells while a team of detectives went to his apartment and arrested Petra Schumacher on charges of acting as an accessory after the fact.

In the meantime, the inspector drove back to the Rheiners' home where he informed the sergeant that the murder had been solved.

'Continue with the investigation as if it hadn't however,' he said. 'I'm not convinced that Mr Splett has told us the truth, the whole truth and nothing but the truth. I'll be interested in hearing Miss Schumacher's statement.'

Petra Schumacher's statement was identical to that of her fiancé.

'Which means,' said the inspector, 'that they cooked it up between them. It may be true, but it's not an independent statement. No two persons involved in such an incident would have completely identical versions of what happened unless they had discussed it and agreed upon it.'

It was Monday morning and the investigations at the Rheiners' house had been completed. The body was at the police morgue where Dr Hammerstein was carrying out the autopsy. Mrs Rheiners had been contacted and would be arriving with Thomas from the Tirol at noon.

'It isn't entirely the true version, in any case,' said Sergeant Froebes. 'I just stopped by the morgue and Hammerstein says that she wasn't fighting him. The girl's got nails like a cat, but the only marks are on Rheiner's back and they're not from fighting. He also says that she was sufficiently aroused that she left traces of her secretions on Rheiners' body.'

'Well, of course, Splett didn't say that Rheiners was raping her in his confession,' said the inspector. 'He said he thought he was raping her and it would be impossible to prove that he didn't think that. Give the lab a call and see if they're ready to report yet.'

The lab was not yet ready, but they were by noon, just shortly before the arrival of Mrs Rheiners.

'I think you'll be able to pin Splett on one point,' said the chief of the laboratory technical section. 'According to his statement, he just stuck the spear into Rheiners' back, but, in actual fact, it was wiped afterwards. There are no prints on it of any kind.

'Plenty of prints of all three participants everywhere else

in the room and there are sperm and female secretion traces on the carpet where they were sitting playing cards. The indications are that that was not all they were playing.

'It wasn't a real orgy or group sex, but everybody was getting pretty excited. There are also indications that somebody went through most of the house looking for something. There's no indication as to whether they found it.'

'Money perhaps,' said the inspector. 'We may be able to tell something when Mrs Rheiners gets here. She's due shortly. You didn't find any money or valuables in the house? Rheiners was comfortably well-off.'

'Valuables yes,' said the technician. 'Money no. There were a few coins in the drawers in the kitchen, but no real money.'

'The Ant, the tavern where Rheiners hung out, says that he was free with money and carried quite a sum of it on him most of the time,' said the inspector. 'The owner is pretty sure he had at least a couple of hundred marks on him when they left.'

'He didn't have it when we got there,' said the technician. 'Of course, half the population of Hannover had run through the place by then. The fellow who found him, this Bruggemann, admitted that he'd picked up Rheiners' trousers, didn't he?'

'Yes,' said the inspector. 'But I doubt very much that he took anything out of them. We checked him out and there's no reason to suspect him of anything. Willi says he was on the verge of collapse when he got there.'

The technician looked at his notes. 'Let's see,' he said. 'That's about it. You wanted to know if there were traces of vomit in the lavatory. Negative. We took it apart. No vomit.'

'Is it possible that the flush would have cleaned it so thoroughly that you couldn't find traces?' said the inspector.

'Possible, but highly improbable,' said the technician. 'The fellow would have had to be a very tidy vomiter. Less than one per cent chance that anyone vomited in that lavatory within the past twenty-four hours.'

'All right,' said the inspector. 'Now, all we have left is Mrs Rheiners.'

A short time later Mrs Rheiners arrived alone, having dropped Thomas off with her mother.

The inspector immediately summoned Dr Hammerstein. He was going to have to tell Mrs Rheiners the circumstances of her husband's death and he was not at all sure how she would react.

As it turned out, her reaction was one of mixed sorrow and anger.

'It's all this stupid sex business,' she sobbed. 'Kurt was a good husband and I know he never cheated on me before. We were happy. But every time you pick up a newspaper or a magazine now, all you read is about the sex revolution and, if you go to the movies, all you see is sex films. Men like Kurt think they're missing out on something and they do foolish things. Did they rob him too?'

'That's what we're trying to determine, Mrs Rheiners,' said the inspector. 'Do you know if there would have been any substantial amount of money or valuables in the house?'

'There should have been around thirteen hundred marks,' said Mrs Rheiners. 'Kurt always drew a thousand marks out of the bank on Friday and he usually had three or four hundred left over from the week before. He might have spent a little more at the Ant because we were away, but he'd also have spent less on the groceries so it should have been about thirteen hundred marks.'

'There wasn't a penny in the house,' said the inspector.

Nor could the subsequent investigations turn up any place where Kurt Reiners might have spent the money which he had drawn out of the bank on the Friday preceding his death. It was quite simply missing.

On May 22, 1973, Norbert Splett was found guilty of unpremeditated murder with extenuating circumstances and sentenced to ten years imprisonment. The charges against Petra Schumacher were dropped and she was not brought to trial.

3

REPEAT PERFORMANCE

It was a golden autumn morning, on Tuesday October 23, 1973, in the great West German seaport of Hamburg and Inspector Frank Luders was standing at the window of his office nursing a cup of black coffee and gazing glumly down at the office workers scurrying past on their way to work.

Autumn is one of the better seasons in Hamburg, the spring tending to be raw and wet, the summer hot and sticky and the winter too cold for anyone but hardy north Germans.

The inspector's glumness was, therefore, not due to the weather, but rather to a profound conviction, well-based on personal experience, that the day was liable to bring some quite unpleasant surprises.

This is, of course, equally applicable to any other senior investigations officer attached to the Criminal Investigations Department of a large police force, but on this particular morning the inspector's forebodings were realized with distressing speed.

'Communications on the line, chief,' said Detective-Sergeant Max Peters, putting his tousled blond head in through the open door to the outer office. 'They think they may have a homicide. You want me to take it?'

'They think,' said the inspector without turning around. 'What do they mean by that? They have a corpse, but they don't know whether it was a natural death or an accident or murder?'

'No,' said the sergeant. 'They don't know whether they have a corpse.'

The inspector turned around and took a long pull at the coffee cup, looking reproachfully at his assistant over the edge.

'It's like this,' explained the sergeant hurriedly. 'A Dr Harold Gross came to the sub-station in Barmbek this morning early and asked for a patrolman to accompany him. He apparently owns a number of apartment houses and he couldn't locate the building superintendent in one of them. He had a locksmith with him and he was going to open the door and go in, but he wanted a police officer present.'

'Why?' said the inspector, putting the empty coffee cup down on the desk.

'I don't know,' said the sergeant. 'Maybe he thought something was wrong. Anyway, the station sent an officer with him and they're now at the apartment of the building superintendent. He's just called the sub-station to say that there's a big patch of blood on the wall and something that looks like a body wrapped up in a sheet in the utility room. The sub-station transferred the call to Communications and they've passed it on to us.'

'Tell Communications to send a car and then have them check whether there really is a body,' said the inspector. 'We've got enough things going without chasing off after any false alarms. Talk to the car yourself when they reach the scene.'

The sergeant nodded and disappeared. In something under ten minutes he was back.

'We've got a radio car at the scene,' he reported, 'and it's a body. I talked to the patrolcar officer myself. He says it's definitely homicide.'

'All right,' said the inspector, getting to his feet. 'Get Ludwig and meet me with the car at the front door.'

The sergeant looked mildly startled and made off down the corridor in the direction of the office of Dr Ludwig Strauss, the department's medical expert. He had not expected that the inspector would be going out personally on what seemed a more or less routine case.

There was, of course, no way that he could know that behind the dark, morose and haggard features of his superior, there lurked a spirit which could enjoy a fine autumn day as well as anyone else.

The police party was not long in arriving at the apartment

house at Buckelweg 4 which turned out to be a new, modern building five storeys high.

The building superintendent's quarters were on the ground floor next to the front entrance. Inside were Dr Gross, the locksmith, the patrolman from the Barmbek substation and the two officers from the patrolcar parked in front.

The inspector found this too much of a crowd and began by sending everyone with the exception of Dr Gross about his business.

'Once we've finished here, I'd like you to step down to the station with us and make a statement,' said the inspector. 'Do you know what happened here?'

'Not the faintest idea,' said Dr Gross. 'Kapfenberger didn't answer the door and there was this sign hanging on it so I got a locksmith and a policeman and came in. There was no one here and while we were looking through the apartment, the policeman found the blood on the wall. I didn't know. I thought it was ketchup.'

'Where?' said the inspector.

The apartment house owner silently led the way into the bedroom. A blanket had been nailed up to the plaster wall above the bed and one of the upper corners had been pulled loose so that it hung down, exposing an irregular, dark brown patch on the plaster.

'Blood all right,' commented the inspector who had seen enough of it to know.

He walked back out of the bedroom and across the kitchen to where a door opened into a small utility and laundry room. Dr Strauss and Sergeant Peters were engaged in trying to remove a blood-soaked sheet from what was obviously a corpse. They were having difficulty as the blood had dried, glueing the sheet to the body in many places.

'Why don't you cut it?' suggested the inspector. 'We can always put it back together again if it's necessary for the investigation.'

The doctor nodded briskly, got a scalpel out of his case and with a few deft cuts laid bare the body. It was that of a totally naked young woman with long black hair.

The sergeant stepped back out of the way and the doctor knelt beside the corpse and began his on-the-spot examination without which the corpse could not be moved to the morgue.

'Do you know this woman?' said Inspector Luders to Dr Gross who had turned very pale.

'Yes,' said Gross. 'It's my building superintendent's wife, Mrs Martha Kapfenberger.' He turned his head away from the corpse. 'Do you mind if I go in the other room? I'm not used to this.'

'Go into the living room,' said the inspector. 'I'll join you in a few minutes.'

He turned to the doctor who was going busily over the corpse.

'Well?' he said.

'Several blows over the head,' said the doctor. 'From the marks, a hammer. Minor skull fractures and a split scalp. That's where the blood came from. Cause of death was apparently manual strangulation while she was unconscious from the blows on the head.'

He bent the limbs, pressed his thumbs into the flesh of the thigh, lifted the corpse to check on the progression of the dark spots of blood which settle under the skin once circulation has ceased, turned back an eyelid and said, 'Seventy-two hours at least.'

'Uh-huh,' said the inspector. 'Anything else? Raped?'

'She seems to have engaged in intercourse shortly before death,' he said. 'No indication that it was forced.'

'All right,' said the inspector. 'Max, get on the radio and tell headquarters we want the corpse transporter and a squad from the lab. You take over here. I'm going to take Dr Gross back to the office and get his statement.'

'I'll come with you,' said Dr Strauss. 'There's nothing more I can do here and I've got some things I'll have to clear away before I can start the autopsy.'

All three men started out through the kitchen to the entrance hall, but came to a halt when Dr Gross suddenly rushed out of the living room.

'Oh my God!' he shouted. 'The poor child!'

'She wasn't a child,' snapped the inspector. 'She was a grown woman. Don't be so emotional.'

'Not her! Not her!' cried Gross in a state of great excitement. 'I just remembered the child. The Kapfenbergers have a little six-year-old daughter named Birgit. Where is she?'

The three investigators exchanged glances.

'All right,' said the inspector. 'Let's start looking.'

Fifteen minutes later they were all back in the entrance hall. The apartment was not large and there was no trace of a little girl in it.

The sergeant telephoned his instructions to headquarters from the police car and then went back to the apartment to wait while the inspector drove to headquarters with Dr Strauss and Dr Gross. Leaving the car standing in front of the building, he hustled the apartment house owner up the stairs to his office, sat him in the chair next to his desk, snapped on the tape recorder and said, 'Now, tell me what you know about this and quick. If the child's in the hands of a murderer, a few minutes could mean the difference between recovering her alive or dead.'

His manner was convincing and Gross began to speak so rapidly that he stumbled over his words.

'I have a number of apartment houses,' he said, 'and I have a building superintendent for each one. I only take men with families for the post and they must have good references because they collect the rents.'

'Whose references did you have for this one?' said the inspector.

'Mrs Inge Foerster,' said the doctor. 'She's a wealthy woman and prominent socially.'

'I know who Mrs Foerster is,' said the inspector. 'What is the man's name, age and so on?'

'Rudolf Kapfenberger,' said the doctor. 'Aged forty-five and an upholsterer by trade, if I remember rightly. The wife, the dead woman, was thirty-two I think. The little girl was six. I know that.'

He paused for an instant.

'I have the feeling that she wasn't Kapfenberger's child,' he said.

'You mean she was illegitimate?' said the inspector. 'How could you know that?'

'No, no, that wasn't what I meant,' said the doctor. 'I meant that I thought she may have been the child of a previous marriage. She didn't look very much like Mr Kapfenberger and she didn't seem that close to him, if you know what I mean.'

'I see,' said the inspector. 'You say that Kapfenberger collected the rents. When? On the first of the month?'

'That's right,' said the doctor. 'He was very conscientious about it and about everything else too for that matter.'

'When did you see him last?' said the inspector.

'On Sunday,' said Dr Gross. 'I was in South Africa for a month's vacation and I just came back on Saturday, so on Sunday I went around to all the apartment houses to see that everything was all right and to pick up the rents they'd collected on the first of October.'

'So you saw Kapfenberger on Sunday and picked up the rent,' said the inspector.

'No,' said Dr Gross. 'I saw Kapfenberger, but I didn't stop to pick up the rent money and go through the books because it was late and I was tired. I told him I'd be along the next day.'

'And?' said the inspector.

'I came the next morning and nobody answered the door and there was a sign hanging on it saying simply "Travelling" ', said the doctor. 'I didn't know what to make of it, but I thought maybe Kapfenberger had had a death in the family and had gone to the funeral. When he still wasn't there the next day, I got the locksmith and the policeman and went in.'

'Did you see Mrs Kapfenberger or the little girl on Sunday?' said the inspector.

'No,' said the doctor. 'I didn't go into the apartment. He invited me in, but I didn't go.'

'And you have no theory at all as to what may have happened?' said the inspector.

Dr Gross looked thoughtful.

'Well,' he said. 'There is a sort of precedent. Three years ago, one of my building superintendents in another building was hit over the head and robbed and it also happened while I was on vacation. The culprit was never caught.'

'What would your being on vacation have to do with it?' said the inspector.

'The superintendents have the money from the rents in their possession longer,' said the doctor. 'Normally, I would pick it up on the second or, at the latest, on the third of the month, but if I'm on vacation they may have to hold the money for several weeks. I suppose that someone might know about this and if they were successful the first time . . .'

'They might try it again,' said the inspector, completing his sentence. 'How much of your money would Kapfenberger have had on him?'

'One thousand, nine hundred and thirty-five marks,' said the doctor. 'I called the tenants yesterday. He hadn't collected from two and one was on vacation.'

'I thought you said he was very conscientious about the rent collecting,' said the inspector. 'Wouldn't it be better to handle all this through a bank?'

'Too many tricks,' said the doctor. 'The tenants claim they've transferred the money when they haven't or they send in incorrectly made-out cheques. Cash is better and if I have to employ a building superintendent anyway, he might as well collect. I can't imagine what went wrong with Kapfenberger. I've always had a very good impression of him. Charming person, really.'

'No doubt,' said the inspector dryly, 'but if the autopsy shows that Mrs Kapfenberger died before Sunday evening, then I'm afraid he's also a murderer. What time exactly was it that you saw him on Sunday?'

The doctor thought it over.

'Five-thirty,' he said finally. 'It was five-thirty or within a few minutes of it.'

'Close enough,' said the inspector. 'Our medical expert won't be able to fix the time much closer than an hour either way in any case.'

An hour either way, was, however, more than ample to establish Rudolf Kapfenberger as suspect number one in the murder of his wife, Martha.

Following the interview with Dr Gross, the inspector had called Dr Strauss at the morgue to advise him of the importance of determining the time of death and to ask for as speedy a report as possible.

The doctor called back at just before three in the afternoon.

'They only brought the body in a half hour ago,' he said apologetically. 'However, she was definitely not alive at five-thirty on Sunday.'

'I suspected that,' said the inspector. 'She was lying there dead in the apartment when Gross called. It could be that he's only alive because he found it too late to go in. Kapfenberger seems to be our man, but we've got a problem.'

'You don't know where he is,' said the doctor.

'Well, that too,' said the inspector, 'but the big problem is the child. Max has just come in from the apartment and the little girl's name is Polarek, not Kapfenberger. She's the daughter of the dead woman by a previous marriage. I'm afraid to put out a general alarm and pick-up order because I don't know what he might do to the child if he's pushed or cornered.'

'I see,' said the doctor. 'You're right, of course. The very fact that he took the girl with him would indicate that he intends to use her as a hostage or something like that. What are you going to do?'

'Sneak up on him quietly, if possible,' said the inspector. 'The only lead of any kind that we have is that Mrs Inge Foerster provided his references so maybe she'll know where he comes from or where he might be going. I've sent Max over to ask her.'

The inspector was still waiting in the office at six that evening when Sergeant Peters returned from his interview with Mrs Foerster.

The sergeant was wearing a very disgusted and discouraged expression on his normally cheerful face. Without a word, he went over to the coffee-making equipment behind the screen in the corner, made himself a large mug of strong, black coffee and returned to his desk.

'Well?' said the inspector impatiently.

'The little girl's probably dead,' said the sergeant.

'What makes you think so?' said the inspector.

'Aside from being Mrs Foerster's protegé, do you know who Mr Rudolf Kapfenberger is?' said the sergeant. He sounded bitter.

The inspector shook his head silently. It occurred to him that the sergeant was acting very strangely and he could not recall ever having seen him so emotionally involved in a case. He was aware, however, that the sergeant had a great many little brothers and sisters and that he was very fond of children.

'Mr Kapfenberger,' said the sergeant, 'is, or was, the lead tenor in the Celle church choir, the most promising pupil in his upholstery class, first violin in the Celle chamber music quartet and the godson of the District Attorney of Hannover.'

'Are you drunk, Max?' exclaimed the inspector in great astonishment. 'I know who the D.A. of Hannover is. He's younger than Kapfenberger. And besides, what the devil does this all have to do with the case?'

'I'm not drunk,' said the sergeant, 'but I'm going to be this evening. What famous institution is located at Celle?'

'The penetentiary,' said the inspector without hesitation. 'You mean . . .?'

The sergeant nodded. 'Life term for premeditated murder of his first wife,' he said. 'He was pardoned three years ago. While he was in prison, he was such a good boy that the D.A. offered to be his godfather when he got baptized for the first time and Mrs Foerster practically guaranteed his good behaviour to help get the pardon through. She is certain, she says, that he can become a useful member of society.'

'Useful in coping with the population explosion,' grunted the inspector. 'Did you tell her anything?'

'No,' said the sergeant. 'I said we wanted to give him the police medal for good behaviour. She believed it.'

'You know where he murdered his first wife?' said the inspector, reaching for the telephone.

'Hannover,' said the sergeant, 'on October 21, 1950.'

The inspector lifted the telephone and said into it, 'Communications? Luders. Get me the Hannover C.I.D. top priority. I want somebody with authority, even if you have to pull them away from their television set.'

'We could send somebody down to pick up his record,' said the sergeant as the inspector put down the telephone. 'Even if they mail it tonight, we won't get it until morning at best.'

'I'm not willing to wait that long,' said the inspector. 'I want them to read it to me over the telephone. Running around out there somewhere is a man who's killed two women and he's got a little girl with him. I want to know what offences he may have committed against children in the past and then I've got to make a decision. Either we come out in the open, order a nation-wide pick-up and alert, broadcast an appeal in the newspapers, radio and television and go after him with everything we've got or we lay low and try not to get him upset so that he'll harm the child.'

For nearly an hour the inspector and his assistant sat waiting in the office, drinking coffee and working on other cases in progress, of which there were quite a number. Finally, Communications called back. The officer in charge of the records at police headquarters in Hannover was on the line.

'You want me to read you this over the telephone?' he said incredulously. 'Have you got any idea of how long a record this bird has?'

'None,' said the inspector, 'but your District Attorney should. He's his godfather.'

'Ah well,' said the officer. 'He's a pretty progressive type. Does a lot of work on rehabilitation of criminals and so on. Wants to make useful members of society out of them.'

'This one needs a little more work,' said the inspector grimly. 'Start reading.'

Thereafter, he sat silently listening, the telephone propped up on one shoulder and his long, thin hand making small, precise notes on the block of lined paper in front of him. Occasionally, he said, 'Uh-uh' or gave a low whistle.

As the time continued to pass and the conversation showed no signs of ending, the sergeant laid down his own pencil and stared at the inspector in open astonishment.

It was a good twenty minutes before the inspector finally said, 'All right. Thanks a lot. Send us the works in the morning, will you?' and hung up. He had filled two pages of his pad with notes.

'Not a first offence, I take it?' said the sergeant cautiously.

'Well, no,' said the inspector. 'Not exactly. Here, I'll read you a short summary.' He read rapidly down the sheet of notes, ticking off certain items with his pencil as he went.

'Rudolf Kapfenberger, born October 20, 1929 in Chemnitz, now Karl-Marx-City in East Germany, illegitimate. Raised by his grandparents. According to the record, he could steal before he could walk. Stole from grandparents, aunts, uncles and, as he was able to get out and around more, anybody with whom he came in contact. He served three prison sentences before he was sixteen and, all told, has twenty-two convictions for theft, breaking and entering, burglary, robbery, armed robbery, assault and grievous bodily harm.'

'Dr Gross could hardly have picked a better man to collect his rents,' remarked the sergeant.

'Then,' continued the inspector, 'we have the little matter of the murder of the first Mrs Kapfenberger. According to the findings of the investigation, on October 21, 1950, Kapfenberger murdered Mrs Martha Kapfenberger, aged nineteen, by striking her over the head with a hammer and then strangling her to death.

'The naked body was found in the laundry room of their apartment and Kapfenberger had hung a "Gone travelling" sign on the door.

'Prior to his crime, he had embezzled the sum of one thousand four hundred and thirty-five marks from his employers. However, this appeared to have nothing to do with the murder.'

'Well, what was the motive then?' said the sergeant. 'That case sounds almost identical to this one.'

'It is practically identical, assuming that Kapfenberger is the murderer,' said the inspector. 'Nobody knows what the motive was except the murderer because he never admitted to the crime, even after he was convicted.

'Mr Kapfenberger has another peculiarity. He never confesses or admits any knowledge of a crime even when he is arrested in the very act.'

'He sounds as crazy as a bat to me,' said the sergeant in bewilderment. 'He should never have been released.'

'That's what the court thought too when they sentenced him to life imprisonment,' said the inspector. 'It was with a recommendation that he be at no time in the future considered for parole or pardon. It was the opinion of the medical experts that he constituted a permanent danger to society.'

'Well then, why in the name of God did they pardon him?' demanded the sergeant in considerable indignation. 'And what about the little girl? Does he have a record of offences against children too?'

'God knows what offences he's guilty of,' said the inspector. 'The only ones known are where he was taken in the act or where the evidence was sufficient to convict him. In all his twenty-two convictions, he's never once admitted to committing so much as a misdemeanour. However, he's known to be a transvestite and he's been charged with molesting children although not convicted.'

'I just don't understand it,' said the sergeant. 'How could a man like that with twenty-two convictions, plus one for murder, have the district attorney for a godfather, enjoy the support of a prominent and wealthy woman, marry an attractive mother of a small child and obtain a well-paid position where he handled substantial amounts of other people's money?'

'It's in the record too,' said the inspector. 'According to Hannover, Kapfenberger has one of the most engaging personalities a man could have. He simply oozes goodness, decency and respectability. You know as well as I that criminals seldom look like the popular idea of a criminal. They're just ordinary people and sometimes they have attractive personalities. Being a criminal has nothing to do with it.

'Kapfenberger, it seems, has such a pleasant personality that he could have been a successful entertainer or a politician or in almost any profession that depends upon making a good impression with people. By chance, he's a born criminal, apparently lacking the ability to distinguish right from wrong.

'Or so says Hannover, at any rate. They knew that he was pardoned and they were expecting to hear from him again.'

'So what's your decision?' said the sergeant. 'Do we go all out after Kapfenberger or do we try to sneak up on him?'

The inspector leaned forward, rested his elbows on the top of the desk and cupped his forehead in his hands. For several minutes he sat quietly, his fingers pressing his temples.

Then he straightened up, leaned back in the chair and sighed.

'I can't decide,' he murmured. 'I hadn't expected anything like this. The man is completely unpredictable . . . if I'm wrong . . . Maybe I'm just tired. I don't want to have to make a decision that could cause a child's death.'

The sergeant fumbled with his papers.

'I wouldn't either,' he muttered. He got up and went over to the coffee pot. 'You want another cup of coffee?'

The inspector shook his head.

'Look at it this way,' said the sergeant, coming back to his desk with an empty coffee cup. 'He's had her since Sunday at least, so if he was going to do anything to her, he's probably done it by now. On the other hand, if he hasn't . . .'

'. . . we don't want to stir him up,' finished the inspector. 'Yes, that's probably the most logical approach. There's no possibility of moving in on him quickly. Hannover says he could be anywhere in Germany, that he's not particularly attached to any one place. If we show our hand, he'll know we're after him and God knows what he'll do. Maybe he's crazy enough to believe that we don't suspect him.'

'Could we play on that?' said the sergeant. 'Plant a false story in the newspapers and the radio that we believe Kapfenberger and his daughter to have been kidnapped by robbers and that the kidnappers' identity was known?'

The inspector considered.

'It's a brilliant idea, Max,' he said finally. 'And I don't see what harm it could do, even if it doesn't work. However, there's not a great deal we could do with it yet tonight so let's sleep on it. We'll both have clearer heads in the morning.'

'Right, chief,' said the sergeant. 'Do you think I could borrow your notes there on Kapfenberger? I'd like to take a look at them before I go to sleep.'

The sergeant knew perfectly well that he was not going to sleep, or if he did, it would be poorly and not for long. In the Kapfenberger apartment that afternoon he had come across many pictures of little Birgit Polarek, a pretty little girl with big, dark eyes and a black fringe across her forehead.

The sergeant was, however, more tired than he realized and, lying down fully clothed on his bed after dinner, fell sound asleep and never awoke until half-past four in the morning.

He then got up, washed, shaved, changed his shirt and went back to the office where the inspector found him busily working when he came in at seven-thirty.

'You know,' said the sergeant, 'the coincidences and parallels in this thing are beyond belief. If Kapfenberger could have got the government to abolish the month of October, he could have been spared a lot of trouble and so would we.'

'Yes, I noticed that too,' said the inspector. 'Just about all the dates in his record are in October. I see you've been making up a chart.'

The sergeant nodded.

'Listen to this,' he said. 'Kapfenberger was born in

October 1929. He got his first conviction in October of 1942. He was married for the first time in October of 1949 and he killed his wife in October of the following year. One year later, again in October, he was sentenced to life imprisonment. In October of 1970 he was pardoned and in October 1971, he married the second Mrs Kapfenberger. Now it's October of 1973 and he's murdered her.'

The inspector dropped into the chair behind his desk.

'He must be aware of the significance of the month of October in his life,' he mused. 'There's a week yet to go in October. I wonder if that might mean that after the first of the month, the child would be safe?'

'I don't think so,' said the sergeant. 'He's had offences and convictions in other months too. It's just that October predominates.'

'Did you come to any other conclusions with the notes?' said the inspector. 'You weren't down here all night with them, were you?'

'No, no,' said the sergeant. 'I just came in a little early. The only other conclusion I reached was that the two murders were as identical as Kapfenberger could make them.

'Both women were knocked unconscious with a hammer while they were sleeping. Both were stripped naked and had had intercourse, presumably with him, shortly before their deaths. Both were strangled manually and wrapped in a sheet. Both were placed in the utility room and in both cases Kapfenberger hung a sign on the door saying "Gone travelling". Finally, in both cases, he had embezzled money just before the murders took place and, allowing for inflation, almost exactly the same amount. If I were to see this on television, I wouldn't believe it.'

'Nor would anyone else,' said the inspector. 'Well, I've made up my mind. We're going to try your plan first and, if that doesn't produce any results, we're going after him with everything. However, we're going to describe him precisely as the kidnap victim and maybe somebody will spot him and report.'

The plan was immediately put into effect and the first

newspaper and radio news reports carried descriptions of a robbery and kidnapping, during the course of which Mrs Kapfenberger had been murdered.

Whether Kapfenberger was taken in by the ruse or not could not be determined, for he simply ignored it. The descriptions, however, had an effect for two days later, but still in the month of October, Rudolf Kapfenberger was taken into custody by a patrolman in the Hamburg district of Wandbek, less than a half mile from the apartment house where he had murdered his wife.

Kapfenberger had been engaged in one of his favourite pursuits. He had been trying to steal a suitcase from a leather goods store and had been detected by the store owner who had called the patrolman on duty in the block.

Kapfenberger, who was alone at the time of his arrest, was recognized by the patrolman as the supposed kidnap victim and brought to police headquarters where he denied that he had attempted to steal the suitcase or that he knew anything about the murder of his wife.

'Impossible!' he protested. 'I saw her this morning and she was alive and well!'

The inspector had expected no more. Kapfenberger had never admitted to anything in his life and he was not going to now. It was not this which troubled him, but rather the fate of little Birgit Polarek. The mere fact that she had not been with Kapfenberger at the time of his arrest was ominous.

There was, however, still the slim hope she was merely sitting in a room somewhere. Kapfenberger had obviously been staying somewhere since leaving the apartment house at 4 Buckelweg. Perhaps the child was there.

Kapfenberger was, as might have been expected, not cooperative. In reply to the question as to where he had been for the past five days, he stated that he had been living with his wife, Martha, at 4 Buckelweg where he was the building superintendent.

He said this with such obvious sincerity and open honesty that even the inspector and the sergeant, who knew with certainty that this was not true, could hardly believe that he was deliberately lying.

'I wonder if he knows it himself,' said the inspector uncertainly. 'I've questioned thousands of suspects and I'd swear that this man is telling the truth.'

'But we know for a fact that he isn't,' said the sergeant. 'It's an indication of how he came to have such influential friends and how he came to be pardoned. He's the most convincing liar I've ever seen.'

'I'm going to ask him direct,' decided the inspector. 'The man can't be all bad. Maybe if I appeal to his better nature, he'll tell us where Birgit is.'

A few moments later, he straddled the chair in front of Rudolf Kapfenberger and, in as friendly a voice as he could manage, said, 'Mr Kapfenberger. I want you to answer me just one question and then, I promise you, you won't be questioned any more. In the name of all the many people who had so much faith in you and who thought that you were basically a good man, where is the little girl?'

Rudolf Kapfenberger gave him a warm, loving smile.

'What little girl?' he said.

The inspector got wearily up from the chair and without another word went back to the office where the sergeant was waiting.

'Better notify the Water Police and the Forestry Department,' he said. 'The body could be in the Elbe or maybe out in the woods somewhere. Tell the Park Service to keep an eye out too. A little corpse like that could be hidden anywhere.'

The sergeant nodded sadly.

'Right,' he said. 'By the way, Mrs Kapfenberger's sister, a Mrs Emma Fiedler, is coming in. She wants to talk to you about swearing out a charge against the person or persons responsible for Kapfenberger's release from prison. She says her sister knew nothing about his record.'

'She's wasting her time,' said the inspector, 'but I'll talk to her. When is she due?'

'Any time now,' said the sergeant. 'I'll go see if she's in the waiting room.'

He left the office and a moment later there came a sort of a mingled yell, yelp and shout from the direction of the waiting room.

The inspector recognized it as his assistant's voice and ran down the corridor, drawing his service pistol as he reached the waiting room door.

Inside, he was greeted by a strange spectacle.

A dark-haired woman was sitting on the bench staring at the sergeant, who was doing a sort of jig in the middle of the floor, with astonished, somewhat alarmed eyes. Sitting beside her was a little girl with a black fringe and big, black eyes. She was regarding the sergeant with obvious amusement.

'Wait, Max!' shouted the inspector, who had also seen pictures of Birgit Polarek. 'It could be her cousin.'

But it was not. The little girl was none other than Birgit Polarek.

'That Kapfenberger brought her over to me on Saturday morning,' said Mrs Fiedler. 'He said they were going on a little trip. If I'd only guessed what kind of a trip he was going to send poor Martha on . . . Well, anyway, I was so upset when I heard about her death that it didn't occur to me that anybody would be looking for Birgit. I thought you probably knew she was with me. I'm sorry if I caused any trouble, but I didn't read the newspaper accounts of the murder. I couldn't bear to.'

'It doesn't matter, Mrs Fiedler,' said the inspector. 'The main thing is, the child is safe. Kapfenberger apparently brought her to you before carrying out his murder so maybe in a backhanded sort of way he isn't all bad after all.'

The court disagreed. In their opinion, as in the opinion of the Hannover court twenty-three years earlier, Rudolf Kapfenberger was a menace to the general public. He was once again sentenced to life imprisonment with the recommendation that he not be considered for parole or pardon.

The date was, of course, October 21, 1974.

4

THE FUTURE BELONGS TO YOUTH

The waters of Shoreham habour are cold in winter and, if not particularly deep, quite deep enough for drowning even a tall young man.

Late at night on the last day of February 1973, they were also dark and covered with little wavelets running beneath the chill wind blowing in off the Channel.

The little waves slapped mischievously at the gasping mouth of the helpless boy as he bobbed desperately up and down, arching his body in a hopeless attempt to remain afloat.

But only magicians can swim when they are tied securely hand and foot and, perhaps, not even they with a great sack of stones and concrete blocks attached to their feet.

Relentlessly, the weight drew him down until the water closed over his head and still he fought, holding his breath in the hope of some miracle. Death at sixteen is not casy.

In the end, however, the air went out with a whoosh and the salt water rushed in, stinging, suffocating. Bright stars exploded in the dark water before his eyes. There was a great humming sound and all the lights went out.

Standing upright, its motorcycle booted feet pressed to the muddy bottom by the weight of the stones lashed to them, the corpse swayed gently and peacefully in the pull of the outgoing tide.

'Cor!' said the heavy-set young man standing on the pier. 'Did you see the way his eyes glared?'

'Didn't mind that so much as the bubbles,' said his companion with a shudder. 'If you ask me, you've gone too far.'

The corpse on the bottom of Shoreham Harbour did not

go far. It did not go any place at all, but remained where it was, held down by the rocks and nibbled by fish and crabs. Because of the cold water, it did not disintegrate or decompose rapidly and the features were still quite recognizable on April 20, over a month later.

Not of course that they would be recognized by any of the persons involved in the finding of the corpse, because they had never seen the young man while he was alive.

They were not very happy to see him after he was dead either.

'Bloody 'ell!' bawled the mate of the small coastal steamer. 'The flippin' screw's fouled on something!'

The observation, as might be expected from a professional seaman, was quite correct. The screw of the ship was fouled on something, a rope from the looks of it.

Being still in harbour, help was close at hand and presently a small boat rowed out and circled the stern of the ship and a frogman tumbled over the side to follow the rope tangled around the screw down into the depths.

A moment later he came arrowing back up, caught hold of the gunwale of the rowboat, spat out his mouthpiece and gasped, 'Jesus! There's a corpse down there! Call the police!'

The police were called and the body of the young man was brought up from the bottom of the harbour and laid out on the quay. He was a tall young man, a touch over six feet, and he had been rather handsome in the modern manner with long, thick, dark hair reaching to below his shoulders. He was dressed in blue jeans, a blue denim jacket and motorcycle boots.

He had been very firmly tied hand and foot with a length of three-quarter-inch manilla rope, and a plastic bag filled with stones and cement blocks was attached to his feet.

Detective Chief Superintendent James Marshall, Head of the Sussex Department of Criminal Investigations, had been notified and he soon arrived at the scene, bringing with him Police Pathologist Mr Hugh Malseworth Johnson who examined the body and stated that the cause of death appeared to be drowning, but that the body had been in the water for at least a month and it would be necessary to perform the autopsy before any other conclusions were reached.

Chief Superintendent Marshall had, however, already reached one conclusion and that was that this was a murder and a particularly savage and cold-blooded one. It was one thing to murder a man and toss his corpse into the sea, but it was quite another to weight a man down and throw him into the sea to drown. It was the sort of thing that people had once done to unwanted dogs and cats, but it wasn't even done to animals any more.

'I don't suppose you'd care to venture an opinion on whether he was conscious at the time?' he said.

Mr Johnson did not care to venture an opinion.

'I'll have more to say after the autopsy,' he said firmly. 'Only after the autopsy.'

Before having the body removed to the morgue for the autopsy, however, the superintendent had it photographed where it lay. It was not in very good shape and, being deprived of the refrigerating influence of the cold water, it appeared likely to break down rather rapidly. The photographs might well be the only hope of establishing its identity.

Identification was, of course, the first step in the investigation, for the identity of a murder victim often leads to the identification of the murderer. Few males are murdered by total strangers and a stranger would scarcely have gone to so much trouble to dispose of the corpse. Moreover, the cruel manner in which the young man had been killed tended to indicate a murderer with intense emotional motives rather than something impersonal such as robbery.

However, even with the photographs it was possible that identification would be difficult. The victim was young. His dress and hairstyle were trendy. Many such young men lived in a casual manner and without regular employment. What relatives they had might see them so infrequently that they would not even realize they were missing. The superintendent was not at all confident that he would find a corresponding Missing Person report in the files.

Nonetheless, there was one and it matched precisely the

description of the dead youth. It had been filed on March 2, 1973, by a Mrs Pauline Olive in the town of Hove, a scant four miles to the east along the coast.

The corpse was made as presentable as possible and Mrs Olive was brought to the morgue to view it. She immediately and tearfully identified it as the body of her son Clive Olive who had been sixteen years old at the time of his death.

According to her statement, Clive had left school at the age of fifteen and had attempted to enlist in the Navy. He had been refused because of a defect in his vision and had, for a time, done nothing in particular, spending his time hanging around the coffee bars in Brighton, Hove and Shoreham. The week before his disappearance on February 28 he had, however, obtained work in a bakery and had begun to talk about going back to school. This had pleased his mother, who described him as a good boy, but still not certain of what he wanted. She had last seen him on the afternoon of February 28 when he had left the house saying, 'Goodbye Mum. I'll see you later.'

Superintendent Marshall now sent his agents to check out the coffee bars in the three towns and also to check the bakery where Olive had worked.

The bakery provided no information as he had worked there for such a short time that he was hardly known and it was unlikely that anyone would have had such strong feelings about him as to murder him.

In the coffee bars, however, the officers began to pick up possible leads. A boy identified only as 'Ted' told the detectives that he had known Olive well, but had not seen him since the night of February 28 when he had been in a coffee bar in Church Road in Hove. He added that Olive, who was usually called Ollie, Clive or, inexplicably, Paul, had seemed worried and had muttered something about somebody who was going to beat him up.

Asked if he had any idea why someone would want to beat up Clive Olive, Ted replied that it might have been over a woman. Olive, he said, had not been able to keep quiet about any success he had with girls. If he had intercourse with a girl, he told everyone about it, naming names, describing how the girl looked naked, how she had made love and what she had said before, during and after. He thought that this habit might have made Olive unpopular in some quarters.

This appeared, to say the least, logical and the police found confirmation of the theory when, as the investigation continued, reports of such indiscretions on the part of Olive in connection with a girl named Doris began to surface.

At the same time, so did other facts. Clive Olive had, it seemed, not been quite as good a boy as his mother had believed him to be. He had been a small-time drugs dealer and, although apparently not addicted himself, had had the reputation of being able to obtain virtually anything for a price.

It also developed that he had been associated in one way or another with an informal youth organization known as the Hell's Angels Cougars or, alternatively, the Mad Dogs of Sussex.

The exact nature of the association was not entirely clear, but it was known that the Hell's Angels Cougars were motorcycle enthusiasts and the clothing and boots worn by Olive at the time of his death were similar to those favoured by the members of such groups.

In addition, a tattoo of the letters H.A.C. had been found on his right arm at the time of the autopsy and this was thought to represent the initial letters of the club known as the Hell's Angels Cougars.

Aside from the tattoo, the only important facts revealed by the autopsy were that Olive had definitely died of drowning, that the body had been in the water for over a month, presumably since the date of his disappearance on February 28, and that he had been savagely kicked and beaten not only with bare fists but with something resembling a policeman's club as well. There were cuts on his arms from the rope and Mr Johnson was of the opinion that he had been alive and conscious when thrown into the water.

Attempts were made to trace the rope and the plastic sack containing cement blocks and stones and it would eventually be learned that these had been taken from a building site and the demolition yard in Shoreham. In the meantime, however, they only tended to confirm the theory that Olive had been murdered by more than one person. In any case, it was almost certain that more than one person had taken part in disposing of the body as the weight would have been too much for even a very strong man.

The lead in connection with the girl named Doris proved more fruitful. A number of persons reported that Olive had boasted extensively of his sexual experiences with Doris and there had been gossip that a girl known as 'Butch' was angry over this as the girl in question was her brother's fiancée.

'Butch' was eventually traced and turned out to be eighteen-year-old Christine Dorn, born Christine Moore and married to twenty-seven-year-old Albert Edward Dorn. The brother who was supposedly engaged to Doris was twenty-one-year-old Brian Stephen Moore. Moore, his sister and Albert Dorn were all connected in one way or another to the Hell's Angels Cougars, but there was no evidence that any of them had known Clive Olive.

All of the leads were beginning to converge on the Hell's Angels Cougars and the police took into custody a number of the members of that group including Brian Moore and Christine and Albert Dorn.

Interrogation of the suspects produced the information that Moore had been on intimate terms with the girl known as Doris, but that at the time of the supposed affair with Olive, he had been absent picking fruit in Kent. Upon his return, he had gone around asking for information on Clive Olive and, in some cases, had paid for it.

There were reports that Moore had been extremely upset about what he termed the rape of his girl by Clive Olive and that he had threatened to 'get him'. This version of the affair was confirmed by Doris herself who stated that she had been a virgin up until the time that she was raped by Olive.

The motive for the murder was now established and the members of the Hell's Angels Cougars who had been taken into custody were released with the exception of Moore and the Dorns. Questioned individually, they eventually broke down and confessed to varying degrees of complicity in the murder.

Moore, in his statement, said that he had gone to Kent on a fruit-picking job and that, upon his return, he had asked his girl Doris if she still had her 'white wings'. This it seemed was a term meaning virginity.

Doris had replied that she had been raped, but, apparently, had not known the identity of the rapist and Moore had spent some forty pounds in an effort to learn who the man had been.

He could not, he said, forget the incident because it had given Doris complexes which interfered with their sex relations.

He accepted all responsibility for the murder and denied that his sister or Albert Dorn had had any part in it.

This agreed neither with the known facts nor with the statements of Mr and Mrs Dorn themselves and all three were brought to trial at Lewes Crown Court on November 27, 1973 with Mr Justice Thesiger presiding.

Mr Michael Eastham, acting as Prosecutor for the Crown, presented the case for the prosecution.

'The prosecution,' he said, 'will attempt to show that the defendant Moore was obsessed with the belief that his girl had been raped by the victim which is not to say that the defendant is a person of high moral character. Indeed, we propose to demonstrate quite the opposite.

'In his statement to the police he has said that he gave up his job to be with Doris and they had decided to become engaged, but he had felt that something was troubling her and he thought that this might be a former boyfriend of whom he had been told by a certain 'Dopey Joe'.

'He had, consequently, asked Doris directly if she had ever had intercourse with another man and she had replied that she had been raped.

'Having determined the identity of the alleged rapist, Moore resolved to "get" Olive or, at least, give him a beating.

'Still in his statement to the police, he said that on the day of the murder, February the twenty-eighth, nineteen hundred and seventy-three, he and the other two defendants took weights and a plastic sack from a construction site and a rope from a demolition yard. These objects were loaded into the Volkswagen van which belonged to Albert Dorn and they were later found by the police attached to the corpse of the victim.

'In his own words to the police, he said, "I thought I might lose my temper and kill Olive and I would then have to get rid of the body. The idea of attaching weights to it and throwing it in the sea came from the Mad Dogs who planned, at one time, to get rid of one of their leaders in this manner."

'He further stated that he punched Olive in the face and hit him with a truncheon which he had obtained while working as a guard. These actions took place in the back of the van driven by Albert Dorn with Mrs Dorn occupying the front seat next to him.

'Olive was crying and screaming and Dorn panicked, driving around Shoreham in an aimless manner, and Mrs Dorn became ill.

'Finally, Olive lost consciousness and Moore thought that he was dead. He tied him up with the rope, attached the sack of weights to his feet and Dorn drove to the waterfront.

'Moore took Olive's shoulders and Dorn carried the plastic sack of weights attached to his feet. When they reached the water, Dorn threw in the sack of weights and Moore simply let go of Olive's shoulders so that he was dragged in after it.

'Clive Olive was, however, still alive and conscious at this point for Moore says in his statement, "His eyes were open. Al said, 'Look, he's bobbing up and down.' It was the staring eyes that bothered me, but Al thought that the bubbles afterward were worse." '

The prosecutor was followed by Mr Johnson who testified concerning his examination of the corpse and outlined his reasons for believing that Olive had still been alive and conscious at the time he was thrown into the sea.

He was followed by Superintendent Marshall who

described the investigations which had led to the arrest and, subsequently, the confessions of the accused.

The defence, represented by Mr Felix Waley Q.C., then called as first witness the accused Brian Moore.

Questioned on his connections with the Mad Dogs of Sussex, Moore stated that he had joined the group in 1969, the same year that he had begun taking drugs. He had tried LSD, amphetamines, barbiturates, hashish and marijuana. He said that he had done this because he had broken off his relations with a girl and was feeling depressed.

Although this was not brought out during the trial, there were later published accounts that Moore had, at the time in question, attempted to commit suicide by entering a cage containing two leopards at a wild animal park where he was engaged as a trainer. The leopards had, apparently, not been hungry.

Asked if he were still taking drugs, Moore replied that he was not. He had, he said, met the girl named Doris and had found that he did not need drugs after that.

'Were you at any time separated from Doris?' asked the attorney for the defence.

'Yes,' said Moore. 'I went to Kent to pick fruit.'

'And what took place upon your return?' said Mr Waley.

'I went to see Doris and the first thing I asked her was if she still had her white wings,' said Moore. 'She said she had been raped.

'We talked about this a lot and I knew she was telling the truth. I was furious and I wanted to kill whoever had done it because I loved her with all my heart and whatever happens I always will.

'Later, I spent about forty pounds trying to find out who had raped my girl and I was finally given the name of Clive Olive.'

'How did Doris convince you that she had really been raped?' asked Mr Waley.

'We went to the hotel where it happened and took the same room,' said Moore. 'When we entered the room, she was able to convince me. I burned my Hell's Angels jacket and she burned the clothes she had been wearing.'

'What did you decide to do about Olive?' said Mr Waley.

'I decided to kill him.'

'How did you arrange that?'

'I met him on the night of February the twenty-seventh and we talked about drugs. I arranged to meet him on the following night.'

'Will you tell the court, in your own words, what happened that night of February twenty-eighth when you met Clive Olive?' said Mr Waley. 'Take as much time as you need.'

'My sister, Christine, and her husband, Albert Dorn, were with me,' said Moore. 'Al was driving the van and Christine was in the front seat with him.'

Moore paused and looked almost questioningly at the other two defendants. After a moment, he continued.

'Olive was in the back with me and I asked him if he knew a girl named Doris. He said no and I asked him again. He still said no and I said, "The one you raped, you bastard!" He still said he didn't know her and then he admitted that he had raped her.

'I was boiling with rage, furious. He struck out at me and I caught it on my left and hit him with my right. It slammed him up against the side of the van.

'We'd been parked, but when I hit him, Al got nervous and started to drive around. I was fighting with Olive in the back and I thought I'd killed him.'

'With your bare fists?' asked Mr Waley.

'I kicked him and hit him with a truncheon on the head, the hands, the body, any place. I was berserk. I thought I'd killed him.'

'Why did you think that?' asked Mr Waley.

'His eyes were staring and, when I took his pulse behind the knee like I'd been taught with animals, I couldn't find any.'

'You have heard the testimony of the pathologist that Clive Olive was alive and conscious at the time he entered the water,' said Mr Waley. 'What is your reaction?'

'I am shocked,' said Moore. 'I truly thought he was dead.'

'Continue with your account,' said Mr Waley. 'What happened then?'

'I told Al to drive to the harbour,' said Moore. 'I was angry because I hadn't found out what I wanted to know and the only person who could tell me was dead.

'I tied up his hands and feet and I fastened the sack of stones and blocks to his legs. Al backed the van up to the water and I dropped him in and kicked the sack of weights in after him.'

'Didn't you realize what you were doing was wrong?' said Mr Waley.

'I don't feel I have done anything wrong,' said Moore. 'I knew it was against the law, but what he did was against the law too. He raped my girl. Nobody else was going to do anything about that so I had to.'

The counsel for the defence terminated the questioning and moved that the charge be altered from murder to manslaughter on the grounds that the drugs taken by the accused had damaged his brain.

The cross examination was taken up by the prosecutor who wanted to know why he had felt it his duty to kill Olive.

Moore replied that it was so he would not rape any more girls.

The prosecutor then suggested that Moore had not committed the murder by himself, but had been assisted by his sister and brother-in-law.

Moore denied this, saying that Christine had had nothing to do with the murder and that Albert Dorn had only driven the van.

'You say,' said the prosecutor, 'that your motive for killing this boy was that he had sexual relations with your girl. Does this mean that you never had relations with her yourself?'

'No,' said Moore. 'It doesn't mean that. Doris and I made love but, because of what Olive had done, it was spoiled.'

Asked to explain, he said that, on one occasion, they had got into the same position in which Doris had been raped and that this had upset her very much so that everything was spoiled.

Questioned further about their relations, he said that they had taken no precautions as both he and Doris wanted a baby. He was opposed to the anti-baby pill as he had heard that it could produce deformities in the children later. Doris had taken the Pill in order to reassure her mother, but she had kept it under her tongue and had spit it out afterwards. She had, however, not become pregnant.

'Was Doris happy about what you had done to Olive?' said Mr Eastham.

'I don't know,' said Moore. 'We often talked about suicide. If the police got too close, we were going to jump off the cliffs at Peacehaven.'

'You have told this court that you have stopped using drugs,' said the prosecutor, 'but is it not true that you still use them?'

'You shut your mouth or I'll belt you one, mate!' shouted Moore and, seizing a water bottle which was standing on the witness stand, he swung it up over his head.

Two prison officers sitting in the dock rushed forward and, after a brief struggle, Moore was overpowered and disarmed. The trial then continued.

The next witness called by the defence was Dr Arthur Williams, a psychiatrist, who stated that he had spoken with Moore on the subject of his use of drugs and that he was satisfied that his statements concerning the use of LSD and other drugs were essentially correct.

Mr Waley asked if the use of such drugs could bring about abnormalities in the personality.

'My conclusions concerning Brian Moore,' said Dr Williams, 'were that he displayed an obsessional, paranoid and somewhat psychotic personality. It would appear that he suffers from certain mental abnormalities which would have an effect on his actions. This condition may have been aggravated by the use of LSD. I think that his concept of reality has been altered through use of the drug and he may experience difficulty in distinguishing between reality and fantasy.'

'Was he insane to the point where he did not realize that

what he was doing was wrong?' interposed Mr Justice Thesiger.

'In my opinion, he was sane,' said Dr Williams. 'He knew what he was doing was wrong, but he was unable to control himself. The impulse was irresistible. He could not overcome his grievance which became worse and worse until he reached a state where, I think, it was either kill Olive or commit suicide.'

The psychiatrist was then cross-examined by the prosecution who wanted to know if, in his opinion, Moore's conduct prior to the murder was such as to warrant his detention in a mental institution.

Dr Williams replied that, had Moore been his patient, he would have attempted to have him committed.

Dr Williams was followed by another psychiatrist, Dr Peter Noble, who testified concerning his interviews with Moore's parents. He had, he said, been a timid child and easily bullied.

'Moore does not seem to have been a very good Hell's Angel,' he concluded. 'He was always on the fringe. His character was made up of two opposing forces, the tough Hell's Angel on the one hand, and a man with a great love for animals on the other.'

Albert Dorn was then called to the witness stand and gave the following account of the events leading up to the death of Clive Olive.

'Brian was convinced that Olive had raped his girl,' he said. 'I was driving and they were in the back of the van. I could hear Brian say, "I'm going to give you a good hiding for what you did," and then he started hitting him.

'The boy was screaming and Christine started to cry. I didn't know what to do so I drove along the waterfront. I thought the traffic might make Brian stop.

'However, it didn't make any difference and, when I looked in the back, Brian had tied him up and fastened the sack of weights to his feet. He told me to drive to the harbour.

'I backed the van up and Brian carried him down and

threw him in. I thought he was dead. There were no screams or anything. Just a lot of bubbles.

'I told Brian, "I think you have gone too far." '

Mr Eastham took up the cross-examination of the defendant.

'Is it not correct,' he said, 'that your wife, Christine, was seated in the van during the time that all this was taking place?'

Dorn replied that she was, but, upon being asked if she knew what was happening, he replied that he did not know.

He was then asked if Mrs Dorn had seen the weights and rope being put into the van and replied in the affirmative. He also admitted that his wife had been the first person to speak to Olive on the night in question.

'I suggest,' said Mr Eastham, 'that your wife, the third defendant in this case, played an important part in the crime. I suggest that she was the bait with which the victim was lured to his death.'

'That is not true,' protested Dorn. 'She was only in the van because she did not want to be left alone.'

The summing up began on December 4, 1973 and the defence based its case on a supposed temporary or permanent drug-induced mental incompetence of the chief defendant, Brian Moore.

'The murder of this sixteen-year-old boy,' said Mr Waley, 'was performed in a manner displaying all the earmarks of a madman. It was a crime which arose from an insane obsession haunting a deranged mind and it was carried out with the ruthless cunning and remorseless cruelty of a maniac for a reason which could exist only in insanity.

'I ask you to find the defendant, Brian Moore, not guilty of murder by reason of diminished responsibility, but guilty of manslaughter instead.'

The plea was not successful. After six and a half hours of deliberations, the all-male jury found Brian Moore and Albert Dorn guilty of murder and Christine Dorn guilty of manslaughter.

While sentencing the two men to life imprisonment, Mr Justice Thesiger said that he was convinced that no one had minded in the least whether Clive Olive was alive or dead at the time that he was thrown into Shoreham harbour. The case was, he added, that of a most horrible murder.

He then turned his attention to Christine Dorn who had, four months previously, given birth to a child while in detention awaiting trial.

'I feel,' he said, 'that you are deeply implicated in this crime and that you were instrumental in luring the victim. I am certain that you exercised a comparatively strong influence on the other two defendants.

'I hereby sentence you to ten years' imprisonment.'

Christine Dorn responded by fainting dead away and it was some time before she could be revived and led back to the cells. As she left the court room, she turned and screamed, 'You bastard!' at the judge.

In order to avoid embarrassment to an innocent person, the name of Brian Moore's girlfriend has been altered.

5

FROZEN STIFF

It was three o'clock in the morning of New Year's Day, 1971 and Werner Schmidt was driving home to Bensburg with Mrs Schmidt sound asleep beside him in the front seat. Like all good Germans, the Schmidts had celebrated the New Year thoroughly and with enthusiasm.

It was for this reason that Werner was driving the big Mercedes rather cautiously over the snow-covered country road running from Hennef, where the celebrating had taken place, to Much, where another secondary road led off to the north-west and Bensburg.

The way was round about and the roads were not particularly good, but the fast, direct autobahn which led north from Siegburg to pass between Cologne and Bensburg might be dangerous, firstly because of the drunks who would be driving on it and secondly because of the traffic police.

Werner Schmidt suspected that he had taken on enough alcohol to cost him his driver's licence if he were to be picked up now.

His choice of route had, however, been fortunate. There had not been a single other car on the road since leaving Hennef.

The car rolled smoothly through the village of Neunkirchen in which not a light burned. The next village, he knew, would be Wohlfahrt and then, Much.

It was a dark night. There was no moon and the stars glittered like the tips of icicles against the blackness of the sky. A bitterly cold wind swept occasional eddies of snow across the macadam. The temperature was five degrees above zero. Inside the car, however, it was warm and cosy and Werner Schmidt was troubled by drowsiness.

He had just stretched out a hand to turn down the heating when the headlights picked up the figure beside the road. Schmidt's drowsiness vanished and was replaced by astonishment. For an instant, his foot lifted from the gas pedal and the Mercedes slowed.

Then, the foot descended again and the big car surged forward.

'Elsie!' called Schmidt, prodding his sleeping wife in the ribs with an elbow. 'Did you see that?'

'I don't see anything,' grumbled Mrs Schmidt, reluctantly half-opening a bleary eye.

'A man,' said Schmidt. 'A naked man. Standing beside the road and jumping up and down as if he was crazy.'

'Probably is too,' said Mrs Schmidt. 'Bunch of drunken kids. Keep your eyes on the road.' With which she promptly fell asleep again.

Behind the car in the flurry of fine snow thrown up by its passing, the strange figure stood motionless now, the high wail of its voice dying despairingly away. Tears were running from its eyes and freezing onto its cheeks.

The point was almost exactly half way between Neunkirchen and Wohlfahrt. There would not be another car until five in the morning.

The car which passed then was travelling south from Wohlfahrt in the direction of Siegburg where Hans-Dieter Mueller would be going to work on the early morning shift of a steel mill which cared nothing about New Year's Day or any other holiday.

The figure was not hopping now, but lay stretched in the snow beside the road.

Mueller saw it, but he did not stop. The place was lonely, it was still completely dark and he feared some kind of a trap. Such things are not unknown in Europe.

He did, however, do more than Werner Schmidt had done. He turned the car around and drove back to Wohlfahrt where he roused the local constable out of bed and reported the matter.

'Why the devil didn't you stop and help him?' demanded

Constable Gunther Weber. 'I could charge you with failing to assist a person in danger.'

'I didn't think it was safe,' said Mueller. 'I have to go to work.'

He left and Weber quickly dressed and set out in the police car for the place indicated. At five-thirty-four, as would be stated in his official report, he came upon the body of a young man lying beside the road.

The man was wearing only undershorts and his feet were bound together with baling wire. The body was cold and rigid and he was dead.

The discovery left Weber in something of a quandary. In Germany, village constables do not handle murder cases and this was, in his opinion, murder. He could think of no other explanation.

It was therefore essential that the Criminal Police in Cologne be advised immediately and equally essential that nothing at the scene of the crime be disturbed until they had arrived.

Although his car was equipped with a radio-telephone, there was no one in Wohlfahrt to answer it at this hour and he was not equipped to raise Cologne direct.

However, if he drove into Neunkirchen or Wohlfahrt to telephone, someone could very well come by and move the body in a well-intended attempt to help or by trampling around in the snow destroy important clues.

Someone, it seemed, had already been there for there were footprints in the snow leading from the edge of the road to the body. Mueller had, however, stated that he had not got out of his car.

He was standing pondering this problem when, to his astonishment, a police car appeared from the direction of Neunkirchen and came to a halt beside his own.

Three men in plain clothes got out and advanced on the constable.

'Inspector Karl Josef, Cologne Criminal Police,' said one of the men. 'We have a report of a possible homicide here.'

'Constable Weber, Wohlfahrt,' said the constable, slightly confused. 'Is your report from a Hans-Dieter Mueller?'

The inspector shook his head. 'An Adolf Meindorf,' he said. 'He's the bus driver on the Much–Hennef line. He and one of his passengers discovered the body and called us from Neunkirchen.'

'That explains the footprints,' said Weber. 'The driver who reported to me didn't get out of his car.'

While they had been speaking, the other two men from the Cologne police car had gone over to where the body lay and one of them had begun an examination of the corpse.

The inspector walked over to join them.

'Well, Armin?' he said.

Dr Armin Baumgartner, the department's medical expert, got a little heavily to his feet and began brushing the snow from his trousers.

'Homicide,' he said briefly. 'Murder by freezing. He's been beaten, but the cause of death is freezing. He's been dead for several hours now.'

The second man had been examining the marks in the snow.

'There's a trail here leading into the trees, chief,' he said, pointing to the open forest which began some ten yards from the road.

'See where it leads to, Franz,' said the inspector. 'If it goes on for a long way, come back and we'll get a party with dogs out here.'

The trail did not go very far.

'He was tied to a tree about two hundred yards from the road,' called the sergeant, coming back to the edge of the forest. 'Do you want to come and take a look?'

The inspector, the doctor and Constable Weber all went to look, walking carefully in the footprints left by Sergeant Moench.

'See?' said the sergeant. 'There's the tree he was tied to and there are some of the pieces of baling wire he was tied up with. He was apparently able to get loose from the tree and get the wire off his hands, but by then his hands were too cold to get the wire off his feet so he hopped to the road.'

'He was probably exposed here for some time before he could get free,' said the doctor, studying the hop marks in the snow. 'You can see how his strength was failing. The further he went the shorter the hops and there are several places here where he fell.'

'It's a wonder he even made it to the road,' said the sergeant. 'The temperature couldn't have been much above zero out here last night. And then he had the rotten luck that not a single car came along until it was too late. A strange sort of murder, isn't it chief?'

'A cruel murder,' said the inspector. 'The cruellest murder I have ever experienced or even heard of in all my time with the police. It should be easy to solve.'

The sergeant looked at him in astonishment. 'Why do you say that?' he asked.

'A man could not have more than one enemy who hated him so bitterly,' said the inspector simply. 'Once we have the identity of the victim, I think the identity of the murderer will be obvious.'

In this, however, he was gravely mistaken.

The identity of the victim was established easily enough. He was an electrician named Ulrich Nacken who had not come home on New Year's morning and had been promptly reported missing by his parents who feared an automobile accident.

Nacken, who came from Cologne, had just bought his first car in December. He was only eighteen years old.

'Well, so much for theories,' sighed the inspector. 'A boy of eighteen has hardly lived long enough to acquire such deadly enemies. I don't know what to think.'

'The murder was almost professional,' said the sergeant. 'We went over the whole area thoroughly, screened the snow around the tree. Not a thing. No trace of his clothing. No trace of the car.'

'You put out a description of the car to the highway patrol?' said the inspector.

The sergeant nodded. 'Nineteen sixty-six Ford, seventeen-M,' he said. 'Medium grey with a black rose painted on the trunk. The licence number is K-HM 943. Not a valuable car and Nacken didn't have much money on him either, according to the parents. He spent it all on the car.'

'A sad thing,' remarked the inspector. 'I talked to the parents and the picture I got was of a clean, serious, hard-working boy, not one to be mixed up with a tough crowd of any kind. Of course, that's the parents' version so it might be a little on the favourable side. I've got a list of his friends that I want you to check out. See if he was in any kind of trouble and also see if you can find out where he hung out normally. He could have left whatever place it was with his murderers.'

'There was more than one?' said the sergeant.

'Arnim says so,' said the inspector. 'He was hit in the face with two different size fists.'

'Did the autopsy show anything else?' said the sergeant.

'Well, he fixed the time of death at approximately four-thirty,' said the inspector, 'and the stomach contents showed a normal dinner and approximately two bottles of beer. Arnim thinks he was beaten up and tied to the tree shortly after midnight. It's important therefore that we find the last place he was seen.'

This did not turn out to be very difficult. Ulrich Nacken had had a large number of friends, young men and girls of his own age, and they agreed unanimously that his favourite spot when he was not working was the Toeff-Toeff Discotheque in Cologne.

'Incidentally,' said the sergeant, reporting on this matter to the inspector, 'his friends agree with his parents' assessment of his character. He was a clean, serious, hard-working boy and nobody I spoke to could believe that he had any enemies.'

'I know the Toeff-Toeff,' said the inspector. 'It's a pretty harmless place. Did you check on whether he was there the night he was killed?'

'Yes,' said the sergeant. 'He was. A lot of people there know him. They say he left shortly before midnight and alone.'

'Then he must have been picked up almost immediately after he left the place,' said the inspector. 'Could have been some kind of a stick-up trap. Girl standing beside the road waving for help and when he stopped a couple of accomplices jumped out of the bushes. It's happened before.'

'It happens all the time,' said the sergeant, 'which is why people are reluctant to stop and help someone in distress now.

'On the other hand, why Nacken? His car wasn't new or worth much and anyone only had to look at him to see that he wasn't likely to be carrying much money.'

'True,' said the inspector, leaning his long, lean body back in the swivel chair. 'And then there's the savagery of the crime. Robbers might have killed him to avoid being identified later, but they wouldn't bother to strip him and tie him to a tree and all that business. I find it hard to believe that there wasn't a personal element in the killing.'

'So do I,' said the sergeant, 'but I don't know what it would be. Frankly, I don't know where we go from here.'

'I've assigned a stake-out for the spot where he was found,' said the inspector.

The sergeant looked startled. 'The murderers returning to the scene of the crime?' he said sceptically. 'That's only in detective stories.'

'Well, perhaps, but you must also consider that we've kept all news of this out of the papers. No one knows that Nacken is dead except the police, his parents and the persons you questioned. The murderers are almost surely not from any of these groups and I would think they must be growing curious. After all, someone could have come along, Nacken could have survived and the police could be in possession of a good description of the attempted murderers. If I were in their position, I'd want to know.'

The sergeant thought this over. 'It's logical,' he said finally, 'but I'm still more inclined to think that it was someone who knew Nacken well enough to check on whether he survived or not without going back there. For example, they could simply wait at his place of work and see if he turned up. Or they could call his home and ask for him.'

'You might check with the parents and see if anyone has called,' said the inspector. 'However, if your theory is correct then there would have been a motive. Any idea where to look for it?'

'Not really,' said the sergeant. 'All I can think of is the Toeff-Toeff. Whatever contacts he had, he had them there.'

'Go to it,' said the inspector. 'We have to follow any line of investigation that we can.'

The sergeant left the office and was not seen again until the following evening when he returned just as the inspector was preparing to leave for home.

'I think I have a possible motive in the Nacken case,' said the sergeant.

The inspector, who had been reaching for his overcoat, drew back his hand and returned to his desk.

'Yes?' he said.

'Nacken may have been mixed up in drugs,' said the sergeant. 'There are a couple of characters named Abie Frankenthal and Klaus Harker who sometimes hang out in the Toeff-Toeff. They're both pushers. Never been arrested, but Narcotics carries a file on them. They were drinking beer with Nacken the night he was murdered.'

The inspector considered. 'Pretty feeble,' he commented finally. 'Granted, the men are pushers. Granted, they were drinking beer with Nacken the night he was murdered. But, even so, that doesn't automatically implicate them as murderers. What would have been their motive? Professional criminals like that don't kill anyone unless they have to, and then they go about it more directly.'

'The only thing that's occurred to me is that Nacken may have been double-crossing them,' said the sergeant. 'I've been talking to Narcotics and they say that the reason that Frankenthal and Harker haven't been busted before is that they don't make the actual sales themselves. They supply a ring of teenage pushers who do the actual selling and take the risk. Could be that Nacken was one of them and didn't come across with the money so they decided to make an example of him.'

'It's possible,' admitted the inspector. 'And it would explain the cruelty of the murder, but wouldn't Nacken have had to be an addict in that case? Arnim didn't say anything about indications of drug addiction in the autopsy and he would have if they were there.'

'Narcotics says most of the kids are addicts, but some of them are doing it just for the money,' said the sergeant. 'He needn't have had to be an addict. On the other hand, Narcotics also has sources of information on these kids and they say no one is spooked or even seems to know that Nacken is dead. Unless they did, it wouldn't be much of an example.'

'That could be explained by the fact that there's been no publicity on the murder yet,' said the inspector. 'Whoever the murderers are, they wouldn't be stupid enough to go around telling people that they'd cruelly murdered Nacken. They'd wait for it to come out in the newspapers.'

'I suppose so,' agreed the sergeant. 'You want me to bring in Frankenthal and Harker for questioning?'

'Why not?' said the inspector. 'Even if it doesn't do anything else, it may throw a scare into them about their drug pushing.'

The inspector and his assistant left the office and went home. It was past seven in the evening and already pitch dark. Twenty miles to the east, the day shift of the police stake-out in the forest between Wohlfahrt and Neunkirchen where Ulrich Nacken had died was just approaching the end of their duty.

Sitting inside the police car, parked just off the road and screened by a copse of young firs, were two very junior patrolmen named Arnold Klein and Leopold Brettweiler.

They were not very happy with their duty, and they were cold. The only way that it would have been possible to heat the car would have been to leave the motor running and this was not permitted.

'Fifty-six more minutes,' said Brettweiler, looking at his wrist watch. 'I wonder how many more years we're going to spend out here in the woods? I thought when I got off foot patrol, I'd have it made.'

'Cheer up,' said his partner, who was behind the wheel. 'Soon it will be spring and we can take sun baths and pick flowers. We can bring along some sausages and roast them over a camp fire and then, as autumn descends . . .'

'Oh shut up,' said Brettweiler. 'You say things like that, they could come true. Besides . . . Holy Moses!'

'Holy Moses?' said Klein.

'Look! Look!' whispered Brettweiler. 'There it is! The grey Ford!'

Out on the highway, a car was cruising slowly past.

'It's a Ford, all right,' said Klein, 'and it looks like a sixty-six. But I can't see the colour.'

He switched on the ignition.

'It's grey!' insisted Brettweiler. 'Watch for the licence plate when he gets past.'

The car was now abreast of them and as it moved slowly on past, both patrolmen could plainly see the lighted numbers, K-HM 943.

Klein let out the clutch and his thumb descended on the button of the siren. With a snarl like a starving tomcat, the police car lunged out into the highway, the siren rising in an urgent scream and the blue Martin's light on the roof revolving and flashing.

The driver of the grey Ford floored the gas pedal and pulled rapidly away from them. The police car with its cold engine sputtered and misfired as Klein nursed it through the gears.

'Get his tyres!' yelled Klein. 'He's going to run away from us altogether!'

Brettweiler drew his service pistol and leaning out of the window, emptied the magazine in the direction of the fleeing car.

With his first shot, the car's lights went out.

'You never touched him!' shouted Klein. 'Watch if he turns off. He's doused his lights and he's going to break into one of the side roads. If we miss him, he'll give us the slip.'

Off the highway were a number of smaller roads leading back into the forest. Some of these went on through and joined up with other roads and some were no more than logging tracks ending in a few thousand or even few hundred yards.

The Ford was now some considerable distance ahead and still gaining. It could, however, be seen as a black, fleeting shadow against the snow-covered shoulders of the road.

'There! There he goes!' shouted Brettweiler. 'He swung in to the right!'

'Are you sure?' yelled Klein, torn with the necessity of an instant decision. 'If you're wrong . . .'

'He went right!' insisted Brettweiler, snapping his reserve cartridge clip into the pistol.

The entrance to the forest road loomed up on the right, Klein slammed on the brakes, fought the wheel around and the police car plunged into it with screaming tyres. Gunning the motor, he shot the car down the double track and around a curve – and slammed on the brakes again just in time to avoid crashing into the back of the grey Ford, its nose buried in a snowdrift.

The driver of the Ford had made a bad mistake. The road he had chosen was a logging road and led nowhere.

He was now trying to struggle out of the driver's seat, a tall, dark and remarkably handsome man, but his overcoat had caught on the door handle and he could not free himself immediately.

'Stand where you are!' roared Brettweiler, piling out of the police car with the pistol in his hand. 'Hands over your head!'

The man sullenly complied.

'There must have been two of them,' said Klein, getting out of the car. 'The passenger side door is open and here are tracks.' He turned to the prisoner. 'Was there someone with you?' he demanded.

The prisoner did not answer.

'Never mind,' said Klein. 'He won't get far. And, just to make certain that you don't try anything, . . .' He produced his handcuffs and handcuffed the prisoner to the steering wheel of the Ford.

'Do you think we should try and follow the other one, Arnie?' said Brettweiler.

Klein shook his head. 'I'm going to get on the radio now and raise Cologne. They'll come out with a party and dogs and they'll have him in no time. If we go running around out there in the dark, there's no telling what might happen. See if our silent friend here has any kind of identification on him.'

Brettweiler went through the man's pockets and came up with an identity card.

'Yugoslav,' he said. 'Maybe that's why he doesn't answer. He can't speak German. The name's Slobodan Vucetic, aged twenty-seven, construction worker. And here's something else. A driver's licence in the name of Ulrich Nacken and the ownership papers to the car.'

At five minutes to eight that evening the inspector and Sergeant Moench were torn from their television sets by the news that the stake-out had made an arrest. At least one more man had fled and a search party with tracking dogs was being got together at the station. The dispatcher wanted to know if the inspector would be taking personal charge.

The inspector would. Ten minutes after the call, Sergeant Moench picked him up in his private car and the officers drove to the scene of the arrest.

Slobodan Vucetic was still handcuffed to the steering wheel of the Ford and the police search party had just set off into the woods, led by two tracking dogs on leash. The dogs were hardly necessary as the footprints could be easily followed with a flashlight.

'Well, is this our murderer?' said the inspector, walking up to Vucetic.

'He doesn't speak German, inspector,' said Klein.

Vucetic promptly made him a liar.

'Simic kill boy!' he said in broken German, speaking for the first time. 'I no hurt boy. Simic kill boy.'

'Is Simic the man who was with you?' said the inspector.

Vucetic nodded. 'He also Slobodan, Slobodan Simic. He kill boy. I no do nothing.'

'We'll see,' said the inspector. 'Take him down to headquarters and book him on suspicion of murder. We'll bring the other one in when the party gets back with him.'

The inspector was obviously not expecting a long wait and he did not have one. In less than an hour the search party returned with Slobodan Simic who the dogs had found hiding in a rack of hay, put out by the forestry department for feeding deer.

He corroborated Vucetic's statements completely with only a slight difference in detail.

Vucetic, he said, had killed Ulrich Nacken. He, personally, had done nothing.

Simic was only twenty-two years old and he was badly frightened. By the time he had reached the police station, he had already implicated still a third Yugoslav, twenty-nine-year-old Vjekoslav Potkonjac.

A team of detectives was dispatched to his address and soon brought him to headquarters where he added his voice to the mutual accusations and denials of personal guilt.

The confusion did not last long. The inspector was very skilled and very experienced in sorting out the true statements from the false and none of the Yugoslavs was particularly clever.

Long before midnight, Slobodan Vucetic and Slobodan Simic had confessed to the actual crime, exonerating Potkonjac who had been present, but who had not taken part.

Determining the guilt proved to be the simplest part, for the motive was so tenuous that the inspector feared a jury might not believe it. Strictly speaking, there had been no motive at all, not even the one of stealing Nacken's car. All of the Yugoslavs earned more money than Ulrich Nacken did and could easily have afforded better cars. Queried as to their reasons for murdering the young electrician, they seemed puzzled themselves. It was, they said, just something that happened.

'We were in Toeff-Toeff,' said Vucetic. 'We drink three, four beer. Not drunk. Little happy. After, we come out, there is boy. He is getting into car. Simic say, "I have girlfriend in Siegburg. We take car. Go Siegburg."

'I put knife on boy's throat. Simic look in back of car and find wire. We tie up boy and put him in trunk. Then, we go Siegburg.'

After visiting Simic's girlfriend in Siegburg, the three Yugoslavs, for no reason that any of them could explain, had decided to get rid of Ulrich Nacken by leaving him in the woods and had driven to the point half-way between Wohlfahrt and Neunkirchen where they had tied him to the tree.

'We take clothes first,' said Vucetic. 'He didn't like so we hit him a little. Then, we tie to tree and go away.'

'You understood that he would die there within a short time, did you not?' said the inspector who was anxious to establish premeditation and deliberation in the crime.

'We know,' said Vucetic. 'Then, I look newspaper every day. No boy in woods. I think, "They still no find or he get away?" He get away, maybe more better go back Yugoslavia. Simic say, "We go look." '

'We go look. We get caught.'

The following morning the story, which had been suppressed up until now, appeared in all the newspapers and that afternoon Werner Schmidt called the newspaper in Cologne to say that he had apparently been the last person to see Nacken alive. He was prepared to grant an interview and, if they liked, they could take a picture of him at the scene.

The newspaper, which was more aware of the legal implications of this publicity, informed the police and immediately following his interview Schmidt was arrested and charged with failing to assist a person in danger, a serious offence under German law.

He was eventually tried, found guilty and sentenced to six months imprisonment and a fine of three thousand marks.

Slobodan Vucetic, Slobodan Simic and Vjekoslav Potkonjac were brought to trial on November 30, 1971, found guilty of premeditated murder without extenuating circumstances and sentenced to life imprisonment in all three cases.

6

MAD DOG!

Paris is a state of mind.

For the romantic, it is Montmartre, la Rive Gauche and the Boul Miche.

For the tourist, it is Notre Dame, the Tour Eiffel and the Champs-Elysées.

For the millions who each morning and evening pack the Metro on their way to and from the offices, shops and factories, it is more often than not the dreary, concrete forest of apartment houses rising in shoddy, concentric rings around the City of Light.

Paris grows. With every passing year, more of the charming little villages of the Ile de France are swallowed up by the irresistible concrete waves and one such village, some ten miles to the west of Paris, is Villennes on the Seine.

During the week, Villennes is practically deserted. The men and many of the women are at work and the children, except for the very small, are at school. Villennes is quiet, almost peaceful. Sunday is, however, something else. Everyone is home. The children play and yell in the streets. Adolescents race the motors of their motorcycles. Radios blare.

Whatever the good Lord may have intended, Sunday in Villennes is not a day of rest. And September 16, 1973 was a Sunday, an overcast, rainy Sunday where the normal possibilities of escape such as a walk in the surrounding country or an excursion to other less depressing places were lacking.

At approximately eleven o'clock in the morning the residents of the apartment house at 16, rue Clemenceau were startled by the sounds of pistol shots or, at least, what sounded like pistol shots.

A number of the less cautious tenants rushed out into the halls and within a matter of minutes the door to the ground floor apartment of forty-five-year-old René Maréchal and his forty-two-year-old wife, Nanette, was discovered to be standing open.

In the little entrance hall inside, the bodies of the Maréchals lay sprawled on the floor, René with a bullet through the right eye which had penetrated into his brain, killing him instantly, and Nanette, mortally wounded in the chest and abdomen.

She was still alive as the neighbours bent over her and she managed to gasp out, 'Grasso! He's mad! He rang the bell and started shooting. Help René. He's . . .'

The blood gushed from her nose and mouth and she died.

In the meantime, someone had already called the ambulance, and the emergency services of the Paris region being excellent as the result of much practice, it soon arrived.

A medical intern had come with it and he conducted a brief examination of the Maréchals and pronounced them dead.

'Has anyone called the police?' he asked. 'I'd advise you all to stay away from the bodies. The Criminal Investigations people don't like it when they've been disturbed. Were there any witnesses?'

There had been no witnesses apparently, but several of the neighbours had heard Mrs Maréchal gasp out the name of Grasso before she died and they said as much. They also indicated the door of the apartment next door, with the name Santo Grasso written with pencil on a scrap of paper and stuck beneath the bell with scotch tape. Then they all backed away, apparently believing that the intern would rush in and arrest the suspect.

The intern, of course, did no such thing, but lit a cigarette and went out to the ambulance to call the police. This action, or lack of it, apparently gave rise to some thought, for the people nearest the door to Grasso's apartment began to disperse and by the time the police arrived there was no one in the hall. Two of the neighbours who had heard Mrs Maréchal accuse Grasso of the murders were, however, waiting with the intern at the front door.

As in all big cities, the report of a homicide in Paris sets in motion a huge and complex machine of which the parts are patrol cars, radio-telephone dispatchers, technicians, finger-print and weapons experts, specialists in forensic medicine and criminal investigations officers.

The spearhead of this small army of men and women is, in almost all cases, the patrol car for the simple reason that there is usually one within a few blocks of the scene of the report. The patrol car's most important function is to determine that a crime has actually taken place.

This was easily ascertained by the two young patrolmen from the car which arrived at 16, rue Clemenceau and, upon being informed that the presumed murderer was in the apartment next door, one of the patrolmen drew his service pistol and took up station at the corner of the hall where he could cover the doorway to Grasso's apartment while the other went back to the patrol car to report to headquarters.

After a moment or two he returned, drew his gun and took up a position next to his partner.

'Charge room officer authorizes use of firearms if necessary,' he said. 'We're not to disturb him, but wait. Headquarters is sending out the specialists.'

The officers were calm, efficient and very wary. It is the only way to remain alive as a police officer in a city the size of Paris.

The specialists arrived promptly in a small, fast van containing six men and enough sophisticated weapons to overthrow the governments of a number of smaller states.

While three of the men took up positions covering the windows outside the house, the leader, a stocky, cat-faced man in his forties, went directly to the door of the Grasso apartment, the remaining two men fanning out to left and right with their automatic weapons at the ready.

The leader, whose name was Jules Lacat, was wearing complete body armour, a protective helmet and a face shield.

The full-automatic machine pistol lay easily along his right forearm, his finger resting lightly on the trigger.

Using his left hand, he pressed the doorbell, waited a moment and then called out in a loud voice, 'Criminal Police. Open the door and come out slowly with your hands over your head.'

There was no sound from the apartment.

Lucat tested the knob and finding the door locked, stepped back, jerking his head to the men on his left and right.

There was the deafening rattle of automatic weapons fire within the narrow confines of the hall and a torrent of lead ripped through the door, tearing out sections of the panels and smashing the lock to pieces.

The squad leader kicked the remains of the door back against the wall and went through, the machine pistol now held in both hands at waist height.

Behind him, his men moved in to either side of the door.

There was no sound within the apartment and, a few moments later, Lucat reappeared, working the slide of the machine pistol to throw the live round out of the chamber.

'Nobody home,' he said emotionlessly.

'Zut!' said a tall man with a spiky black moustache, who had been waiting just inside the front door. 'In you go, François. See if you can turn up a picture for the pick-up order.'

A slightly-built, young man with sandy-brown hair and sharp features, dashed into the apartment.

'Can I take the ambulance back now?' said the intern to the man with the moustache.

'Why not?' said Inspector Pierre Dupont, Senior Investigations Officer of the Paris Criminal Police. 'We will arrange for transport of the bodies to the morgue. Do you have any information on the case?'

'None,' said the intern and left.

Detective-Sergeant François Renard came out of the apartment with a number of photographs in his hands.

'This is him,' said the sergeant. 'One of these is his

Foreigners' Registration Card. Santo Grasso, aged thirty-eight and an Italian citizen. Comes from Sicily.'

The inspector sighed. 'They all do,' he said. 'Call head-quarters and give them the description. General pick-up order to all units. Detain and hold. Dangerous. Presumably armed. Use of firearms authorized.'

The sergeant went down the hall to the front door and the police car parked at the kerb outside.

'All right, the rest of you,' said the inspector to the little group of detectives awaiting orders. 'Go through the building and see if anyone here knows him or knows where he may have gone.'

The detectives made off silently. Forty minutes later, as the bodies of René and Nanette Maréchal were being loaded into the police ambulance for transport to the morgue, they returned.

No one in the building had known Santo Grasso. No one knew where he might have gone.

While they had been waiting, the inspector and his assistant had gone through the two apartments. They had found nothing to indicate that the Maréchals had known Santo Grasso any better than the other tenants and they had found nothing to indicate a motive.

'It was not robbery,' said the inspector. 'There are valuables and cash in the Maréchal apartment lying about openly and he didn't touch them.'

'He didn't even take his own money,' observed the sergeant. 'The impression I get is that he left without taking anything.'

Santo Grasso had, however, taken something. Two pistols, a rifle, a shotgun and close to a thousand rounds of ammunition.

It would have disturbed the inspector a great deal had he known this, but he was not going to find it out until nearly two hours later when twelve-year-old Patrick Gaumer and his ten-year-old brother, Marcel, returned home from a rather soggy game of touch-football in the park of the suburb of Ecqueville, less than five miles from Villennes.

Patrick and Marcel should actually have been home

considerably earlier, but they knew that their father, André Gaumer, had gone into Paris on some kind of business and there was no one in the apartment except their mother, Monique, and the seven-year-old youngest brother, Jacques. Monique, at thirty years of age and already the mother of three very exuberant boys, was too harassed to be a very severe disciplinarian.

In this case unpunctuality paid off, for had Patrick and Marcel come home when they were supposed to, it would undoubtedly have cost them their lives.

It would also have cost them their lives if they had been four inches taller, because when they arrived at the door of the fifth floor apartment and pressed the bell to be let in, three nine millimetre pistol slugs passed through the door, over their heads and into the wall of the corridor opposite.

Neither of the boys had the slightest inkling as to who might be doing the shooting, but they were both seasoned television viewers and knew gunfire when they heard it. Also, being big city French children, they were intensely practical. They therefore threw themselves flat on their stomachs, wormed their way to the stairs and descended the first flight headfirst. Following which, they took the elevator to the ground floor and ran to the nearest intersection where they found a traffic policeman on duty.

Sceptical, but ready for anything, the policeman followed them back to the apartment building and inspected the door with the three bullet holes from the safety of the head of the stairs.

Oddly enough, no one else in the building seemed to have heard the pistol shots for none of the other tenants had come out.

It would later be determined that the reason for this was that no one else on that floor was at home, but now the lack of onlookers made the policeman suspicious that the boys were pulling some kind of a trick.

He therefore walked quietly over to the door, drew his gun and standing to one side with his back to the wall, cautiously pressed the doorbell.

Three more nine millimetre slugs passed through the door.

The policeman quickly holstered his gun, laid down flat on the floor and wormed his way across to the stairwell, precisely as the boys had done.

Five minutes later, the communications centre at police headquarters in Paris knew that someone was shooting through a door in Ecqueville.

They, of course, had no reason to connect this with the murders of René and Nanette Maréchal in Villennes.

The report, however, set off very much the same reaction as had the killings in Villennes, and Specialist Lucat and his men soon arrived at the scene.

Once again, Lucat went to the door under cover of the automatic weapons of his squad, but this time there was a response. Two heavy rifle bullets smashed into his body armour with such force that he was knocked backward and received painful bruises which would remain black and blue for the following week.

This was not the first time that such a thing had happened to him and he got up, blew the door off its hinges with machine pistol fire and would have charged through had the hall beyond not been stacked to the ceiling with what was apparently all the furniture in the apartment.

While withdrawing, he was struck by a charge of buckshot from Santo Grasso's shotgun which, had it been at a little closer range and not partially deflected by the furniture barricade, could very well have broken his spine despite the body armour.

Limping slightly, the squad leader joined his men at the head of the stairs.

'Get the tear gas gun,' he ordered shortly. 'We'll have to smoke him out.'

He had not spoken in a particularly low voice and from the apartment across the corridor, there came a response.

'No tear gas,' said a man's voice. 'You shoot tear gas, the woman and boy die!'

The squad leader did not change his expression.

'Go get those two kids up here,' he said in a low voice to

one of his men and to another, 'See if Inspector Dupont's got here yet. He's on duty today.'

The two men went off down the stairs and returned in a few minutes bringing with them Patrick and Marcel Gaumer and the inspector and his assistant.

'Listen to this man's voice and see if it's your father,' said the specialist to the two boys and, raising his voice, he called out, 'You there in the apartment! What do you want?'

There was no reply.

'Okay. Hand me the tear gas gun,' said Lucat.

'No tear gas,' shouted the voice from the apartment. 'I kill the woman and the boy!'

'That's not dad,' said Patrick Gaumer. 'This man talks like a foreigner.'

There was a strange note of embarrassment in his voice which was not overlooked by the inspector.

'Whose voice is it, Patrick?' he said.

The boy looked unhappy and did not reply.

'It's mama's boy friend,' said Marcel. 'Old Santo Grasso.'

The police officers looked at each other.

'Your mother has a boy friend named Santo Grasso?' said the inspector. 'An Italian? From Sicily?'

'That's him,' said Patrick a little sulkily. 'He isn't her boy friend no more. That all happened two or three years ago. She doesn't have anything to do with him now.'

'You boys go downstairs and wait for your father,' said the inspector.

'Well, at least we know who we've got in there,' said Lucat, taking off his helmet to wipe the sweat from the bald patch on the top of his head. He felt for his sore ribs underneath the body armour. 'The boy means business.'

'Grasso,' called the inspector. 'This is the police. We know you're in there and we know that you killed René and Nanette Maréchal. Why did you do that, Grasso?'

There was a short silence and then Grasso answered.

'They make too much noise,' he said. 'I can't sleep. Is Sunday and I can't sleep.'

The inspector made a circle with his thumb and forefinger to indicate success. It was important in such cases to be able to engage in a dialogue with the hostage taker. At worst, while he was talking, he was not shooting and, at best, he could sometimes be persuaded to give himself up.

'Have you had trouble sleeping lately?' inquired the inspector sympathetically. 'I also had much trouble sleeping at one time. Perhaps, if you were to talk to my doctor . . .'

He continued to talk and, at the same time, slipped his notebook out of his pocket and wrote on the first page, 'Get some mikes on the apartment walls. I'm going to move up next to the door and see if I can get him to expose himself. Sharpshooters to try to cripple, but not kill. I want report on status woman and child inside as soon as mike's installed.'

'We don't have any body armour to fit you,' said Lucat dubiously, looking at the inspector who was a trifle overweight.

The inspector waved a hand in dismissal. He was now chatting with the gunman about the delights of the climate in Sicily.

Flat on his stomach and with surprising agility for a man of his size and girth, he slowly crossed the corridor until he was lying flat up against the wall beside the door of the Gaumer apartment, keeping up the stream of talk all the time.

Grasso was not doing much talking, but he was at least occasionally responding to the inspector's remarks, which showed that he was listening.

At the head of the stairs, Specialist Lucat's sharpshooters rested the barrels of their rifles on the top step, searching for any sign of movement behind the tangled mass of furniture filling the apartment hall.

Sergeant Renard had gone into the apartment next door with a team of technicians and now he crept out and over to where the inspector lay.

'The bug men say there's three people breathing in there,' he whispered. 'No talk. Just breathing.'

The inspector nodded to show that he understood and then wrote on his pad, 'Tell Lucat to stand by. I'm going to try to bring him out now.'

The sergeant nodded in his turn and crossed the hall to

the head of the stairs. The sharpshooters aimed their weapons.

'Why don't you give this business up and come out, Grasso?' called the inspector. 'You can't get away and, if you had no other reason to kill the Maréchals than what you say, all that will happen to you is that you will go to the hospital. It is a very comfortable hospital and quiet. You will be able to sleep.'

Santo Grasso told the inspector what he could do with the hospital.

The inspector stopped talking and wormed his way back to the head of the stairs.

'He's becoming too excited,' he said. 'I don't like it. I'm afraid all we can do is try to wait him out.'

'We could make a double assault,' said Lucat. 'One party through the front door with fire axes to chop away the furniture and one down ropes from the balcony above.'

'He'd kill the woman and the boy,' said the inspector.

'He will anyway,' said Lucat bluntly. 'That's what he's there for. If he had any demands, he'd have made them by now. He doesn't expect to come out of there alive and he won't leave anyone else alive either, if he can manage it.'

The inspector did not reply. Lucat was a man who had had a great deal of experience with such cases.

As the afternoon and evening passed, Santo Grasso seemed to grow ever more excited and took to firing at cars and pedestrians through the windows of the apartment. Fortunately, no one was hit, but the area had to be cordoned off.

There was also an alarming number of shots being fired in the apartment itself, but the men manning the microphones attached to the dividing wall of the next apartment reported that they could still hear three persons breathing and Monique Gaumer attempting to calm and reason with her former lover.

She was obviously not having much success and at nine o'clock the following morning, the Sicilian, who had apparently not slept a wink throughout the night but was still filled with a frenetic energy, turned his mind to something else.

'No Santo!' screamed Monique Gaumer, her voice rising so that it could be plainly heard even without microphones. 'Don't do that! Not in front of the boy! Oh God! You are mad, Santo! Jacques! Turn your head! Don't look! Santo, you cannot . . .!'

Her voice died away and the microphone men could hear only a scuffling sound and the heavy breathing of the man.

'Set up your assault teams, Lucat,' said the inspector quietly. 'If he doesn't calm after this, we may have to risk it with tear gas. The man's lost all touch with reality.'

There had been a short period of silence following Monique Gaumer's outcry, but now the firing within the apartment resumed. Santo Grasso was apparently shooting with everything he had, the pistols, the rifle, the shotgun.

'He must have a truck load of ammunition in there,' remarked the inspector, 'but, if he . . .'

He was interrupted by the sergeant who came scuttling rapidly across from the apartment where the listening posts were installed.

'There's only one person breathing in there now!' he said.

'Go in and take him, Lucat,' said the inspector sadly.

Five minutes later, Specialist Jules Lucat and his men stormed the Gaumer apartment behind a barrage of tear gas. They met no opposition and the shooting within the apartment ceased abruptly as the first tear gas shell arced through the window.

As Lucat had predicted, Santo Grasso had left no one alive.

Sprawled on the living room floor, her half-naked body surrounded by the torn shreds of her clothing, Monique Gaumer lay dead with a nine millimetre bullet fired at close range through her brain.

At the other side of the room, seated at the table with his face obediently turned to the wall, was the corpse of little Jacques Gaumer. He had been killed with another nine millimetre pistol bullet fired into the back of his head at close range.

Santo Grasso was not in the living room. He lay in the front hall just behind his furniture barricade and, for his own execution, he had not made use of either of the pistols. Instead, he had placed the muzzle of the shotgun in his mouth and had stretched down to pull the trigger.

The charge of buckshot had blown his head off completely.

7

A FAMILY AFFAIR

It was January 7, 1974 and through the streets of Frankfurt am Main a Mercedes 250S was rolling slowly although the traffic was not heavy.

The man at the wheel was young, dark and had long, drooping moustaches in the style currently popular with younger Germans. His companion in the passenger seat beside him was older, heavier, clean-shaven and short-haired.

In a way, each of the men was a symbol of modern Germany in the seventies, the clean-shaven, ambitious striver after material success and the long-haired, liberal easy-rider of the new wave. Both spoke German, but there was scarcely more real communication between them than between an Eskimo and a Zulu. The worlds in which they lived were parallel and contiguous, but totally alien and incomprehensible the one to the other.

Perhaps in no other part of Germany is this division of society so marked as in Frankfurt where hippies and students share communes, fight pitched battles with the police and search for a new society in experiments with drugs and permissive sex while others work frenziedly to pile up still more millions, to buy more expensive cars, to hang still more jewellery on their expensive women.

The division is less by age than by philosophy.

On this particular evening a representative of still a third group was walking briskly along the sidewalk a hundred yards in front of the Mercedes.

Mrs Elly Bender was walking rapidly, not because she was in any hurry, but because she always did things rapidly.

By a coincidence, her age was exactly the total of those of the two men in the car.

Mrs Bender did not know this, nor would she have been interested if she had. A widow on a pension, she was on her way home and her thoughts were largely occupied with the possibilities of the evening's television programme.

As the Mercedes whispered past her, she did not even glance at it. There is nothing unusual about a Mercedes in Frankfurt.

Suddenly, however, there was a sharp explosion.

Looking up, Mrs Bender saw the Mercedes swerve slowly in towards the kerb and it occurred to her that it had blown a tyre.

Then, to her astonishment, she saw the door on the driver's side open and the driver half roll, half fall out into the street.

As he struggled to rise, the man in the passenger seat reached across and, lying half out of the open door of the car, fired two shots from a pistol at the young man with the moustache.

Mrs Bender clearly saw the man's body jerk as the bullets drove into his torso and then go limp.

Squinting through the smog of pollution which lies in a permanent blanket over the city, Mrs Bender could see a dark pool of blood beginning to form around the motionless figure.

In the meantime, the Mercedes rolled on and came to a noisy halt with its crushed fender flattened against the brickwork of a building foundation.

There was silence.

It was only when the tall, husky man who had fired the shots stepped out of the car and walked off a little unsteadily down the street that Mrs Bender realized that she had just been a witness to murder.

Being a responsible woman and conscious of her civic duty, she immediately made off in the direction of the nearest police station at a speed remarkable in view of her age and lack of athletic training.

She could have saved herself the trouble for there were

people living and working in the buildings along the street and they had informed the police by telephone very shortly after the incident took place.

By the time that Mrs Bender arrived back with a foot patrolman a sizeable crowd had gathered and two officers from a patrol car were at the scene and attempting to locate witnesses.

As it turned out, Mrs Bender was the only actual eye witness or, at least, the only one who would admit to it. Frankfurters are not any more inclined to become involved in criminal matters which do not concern them than the residents of any other big, violent city.

Mrs Bender was still in the process of making her statement to one of the patrol car officers when the Homicide Squad arrived from police headquarters. An advance team, it consisted only of Inspector Hardy Kastner and Detective-Sergeant Max Ochs.

Other patrol cars were also now arriving and, while the stolid sergeant took charge of operations, setting up a cordon of police around the area and blocking off the street, his chief went to inspect the body and then the stationary car, returning finally to listen to Mrs Bender's account.

'Get the tape recorder and take down this lady's statement,' said the inspector as the sergeant came up to where he and Mrs Bender were standing. 'And while you're at the car, check and see if the ambulance is on its way yet. We're going to need Adam.'

Adam was Dr Adam Zobeljaeger, the department's medical expert, who appeared with the police ambulance before the sergeant had had time to make the call over the car's radio-telephone.

'Well?' said the inspector who had followed him out to where he was kneeling beside the body.

'He's dead, if that's what you mean,' said the doctor. 'Three bullet wounds in the upper chest. One was very close range. Seven-sixty-five calibre, it looks like.'

'Gang killing perhaps,' remarked the inspector. 'We have a witness and she says it was a big man and very cool. Stepped out of the car and simply walked away.'

'This boy here wasn't any gangster,' said the doctor. 'He's got callouses and cuts all over his hands. Some kind of a hand worker, garage mechanic maybe.'

'See if there are any papers in his pockets,' said the inspector. 'I don't want to go through the car until the technicians have dusted it for prints.'

The doctor searched through the dead man's pockets. There were papers, money, a pocket comb and a picture of a very young girl.

'Dieter Poeschke,' said the inspector, reading from the personal identity card carried by most Germans. 'He was only just turned twenty-one. You were right. He was a garage mechanic. Lived in Frankfurt-Sachsenhausen. Says here he was married. My God! This couldn't be a picture of his wife, could it? She doesn't look a day over sixteen.'

But in this he was mistaken.

Sitting in her neat two-room apartment in Frankfurt-Sachsenhausen, a scant two miles distant from where her husband's body lay in a pool of blood in the street, the widow Silvia Poeschke was several days over sixteen, although not enough to make up six months, the length of time that she had been pregnant.

Silvia was feeling a trifle left out of things because she was sitting alone on her bed in the bedroom and listening to some remarkably strange sounds through the paper-thin partition between bedroom and living room.

She had been married only two weeks now and she was beginning to think that she had married into a very unusual family. Not, of course, that she was narrow-minded or anything like that, but the couple in the room next door were her brother-in-law and his sister and, unless she was greatly mistaken, they were engaged in sex.

Silvia was a very modern, very enlightened girl and she had taken it as completely natural that she and Dieter should have sex together and even that they should produce a child without benefit of clergy. It had been Dieter who had insisted on the marriage. She had not pressed him.

However, sex with one's own brother?

Silvia was not quite sure just how she felt about that. As it happened, she had no brothers, but still . . .

She was also feeling slightly embarrassed. It was the height of bad taste among modern young Germans to show sexual jealousy, but she was, she realized, jealous of Dieter and his sister.

All yesterday evening she had lain awake in the darkness, listening to the sounds which the two brothers and their sister were making beyond the wall, the giggles, the moans, the sound of flesh slapping naked flesh and Renate's whispered instructions.

'All right,' pouted Silvia, alone in her bedroom. 'If they're going to have group sex, they could at least count me in too.'

But, of course, she was six months pregnant and group sex might not be good for the baby. The widow Silvia was beginning to feel quite maternal.

Well, perhaps not completely maternal towards her brother-in-law. It was a strange sensation to have someone similar to Dieter in the same apartment and yet know that they were total strangers.

As a matter of fact, she might never have met Juergen Poeschke if it had not been for the amnesty.

Dieter had told her about his five year older brother who had been left behind in Communist East Germany with the grandmother when, sixteen years earlier, Mrs Anna Poeschke had fled with her son Dieter and her daughter Renate to the West. Juergen had been something of a legendary figure who had never accepted the restrictions of a Communist State. He had been jailed for escape attempts, beating up police officers and, on this last occasion, for assaulting a major of the Russian army on a visit to East Berlin.

The whole family had thought that Juergen was now lost forever and that, if he did not simply disappear entirely, he would surely spend the rest of his life in prison. But then there had been the amnesty two months earlier and Juergen had not only been released, but kicked out of the Worker's Paradise altogether. It was the perfect solution because it had pleased everyone: Juergen, his mother, brother and sister in the West and, of course, above all, the East Germans.

If anyone had not been pleased, thought Silvia, it was Renate's husband, Hans Appel. He was thirty-four, ten years older than Renate, and as square as an ice cube. Silvia could not understand why Renate had married him, unless it was the money.

Hans had plenty of money. He had started out as a simple stone mason and, through sheer hard work and persistence, had become the owner of a good-sized construction company. He had loaded Renate with presents, jewellery, clothing, anything that she might want.

On the other hand, she did not see very much of her husband. He was practically always working and Renate was at home alone with the three children. Two of the children were her own. The six-year-old Claudia from her first marriage, and Tanja, the daughter which she had borne Hans a year ago. The third child was four-year-old Lydia, Hans' daughter by his first marriage.

'Three daughters,' mused Silvia. She was rather hoping for a boy, but then girls were nice too, of course.

In the room next door, Renate was making remarkable sounds. It was as if she was laughing and crying at the same time.

The laughing and crying was, however, all over and Renate and Juergen were sitting decorously listening to music on the record player when Sergeant Ochs knocked on the door.

The sergeant was always the one to notify the next of kin, not because his chief was inclined to push all of the unpleasant details onto his assistant, but because his appearance and personality were so reassuring that it tended to lessen the shock. The sergeant did not look very much like a police officer or even an official.

This time, the sergeant needed all his powers of reassurance and, having noted that the widow was in an advanced state of pregnancy, first took her sister-in-law into the kitchen to inquire whether the family doctor was immediately available before stating the purpose of his visit. The sergeant did not want to be responsible for bringing on a miscarriage.

As it turned out, there was a doctor in the same building and the sergeant proceeded to break his unpleasant news.

For a moment, the three survivors simply stared at him in disbelief and then, grasping that what he said was true and that Dieter had been murdered, burst into a simultaneous orgy of weeping, throwing themselves into each other's arms and sobbing uncontrollably.

There was no doubting the sincerity or depth of their grief and it was some time before the sergeant could calm any of them sufficiently to ask the questions which he had to ask.

Even then, the statements which he received threw no light at all on the identity of Dieter's murderer.

Dieter Poeschke, it seemed, had been a completely ordinary, reasonably hard-working garage mechanic, who, although he wore his hair and moustache long, was involved with neither drugs nor promiscuous sex and certainly not with any underworld activities.

He and Silvia had married only a month earlier, at Dieter's insistence, and his brother Juergen, who had arrived from East Germany two months earlier, had been staying with them for the past two weeks. There had been no trouble of any kind and, in so far as any of them knew, Dieter had had no enemies.

The sergeant posed his final question.

'Do any of you know a tall, husky, clean-shaven man among Mr Poeschke's acquaintances?' he asked. 'A man in his early forties or perhaps a little younger?'

It was the description of the murderer which Mrs Bender had given, but the sergeant did not mention this or even reveal that there had been a witness to the killing. It is the policy of the German police not to release any more information than necessary until a case has been solved.

Silvia's eyes opened very wide and she seemed on the point of saying something, but both Renate and Juergen said almost simultaneously, 'He had no friends like that.'

The sergeant looked at the widow who lowered her eyes and said nothing.

'I'm almost certain the girl knows who the murderer is,' the sergeant told the inspector upon his return to the office, 'but she's covering up.'

'You think she might have something to do with it?' suggested the inspector.

The sergeant shook his head. 'I can't believe it,' he said. 'No sixteen-year-old girl could simulate such shock and grief. None of those people were expecting to hear anything like that. They weren't even startled when I said I was from the police, just curious. And besides, what motive could she have? They've only been married a month and she's six months' pregnant.'

'The motive certainly isn't apparent,' agreed the inspector. 'However, we can worry about that when we have the murderer in custody. It shouldn't be too difficult to locate him. We've got a reasonably good description from the witness.'

'A description that could pass for a few thousand men in Frankfurt,' observed the sergeant.

'True,' said the inspector, 'but we can also deduce certain other things. For example, the murderer must have been known to the victim for they were riding together in the same car. What we have to do is check out every male between the ages of twenty-five and forty-five that Poeschke knew and the one who answers the description is our man.

'We then bring him in for a line-up and see if Mrs Bender can pick him out.'

'Sounds easy,' said the sergeant doubtfully, 'but what if it was somebody that he just met or simply a hitchhiker he gave a ride to?'

'If they didn't know him, why did they kill him then?' said the inspector. 'There wasn't any attempt at robbery and to shoot the driver of the car you're riding in seems to me to indicate a something more than casual intensity of feeling on the subject.'

'I suppose so,' said the sergeant, 'but I have the feeling myself that the investigation isn't going to be all that easy. For some reason or other, the widow and his brother and sister aren't co-operating.'

'Then try his mother,' said the inspector. 'She lives here in the city too and I've just turned up her address from Poeschke's papers.'

'Now?' said the sergeant. 'The others will undoubtedly already have told her that he's dead. She may not be in much shape for questioning.'

'Nonetheless, we have to do it,' said the inspector. 'Since there's no hint as to who the murderer is, for all we know he could be clearing out of the country right now. If there's any lead to be picked up, we want to pick it up immediately.'

The sergeant, who had not had any dinner and who had been coping with grief-stricken relatives for the past two hours, got rather unhappily to his feet and was heading for the door when Dr Zobeljaeger appeared.

'Hold it a minute, Max,' he said. 'I have a little information for you. The victim was shot three times with a seven-thirty-five calibre automatic. I got out two of the slugs and ballistics says it's Baretta ammunition. No record of the gun here and they're checking the central registry in Wiesbaden. Does that help?'

'Not in the least,' said the sergeant stolidly and continued towards the door.

Mrs Anna Poeschke proved to be no more helpful than had been her children and her daughter-in-law.

'There's just no one who could possibly have wanted to harm Dieter,' she sobbed. 'He was such a good boy and so loving to his wife and his brother and sister. Why would anybody kill him?'

'That's what we're trying to find out,' said the sergeant patiently.

Contrary to his expectations, Mrs Poeschke had not been informed of the death of her youngest son by the others and she took the news nearly as badly as they had.

'My children have always been so affectionate with each other,' she mourned. 'Dieter always used to say that he wanted to marry Renate when he grew up and so did Juergen for that matter.'

The sergeant cleared his throat. 'A lot of children get those ideas when they're little,' he said.

'Oh, they weren't so little,' said Mrs Poeschke. 'They knew what marriage was, but, of course, there are those silly laws here and even in Sweden where they do let the brothers and sisters marry now, they won't let a sister marry both brothers at the same time. It seems so foolish. After all, what business is it of the government?'

The sergeant did not answer. As an old and seasoned investigator with the criminal police in one of Germany's most violent cities, he had experienced some weird and wonderful things in his time and he regarded them all with his customary stolid, emotionless composure.

Now, for the first time in his career, he was literally struck dumb. There was no mistaking Mrs Poeschke's words. Her children were very attached to each other, so attached that, even in liberal Germany with its almost total lack of laws governing sexual behaviour, the attachment was illegal.

And with this realization, the conduct of the widow and the brother and sister whom he had interviewed previously took on new meaning. The question of the motive seemed to be answered.

'I understand your daughter is married to a Mr Hans Appel,' said the sergeant, making use of the information that he had received during the earlier interview. 'Is he a tall, husky, clean-shaven man in his forties?'

Mrs Poeschke caught on quickly.

'Hans is only thirty-four,' she said, 'but he wouldn't hurt Dieter. They were great friends.'

'But he is tall and husky and clean-shaven, isn't he?' said the sergeant.

Mrs Poeschke nodded grudgingly. 'But why would he kill poor Dieter?' she whispered. 'He didn't have a reason in the world.'

The sergeant did not attempt to explain to her what reason he had in mind, but thanked her for her co-operation and returned to the station where he found the inspector preparing to leave for home.

'Better stick around for a while,' said the sergeant. 'I think I know who killed Poeschke and I think I know why.

With your permission, I'm going over to Wiesbaden to make an arrest.'

The inspector listened to what he had to say and then decided to come with him. Forty-five minutes later Hans Appel ushered them into the living room of his comfortable apartment in Wiesbaden, twenty-five miles west of Frankfurt.

'I've been waiting for you,' he said. 'You took your time coming.'

'Did you murder your brother-in-law, Dieter Poeschke?' said the inspector who believed in coming directly to the point.

'Yes,' said Hans Appel flatly.

Appel was placed under arrest, cautioned as to his rights and taken to police headquarters in Frankfurt where he voluntarily made a full confession to the murder of his brother-in-law, Dieter Poeschke.

'I always liked Dieter and I got on with him well,' said Appel. 'Of course, we were different generations and he had different ideas to mine, but I didn't think that that really mattered so much. I thought it was all trendy stuff whipped up by the media and that underneath there wasn't all that much difference either.

'Dieter wasn't like a lot of the kids nowadays who lay around in the streets and kill themselves with drugs and things. He was a good worker and he made good money. I'd even thought of taking him into the company some day, if he wanted to.

'I liked the way he handled himself with Silvia too. A lot of young fellows his age would have just let things go, but Dieter said that now Silvia was pregnant they were going to get married, and they did.

'The trouble all started about a month before the wedding when Renate's older brother, Juergen, came over from the East Zone. I'd heard a lot about him from Renate and Dieter and I could understand that they were happy to see him. As I understood it, they'd been separated for over sixteen years.

'Dieter wasn't married yet at that time and he only had a single room and Mrs Poeschke only has a very small apartment too so Juergen moved in with us. I thought that was only natural. We had a big place and lots of room and it was going to be a little while before Juergen could get on his feet financially. As a matter of fact, I guess I was the one who suggested it.

'Well, everything was just fine. I got along well with Juergen and it was no trouble at all having him. As a matter of fact, I'm not home too much of the time. If you want to be successful in the contracting business today, you've got to look after everything yourself and some of our jobs are out of town.

'As I say, everything went well until about two weeks ago and then I came home late and Renate and Juergen had both gone to bed, Renate in our bedroom and Juergen in the guest room naturally.

'I went into the children's room to see if they were all right and Claudia was still awake.

'I started to tuck her in and she said, "If you won't tell anybody, I'll tell you a secret."

'I thought it was just some child's game so I said, "I won't tell. I promise." And then she said, "Mommy and Uncle Juergen were in bed all afternoon. They were all naked."

'I couldn't believe my ears. Claudia is a bright little girl and she doesn't make things up, but even if she did, I didn't see how she could think of something like that.

'I asked her if she was sure that she wasn't telling me a fib and she said no, that Mommy and Uncle Juergen took off all their clothes and got into bed and then they made a lot of funny noises and she thought they were tickling each other. They wouldn't let her into the bedroom.

'I was confused. I went out into the kitchen and I drank two or three brandies, something that I never do otherwise, and I thought about it.

'All I could think of was that Juergen really wasn't Renate's brother after all and that the whole thing was a conspiracy between her and Dieter and Mrs Poeschke so that she could bring a lover right into my house. I never dreamed that she and her brother were really having sexual relations. It's just something that nobody does except sick people or maybe some place in Scandinavia.

'The next day I went down to the residents' registration office and asked to see Juergen's registration. He'd had to register as soon as he moved in with us, of course, and I made up a story about how he was sick and unconscious and I had to know the address of his relatives.

'Normally, they won't show you somebody else's registration, but they believed me and I got to see it.

'He really was Renate's brother.

'I didn't know what to think then. The information on the registry form had to be correct because they would have insisted on seeing his birth certificate and his other papers and I couldn't see how he could have forged a complete set of documents.

'What was more, I couldn't see why he would bother. If he was Renate's lover, he could just as easily have met her outside or even at the house. God knows, there was plenty of opportunity with me working so much of the time.

'I still didn't want to accept that Renate was actually sleeping with her brother, but I believe in having things out in the open so I went home and had it out with them.

'There was quite a row, mainly between Renate and me. Juergen didn't say too much. But the worst part was that neither of them actually denied it.

'Finally, I said that Juergen had to go. I didn't know what was going on and I didn't care what they said, but I wasn't going to have him in my house for another minute.

'Renate said, "All right, then I'll go with him," and they walked out of the apartment just like that. She didn't even take her clothes with her.

'I didn't know where they'd gone, but then I found out that they'd gone to stay with Dieter and Silvia so I went there a week later and tried to talk to Renate.

'I was convinced by now that there was nothing to my suspicions because I didn't believe that it would be possible for them to have sex relations when they were living with Dieter and Silvia. Silvia was always home and I thought that Dieter would be as shocked by such a thing as I was.

'I couldn't get anywhere with Renate. She wouldn't even talk to me, although I promised her a new fur coat and jewellery and just about anything she wanted if she'd come home.

'I still had the three children with me and I'd had to hire a woman to look after them. My business was going to pieces because I wasn't attending to it. And the only way I could communicate with Renate was through Dieter. I had to wait in the housemaster's apartment and Dieter would take my message up to Renate and come down with the answer, if there was any.

'About the only answer he ever came down with was that she wanted a divorce. I never mentioned the business with Juergen and neither did she.

'Then, finally, on January seventh I had the car in the garage and Dieter came over to Wiesbaden to pick me up. I'd been carrying my Baretta automatic on me ever since Renate had left and I had it that day. I don't know why. I certainly didn't intend to kill anybody.

'We drove to Frankfurt and had the same old business with Renate all over again and then Dieter started to drive me back to Wiesbaden.

'I was feeling pretty bad and I wanted to confide in somebody and I thought Dieter was the right person. After all, he was my brother-in-law and we'd always got on well together. I felt we sort of understood each other.

'So, as we were driving back to Wiesbaden, I told him what Claudia had said and about the row with Renate and Juergen because I was pretty sure that he didn't know anything about all that and I said I was sure that it was all just a misunderstanding.

'When I finished he looked at me sort of bewildered as if he didn't understand and said, "But Hans, both of us (at this point the late Mr Poeschke made use of the German equivalent of that fine, old Anglo-Saxon verb) Renate all the time."

'When he said that it was as if something inside my head snapped. I remember shooting him now, but I don't think I was actually aware of it at the time.

'Afterwards, I walked to the bus stop, took the bus to the railway station and came home. I thought you'd be waiting for me when I got here and I've been expecting you ever since.'

On July 29, 1974, the court in Frankfurt listened to and accepted Hans Appel's version of the events surrounding the murder of his brother-in-law and sentenced him to twenty-one months imprisonment. Even this sentence was not served as Appel was immediately released on bail pending a successful appeal to have the sentence set aside or suspended.

He is, however, a ruined man, his contracting company having fallen apart during his absence, and he apparently no longer feels any strong desire for material success.

Renate and Juergen are living together in a three-room apartment in Wiesbaden, the rent of which is paid by the Welfare Department.

Although police investigations of the charges of incest were initiated, they were subsequently dropped for lack of evidence. Incest is very difficult to prove if neither party is prepared to testify and both Renate Poeschke and her brother have steadfastly denied any relationship more intimate than that governed by brotherly love.

8

TRAVELS WITH A KILLER

Istvan Stefan Hollossy turned the cigar thoughtfully in his fingers, bit off the end, spat it on the floor, lodged it in the corner of his mouth and struck a match with his thumbnail.

'Are you telling me that our financial arrangement is ended, Cornelia?' he asked in a calm, almost conversational tone.

He gazed impassively at the pretty, dark-haired girl seated on the sofa before him, his broad, flat face and slitted cat's eyes making him look vaguely like one of the illustrations in a child's book of lovable animals.

The girl made a nervous gesture with her hands.

'Janos and I want to get married, Stefan,' she said softly. 'We need the money.'

Sitting at the opposite side of the room, Janos Telek was astounded to see a gun suddenly appear in Hollossy's hand.

There was the whiplash report of a 7.65 mm pistol being fired within the confined space of the little attic room and Cornelia Renz' pretty, dark head jerked backward.

A round, discoloured spot no bigger than the tip of a man's finger had appeared, as if by magic, on the white skin over her left eyebrow.

As Janos Telek watched, frozen with horror, the girl that he had been planning to marry pitched forward onto the carpet. Her left leg jerked twice in a reflex movement and she lay still.

Twenty-two-year-old Cornelia Renz had been killed instantly by a 7.65 mm pistol bullet fired at close range into her brain.

The shock nearly deprived the twenty-six-year-old

Yugoslav of his reason and for several moments he lost all touch with reality.

How could Stefan Hollossy cold-bloodedly murder Cornelia? It had been Hollossy who had introduced him to her in the first place. And, although it all seemed long ago now, had only been some two months previous.

Janos Telek had come up to the German city of Luebeck on the Baltic Ocean where he had found work as a driver-salesman for a margarine company. Gifted for languages, he spoke fluent German as well as several of the Balkan languages.

It had been because of the languages that he had met Stefan Hollossy. The Hungarian had been drinking in the bar of the Blue Mouse, a popular Luebeck night spot, and Telek had addressed him in his mother tongue.

Hollossy had been so delighted that he had not let Telek pay for another drink all evening. He was, he said, the same age as Janos and a commercial artist by profession.

Commercial art seemed to pay very well, for Hollossy spent money as if he enjoyed an inexhaustible supply of it and, to an extent he did, as Janos found out two days later.

The inexhaustible source of money was named Cornelia Renz and she was sitting in the Kazoria, a Greek wine bar, when Hollossy and Telek came in.

'I need some money, Cornelia,' said Hollossy calmly, sitting down at the table and lighting one of his ever-present cigars. He smoked a comparatively expensive brand with the ominous name of Al Capone.

To Telek's astonishment, the girl had opened her purse and had given Hollossy several hundred marks. He was not only astonished, but also dismayed. Janos Telek had just experienced that remarkable phenomenon known as love at first sight and the transaction which had just taken place could only mean that Cornelia Renz was a prostitute and that Hollossy was her procurer.

Although it saddened him, the knowledge did not diminish his emotions and, when Hollossy went to the men's room, he quickly made a date with the charming Cornelia.

To his delight, she accepted immediately. The sentiments were, apparently, mutual.

On that first date Janos had learned all about Cornelia's relations with the Hungarian and the matter had not been nearly as bad as he had feared.

Cornelia was a prostitute, but not with her body and she did hand over a good part of her earnings to Hollossy, but he was not her procurer. Cornelia needed no procurer or protector as her clientele was very exclusive and so extensive that she could hardly take care of all of it.

The fact was, Cornelia was a masseuse and not just a self-taught one, but a trained, diplomaed, medically approved masseuse. She was employed at the Little Sea Castle, a luxury hotel catering to the elderly, located at Timmendorf Beach on the shores of Luebeck Bay a few miles to the north of the city.

There she massaged for an adequate, if not magnificent salary, the aching bones and muscles of hotel guests, none of whom would have dreamed of requesting that she massage anything else.

Now, Germany, Holland and the Scandinavian countries are teeming with masseuses, all self-taught and all highly specialized in parts of the body seldom requiring medical massage. Many of them are, however, far from attractive and, lacking Cornelia's formal training, they are inclined to go about matters in a rather heavy-handed manner.

A trained masseuse, such as Cornelia, literally has gold in her fingertips. Although she was fully aware of the potential, Cornelia had never made any effort to exploit her talents until she ran into Stefan Hollossy in the Nautic Bar, another Luebeck night spot.

Like all Hungarians, Hollossy was charming and, although he did not move in with her in the attic apartment in Timmendorf, they became lovers, an expensive arrangement for Cornelia as Stefan was a man with exclusive tastes and seldom or never the money with which to pay for them.

Cornelia's modest savings account was quickly exhausted with purchases such as a light green Fiat 124, so that Stefan could come to Timmendorf to see her without riding the bus, and opulent weekends at the extremely luxurious Sea Horse Hotel.

It was a magnificent scale of living, but Cornelia's salary could not support it. At this point, the savings account being exhausted, Stefan pointed out that for a person of Cornelia's background and training, there were great opportunities of increasing the income. It would only be necessary to drop a few discreet hints in the right places . . .

Cornelia did not even hesitate. Although she retained her job at the Little Sea Castle, she began doing what is euphemistically termed 'special massage' on the side. Her clients were of both sexes and all were unanimously delighted. Cornelia was a very highly trained masseuse.

Why did Cornelia do this? She was a beautiful girl, professionally trained and above average in intelligence. She was not particularly infatuated with Hollossy, as witness the fact that she fell in love with Janos Telek immediately she met him. She was not even afraid of Hollossy whom she believed to be a commercial artist out of work.

There is a theory that victims are destined to the role by their own natures. Aggressor and victim do not play active and passive parts, but join together in a mutually complementary performance of a tragedy grasped by neither.

There was no reason for Cornelia Renz to prostitute her nimble fingers to pay for Stefan Hollossy's expensive cigars and nightclub bills, but she did it and, in so doing, effectively initiated her own death.

There had been, however, a brief period of happiness. Cornelia and Janos were in love. He had moved into the little attic apartment in Timmendorf, they had opened a new savings account into which he paid all of his salary and, on weekends, they had gone to Luebeck to eat dinner in cheap, Italian restaurants and enjoy themselves like two carefree children.

Stefan had not commented on the arrangement and it did not occur to either of them that he might have any objections. It had been a Thursday evening, April 3, 1975, when he had telephoned to say that he was in Luebeck and would like to come out and see them. He said that he had an interesting proposition for Janos, but he would not say what it was.

Janos had told him to do so, they would all have a drink and a little something to eat together.

He had barely hung up when Hollossy appeared at the door. He had, it seemed, not been in Luebeck at all, but right there in Timmendorf.

The conversation which had followed had been short and to the point, so short in fact that Telek could scarcely grasp the fact that his sweetheart was dead.

One moment she had been sitting on the sofa, neat, pretty and speaking in her soft, gentle voice, and the next she had been lying on the carpet, the horrible little hole over her blank, staring eye and her open mouth gaping at the ceiling.

The whole affair had happened so quickly and unexpectedly that it was incomprehensible. Hollossy's appearance, the very short and matter-of-fact exchange of words, the sudden drawing of the pistol, the shot. From the time that the Hungarian had knocked on the door until Cornelia was dead was less than five minutes.

In a novel, Janos Telek would undoubtedly have sprung at the throat of the murderer and would either have revenged his dead sweetheart or died in the attempt.

However, this was real life and real death. Janos Telek was a margarine salesman, not a hero, and at that time he did not believe that he himself had more than another minute or two to live.

Surely, no one in his right mind would murder a young girl in the presence of a witness and then allow that witness to remain alive. He was positively astounded to see Hollossy replace the gun in the jacket pocket from which he had drawn it.

'Come on,' he said pleasantly to the paralyzed Telek, 'Grab hold of her feet and we'll toss her up onto the bed. God knows, this place is small enough as it is.'

Nearly insane with shock and fear, the Yugoslav did as he was told and together they placed the corpse on its back on the bed. There was scarcely any blood coming from the bullet hole, but the girl's eyes were wide open and stared horribly, so that Telek became abruptly and violently ill, vomiting over his own shoes and trousers. Hollossy looked at him solicitously as he might have regarded someone being seasick and then took the corpse by the arm and rolled it over on its face.

Suddenly, he stiffened. 'Say!' he exclaimed. 'Isn't there an old woman lives next door here? If she heard the shot . . . Don't want any witnesses . . .'

The pistol appeared in his hand as if by magic and he slid out of the apartment door, as silent and deadly as a viper.

Janos Telek was as good a Communist as any other Yugoslav, but he fell to his knees and broke into fervent, if unorthodox, prayer. If Hollossy was prepared to kill an old woman simply because she might have heard the shot, what chance did he, an eye-witness, have?

Quite a bit apparently.

After a moment, Hollossy returned, the gun back in his pocket, with the observation that the lady was not at home.

'Get your stuff together and come with me,' he said. 'No tricks now. I mean business.'

Telek was utterly convinced that he meant business and the last thing in the world that he was contemplating was tricks. Gathering up his few personal belongings, he followed the Hungarian down to the courtyard where his own old Opel Rekord was parked.

'You drive,' said Hollossy, getting into the passenger seat in front. 'I'll tell you where to go.'

'I can't drive,' said Telek desperately. 'The cops took my licence last Saturday.'

It was perfectly true, but Stefan Hollossy apparently did not regard driving without a licence as a very serious offence.

'Don't worry about it,' he said jovially. 'If the cops stop us, it'll be a lot more than driving without a licence. You might not believe it, but I'm wanted in five countries and the least thing they want me for is bank robbery.'

Janos Telek did believe it and he had every reason to. As would later be revealed, Hollossy was wanted in Hungary, Austria, Switzerland, Germany and Sweden on armed robbery, assault with a deadly weapon and attempted murder charges. His most recent exploit before arriving in Luebeck had been a jail break in Sweden where he had been serving twenty years for armed robbery.

Oddly enough, up until the murder of Cornelia Renz, he had never actually killed anyone, although he had gravely wounded a number of people. Hollossy was not a killer in the sense that he enjoyed killing and did it for its own sake. Rather, he was a man who was determined to have whatever he set his mind to at all costs. During the course of his robberies, if no one offered resistance, no one was hurt. If anyone did, they were shot down instantly and ruthlessly.

Janos Telek, of course, knew nothing of all this and Hollossy did not go into details about the reasons for being wanted in five countries. However, he had seen what had happened to Cornelia and he was prepared to obey without question whatever orders his strange captor might choose to issue.

The only question that remained was: What did Hollossy want of him?

He was soon to find out. The Hungarian was gregarious and he had apparently become tired of playing the lone wolf. He liked Telek and so he had decided to make him his partner in crime.

'You must be practical in this life,' he explained reasonably. 'We need money for hotel bills, food, drink, women, clothes and travel, but we do not have any. Fortunately, there are people everywhere with money and it is only necessary to take it from them.

'Let us start with a simple example. We go into a store together, a small store where the owner is present. Such people always have money, sometimes quite a lot, sometimes not so much.

'Banks have more money, but they are more difficult. I cannot let you try a bank until you have had more experience. Have you ever killed anyone with a knife?'

Telek shook his head. He was utterly incapable of speech. Not only had he never killed anyone with a knife, he had never been in so much as a fist fight. He was horrified by even the thought of violence and was completely honest, believing that the only happiness comes from money which you have earned yourself. Hollossy could hardly have picked a worse partner.

'Well, never mind,' continued Hollossy. 'Perhaps we can find a drunk for you to practise on.

'Now, listen carefully. We go into the store and I engage the owner in conversation. Then you come up behind him and slip the knife between his ribs.'

He paused and frowned, obviously thinking.

'It might be better if you were to split his head with a hatchet,' he said judiciously. 'If you did not do it properly with the knife, he might call for help or even fight with us. On the other hand, it would be harder for you to hide the hatchet in your coat. I will have to think about it.'

He fell silent and apparently did just that.

Telek was on the verge of fainting. He had grasped immediately why Hollossy wanted him to do all the knifing and splitting of heads.

Once he had killed or injured someone, he would be as much of a hunted criminal as the Hungarian. Whether he liked it or not, he would really be his partner in crime, at least until such time as he was captured and sent to prison for the rest of his life or shot down by the police.

They did not get very far with the Opel that evening for, on the outskirts of Ratzeburg, twenty miles south of Luebeck, they had a flat tyre and Hollossy decided to abandon the car.

He then marched his still shaking captive to the nearest tavern where he bought him three whiskeys, the same number for himself and a fresh supply of Al Capone cigars.

Hollossy seemed in the best of spirits and, after a brief flirtation with the barmaid, ordered a taxi and drove his new partner off to spend the night with what he described as friends.

Telek was astonished that such a man had any friends and he could not decide whether they were ordinary people or criminals like Hollossy. He spent a sleepless night, for every time he dozed off he was tortured by the vision of Cornelia's dead face with its sightless eyes staring at the ceiling.

The next morning Hollossy took him to the railway station where he bought two tickets for Hamburg. It was typical of the man that, as long as Telek was with him, he was never permitted to pay for anything. Stefan Hollossy was an extremely generous man with money, possibly because it was always someone else's.

Arriving at Hamburg at nine-thirty in the morning, Hollossy seemed at a loss as to what to do next and finally took his unwilling partner to see a showing of 'Archie, the Porno Butler', which was playing in a round-the-clock movie house.

This was followed by lunch, naturally at a first class restaurant, and the Hungarian then led the way to a department store where he stole a wig and a raincoat, 'For their work,' as he put it.

The afternoon was spent looking at jewellery stores which appeared to hold a great attraction for Hollossy. Telek made himself as accommodating as possible. He had no wish to die and Hollossy had shown him the three pistols which he carried at all times in his pockets.

'Always keep the pistol loaded and cocked,' he advised Telek earnestly. 'People will tell you that you can have an accident that way, but it is not as grave an accident as you can have if you need the gun in a hurry and it is not loaded.'

That evening, Hollossy rented a double room at the Union Hotel on Paulinus Square and, having locked the door from the inside, put the key in his pocket and fell instantly asleep.

Telek contemplated knocking him out with the table lamp, but was unable to find the nerve. The Hungarian had the reflexes of a cat and, if anything were to go wrong, the result would be fatal for Telek.

Shortly after two o'clock there was a demonstration of Hollossy's reflexes. A police car passing through the street below switched on its siren for a moment.

Instantly and in a single movement, Hollossy was off the bed and the muzzle of the 9 mm pistol, the big one, was pressed against Telek's right ear.

For a moment, they remained frozen, a tableau of a man and his murderer, and then the siren was switched off.

Hollossy relaxed, put the gun back in his pocket, went back to his bed and fell promptly asleep again.

Telek fainted.

The next day was spent in a further survey of the Hamburg jewellery stores, but Hollossy, who never slept twice in the same place if he could help it, did not return to the Union Hotel but took a room in a modest pension on the other side of town.

By this time Janos Telek was so exhausted from the nervous strain that he had no sooner laid down than he fell sound asleep. He was awakened at shortly after midnight by Hollossy shaking his shoulder.

'I've been thinking,' said the Hungarian. 'We're getting short of money. The old woman who runs this place may have some. Why don't you go down and kill her and see what you can find?'

The appalled Yugoslav, his tongue oiled by terror, sat up in the bed and offered one of the most passionate and convincing arguments of his life as to why it would not be advisable to kill and rob the owner of the pension.

'If we do that, the police will be looking for us and it will be impossible to rob the jewellery stores,' he concluded.

Hollossy found this reasonable.

'You are a good partner, Janos,' he said, turned over and went back to sleep.

Telek did not sleep another wink all night.

By morning he had come to the conclusion that he would make a break for it at the first opportunity. If he continued as he was, he was going to end up a hunted criminal or possibly dead in any case. He might as well be shot down by Hollossy as by the police.

The next day was Sunday and Hollossy was, apparently, an observer of the Sabbath for he did not leave the room, having all meals and the Sunday papers brought up by the same woman he had suggested killing and robbing the night before.

To Telek's amazement, although they now had very little money left, Hollossy tipped her generously.

The following morning Hollossy and Telek set off bright

and early to scout out the jewellery stores in Spitaler Street, a pedestrian mall.

Telek was still determined to escape or die in the attempt and, as Hollossy's attention was focused on a particularly tempting jewellery store window display, he edged slowly off until he was near a corner.

Expecting any moment the impact of a bullet in his back, he suddenly broke for the corner of the building, sprinted around it, cut through the nearest alley, doubled back into a department store and out the side door and halted the first taxi by the simple expedient of standing directly in front of it.

'Take me to the police station,' he gasped, throwing himself on the floor of the back seat. 'I've been a witness to a murder.'

Ten minutes later he was pouring out his tale to the not entirely convinced ears of Inspector Frank Luders of the Hamburg Criminal Police while the inspector's assistant, Detective-Sergeant Max Peters, talked to the police in Luebeck and Timmendorf over the telephone.

The fact was, Telek's experiences had so unsettled him that he gave the impression of being drugged, insane or both.

There was no report in Luebeck or in Timmendorf of the murder of Cornelia Renz, but a patrolman dispatched to her address as given by Telek, forced the door, which Hollossy had carefully locked, and found the corpse exactly as Telek had described it.

In the meantime, the records section had been busy with Hollossy's quoted statement that he was wanted in five countries and had found that he was not exaggerating. All of the entries in his voluminous file stated that he was extremely dangerous and to be approached only with the utmost caution.

Minutes after this information reached the inspector's desk, a top urgency red alert went out to all patrol cars and foot units. Road blocks were set up at the edge of the city and teams of officers were dispatched to the railway station and the inter-city bus depot.

The area around Spitaler Street was cordoned off and search parties went through every building. Stefan Hollossy was no longer there.

'Do you have any suggestion as to where he may have gone?' asked the inspector, fixing Telek with a dour eye.

'He's gone to rob a jewellery store,' said Telek. 'Whatever he takes into his head, he does regardless. He won't go back to the pension. He never goes back to the place once he's left it.'

However, Telek could not say which jewellery store Hollossy might have in mind. He did not know Hamburg and he and the Hungarian had looked at a great many jewellery stores since their arrival in the city.

'Get a list of the jewellery stores in the city centre,' said the inspector to Sergeant Peters, 'and try and get at least one man to each of them as quickly as possible. It's probably a wild goose chase. Hollossy must know we're looking for him by now and, regardless of what this Yugoslav says, I doubt that he'll try to pull off a robbery right under our noses.'

The inspector gravely underestimated Stefan Hollossy. At ten minutes to four that afternoon while police officers were being rushed to all jewellery stores in the downtown section of the city, Hollossy walked into the Hoellinger Jewellery Store located at 21 Alstertor Street on the edge of the suburbs. He was carrying the stolen raincoat over his right arm and in the hand beneath it was the cocked 9 mm automatic.

Inside the store were seventy-four-year-old Josef Hoellinger, his sixty-six-year-old wife, Maria, and thirty-eight-year-old Cristel Semmelhack who for twenty years had played the multiple role of salesclerk, manageress, friend and daughter to the childless Austrian couple.

'This,' said Stefan Hollossy, throwing back the raincoat to reveal the gun, 'is a hold-up.'

Like many older people, Hoellinger was a man of great courage. Without the slightest hesitation, he jerked open the cash drawer and brought out a tear gas cannister.

With equal lack of hesitation, Hollossy pulled the trigger.

The heavy slug smashed into Hoellinger's face, completely tearing away his lower jaw and knocking him to the floor.

Coolly and with incredible accuracy, the Hungarian fired two more shots, striking both Maria Hoellinger and Cristel Semmelhack in the head and killing them instantly.

He then pocketed his weapon and sauntered out of the store.

Behind him, Josef Hoellinger, in terrible agony and bleeding heavily from his shattered jaw, dragged himself across the floor and out the front door into the street. He was still conscious and, although unable to speak, made gestures to the passersby who came running that they were to help his wife and salesclerk inside. They were of course beyond help, but Josef Hoellinger was rushed to the hospital where he eventually recovered from his wound.

In the meantime, the dispatcher's voice at police headquarters was calling steadily over the police radio, 'Red alert! Red alert! All units. Istvan Stefan Hollossy believed in area of Alstertor Street. Unrestricted use of firearms authorized.'

In the courtyard at police headquarters, Captain Bernd Wilhelm mustered the Special Squad of which he was in charge. Only twenty-seven years old, most of his men were considerably younger. The Special Squad called for quick reflexes.

'Load,' said the captain.

The bolts of six machine pistols snicked back, throwing the first shell into the firing chamber of the rapid-fire weapons.

'Usual procedure,' said the captain. 'If we go in, I lead the first squad. Karl is back-up.'

The squad nodded in understanding. The captain was always the first man in.

No one would, however, be going in anywhere in the Alstertor Street. Once again, Stefan Hollossy had been too fast for the police cordon and he was now being driven across town by a very nervous cab driver named Werner Novak. Novak was nervous because Hollossy was holding the muzzle of the automatic against his ribs and, having heard the broadcast over the cab radio, he knew who his passenger was.

Roughly a half mile from Alstertor Street, Hollossy suddenly ordered the cab driver to stop and back the cab into a dark entry. Novak did so and, certain that he was now to be killed, leaped out of the cab and ran wildly down the street.

Hollossy ignored him and ran off in the opposite direction, plunging through the door of a machine shop at 84 Iffland Street where twenty-six-year-old Walter Klein was just on the point of going home.

In what seems to have been a purely reflex action, Hollossy raised the gun and shot him in the stomach. He then ran back out of the door.

In terrible pain, Klein staggered after him and was just in time to see him disappear into the basement of number 20 Grauman's Way.

Dragging himself to the telephone, he dialled the emergency police number and gasped out his information. In the meantime, Werner Novak had also called the police and, within minutes, the patrol cars began to pour into the area.

The building at number 20 Grauman's Way was surrounded, but no attempt was made to enter the basement. The rat was, presumably, in the trap, but he still had all his teeth and he had demonstrated that he knew very well how to use them. The job was one for the Special Squad.

Captain Wilhelm and his men rushed to the scene, but they did not make any immediate attempt to enter the cellar either. They were police officers and not desperados. Risks were taken only if they could not be avoided.

A loudspeaker was therefore set up in front of the cellar and, for over an hour, Inspector Luders tried to persuade Stefan Hollossy to throw down his guns and come out.

There was not the slightest sound from the cellar.

'Could he have given us the slip?' worried the inspector. 'Only Klein saw him go in there and he was badly wounded. He could have come back out again while Klein was on the telephone. If so, we're here besieging an empty cellar with half the force while he's clearing out of the city altogether.'

'A little tear gas?' suggested the sergeant.

'Try it,' said the inspector.

The tear gas was unsuccessful. The door to the basement entered into a corridor running parallel to the front of the building and there was no way of getting the tear gas shells back into the basement proper.

'Well, I suppose it's us then,' said Captain Wilhelm, settling his helmet onto his head and pulling down the face visor. 'We've got to know whether he's in there or not, I take it.'

'I'm afraid we do, Bernd,' said the inspector. 'Keep your head down.'

At ten minutes past five, Captain Wilhelm led the charge of his squad through the door and into the basement, his machine pistol at the ready.

Stefan Hollossy was also ready. His first shot ranged upward and struck the captain in the jaw beneath his face visor.

The captain continued to advance, firing his machine pistol on full automatic until the magazine was empty. He was then seized by his men and dragged outside while struggling to reload. Taken to the hospital, he eventually recovered and returned to duty.

The second charge of the Special Squad was led by the back-up man, Karl, and drew no fire.

The lights were turned on and Hollossy was found lying dead at the back of the basement. He had been struck twice by Captain Wilhelm's fire, once in the right shoulder and once in the left leg.

The bullet which had passed through his brain was not, however, from any police weapon. It was from a nine millimetre automatic pistol.

It was still gripped firmly in his very dead, very stubborn hand.

9

ROUGH JUSTICE

It was quiet in the charge room of the Meidling sub-station of the Vienna police. The midnight to eight duty had mustered an hour and a half ago and were now patrolling the streets of the Austrian capital in the gentle darkness of the spring night. The page of the calendar for April 4, 1968 had still not been torn off the block hanging on the charge room wall.

At one-thirty-nine there was a discreet buzz from the switchboard and a red light began to flash. The duty sergeant reached over and pressed the button.

'Charge room,' he said.

'Patrolman four-six-eight,' said a clear, rather high voice from the loudspeaker. 'I am at the Excelsior Garage, forty-seven Stein Street. I have intercepted two robbers.'

'Good,' said the duty sergeant. 'Do you require help to bring them in?'

'I require the corpse transporter,' replied the voice calmly. 'They are both dead.'

'What!' exclaimed the sergeant, startled out of his official manner. 'What happened?'

'They opened fire on me,' said Patrolman four-six-eight. 'I returned the fire.'

'Are you wounded?' said the sergeant.

'No,' said the patrolman.

'Then remain where you are,' ordered the sergeant. 'This will have to be reported to the C.I.D. They'll send someone out.'

He cut off the connection and dialled the number of the Criminal Investigations Department at police headquarters.

'Meidling,' he said when the telephone was picked up.

'We've had a shoot-out in the Excelsior Garage, forty-seven Stein Street. One of our patrolmen and two robbers. The robbers are dead. Do you want to check it out?'

'Right,' said the voice from headquarters. 'On the way, Meidling.'

The only witnesses to the conversation at the sub-station had been two sleepy patrolmen on standby duty, but at police headquarters two reporters covering the night crime beat followed the car from the C.I.D. out to Stein Street.

Next day two of the morning papers carried the headline, 'Heroic Rookie in Shoot-out With Gangsters!'

There was a large picture of Patrolman Ernst Karl, twenty-three years old and four months on duty with the force, and several shots of the two gangsters lying dead on the garage floor in pools of blood, their guns still gripped in their hands.

'Remarkable!' commented Inspector Franz-Josef Alte, the distinguished, grey moustached and side-whiskered senior investigations officer, laying the newspaper down on his desk and opening his silver cigarette case for one of the special, hand-rolled sobranie cigarettes which were the only things that he had ever smoked.

'How so?' said his assistant, picking up the newspaper and retreating to his own desk on the opposite side of the room.

'Are you familiar with the Excelsior Garage?' asked the inspector.

Detective-Sergeant Karl-Gustav Schuhmacher nodded silently, his square-jawed, handsome face bent over the newspaper. After a moment, he pushed it aside.

'Daytime parking garage,' he said. 'Used by the office people.'

'Can you imagine what would be in there at one-thirty in the morning so valuable that two desperate gangsters, armed to the teeth, would be prepared to shoot it out with a police officer to gain entrance?' said the inspector.

The sergeant looked startled.

'There wouldn't have been anything in there at night,' he

said. 'Not even a car. You're right. It's damned remarkable. Let me see who handled it last night.'

He left the office and came back a half hour later.

'The night trick man went out,' he said. 'Boy named Schelling. He's only in plainclothes for eight months. All he did was take the patrolman's statement and have the bodies sent down to the morgue. Their guns are in ballistics. No record on either weapon and neither one had been fired.'

'Let me talk to Igor,' said the inspector, picking up the telephone.

Dr Igor Schminke, the department's medical expert, had nothing to report other than that both men had been shot through the head and that he had recovered the bullets and sent them to ballistics.

'They say that they're pretty badly deformed,' he added, 'but that they're police ammunition.'

'Satisfied?' asked the sergeant as the inspector hung up the telephone.

'Even less so,' said the inspector. 'A four-months-old rookie, under fire for the first time, and he's so cool and accurate that he shoots two dangerous gangsters through the head before they can even fire their weapons. Call the training centre and ask them what kind of a score Karl had at weaponry training.'

The sergeant did as he was told.

'Good,' he said, putting down the telephone. 'Not the top of the class, but good. He's a very enthusiastic cop. Great law and order man.'

'Maybe too enthusiastic,' muttered the inspector. 'I've seen it before. Well, go get me a rundown on the victims now, will you? I want to know if they really were gangsters and, if so, what kind of gangsters.'

The task took the sergeant a little longer, but when he returned to the office, his information was concise and accurate. It was the only kind of information that he ever presented, which was one of the main reasons why he was the inspector's assistant.

'To begin with,' he said, 'the names given in the newspapers are incorrect. The two men were really Walter

Poettler, aged twenty-four and Johann Khisl, aged twenty-three.

'They both have records, but not exactly as gangsters. They're just petty crooks, drunk-rolling, small-time swindlers, blackmail and . . .'

'Ah-ha!' interrupted the inspector. 'Blackmail, you say?'

'You think they may have been blackmailing Karl?' said the sergeant. 'You couldn't get much from a patrolman's salary.'

'But you could get something out of a patrolman if you're a two-bit crook,' said the inspector. 'For example, a patrolman on night duty in the business district goes along trying doors. Every once in a while he finds one that the owner's forgotten to lock. So he calls the station and they contact the owner who comes down and locks it. Supposing he didn't call the station, but somebody else?'

'I see what you mean,' said the sergeant, 'but that doesn't fit in with the picture of Karl at all. His section sergeant says he's got an almost pathological hatred of crime and criminals.'

'Could be faking it as a cover up,' said the inspector. 'Or he could be doing something against his will because this couple were blackmailing him. You talked to the section sergeant? What did he have to say otherwise. What's this Karl like?'

'Tall, skinny kid,' said the sergeant. 'Strong as an ox and earnest as an owl. All spit and polish as if he was in the army rather than the police. Volunteers for everything and they have to knock him out to get him off duty.'

'The last statement is not literally intended, I take it,' remarked the inspector. 'However, I think you'll agree that, if Karl was being forced into some illegal activity, he'd be very liable to kill the blackmailers, given his nature and attitudes.'

'I suppose so,' said the sergeant. 'What do you want to do about it?'

'Exactly what we'd do if the man wasn't a police officer,' said the inspector. 'Murder is murder and I believe we have good reason to suspect that these two men were murdered.

That they may have deserved it, is of no consequence. If we're to permit the murder of everyone who deserves it, Vienna will decimated.'

'Full investigation then,' said the sergeant, getting to his feet. 'Well, it shouldn't be hard to crack if we can find out what it was that they had on him.'

It was, as the sergeant said, not difficult to break the case of the murdering police officer nor was it much more difficult to find out why Ernst Karl had lured his victims to the garage and shot them down in cold blood as they entered.

Ernst Karl, the very tough cop, was homosexual.

'They were blackmailing him,' said Sergeant Schuhmacher. 'He's made a full confession. They threatened to have him kicked out of the force so he's been paying them practically his entire salary plus anything he could borrow. Said he was afraid that it was only a matter of time before they'd force him into doing something crooked, so he killed them.'

'Sort of "I'd rather murder you than commit a crime" thing,' said the inspector. 'I suppose it didn't occur to him that murder was a crime.'

'His defence is that the men were criminals so they deserved to die anyway,' said the sergeant.

'We've been through that before,' said the inspector. 'I can't see the court accepting it.'

The court did not accept it, but the jury was somewhat understanding of Ernst Karl's predicament. The verdict was guilty, but with strong extenuating circumstances.

On December 19, 1968 Ernst Karl was sentenced to twenty years imprisonment and sent to the federal penitentiary at Stein to begin serving it.

In theory, this should have been the end of the career in law enforcement for ex-patrolmen Karl, but Karl did not see it that way. Scarcely arrived in prison, he began holding his own private court proceedings in the exercise yards and recreation rooms. Fellow prisoners whose sentences were, in Karl's opinion, insufficiently severe punishment for the crime concerned were summoned before the court by Police Officer Karl, prosecuted by Prosecuting Attorney Karl, sentenced by Judge Karl and, had the guards not promptly intervened on more than one occasion, executed by Executioner Karl.

There was no attorney for the defence, no jury and no acquittals. Executions were carried out, or would have been had there been no interference, by means of Karl's own two very powerful hands serving as a garotte.

Needless to say, Ernst Karl instantly became one of the most unpopular prisoners to ever grace a penal institution and the warden was constrained to hold him permanently in solitary confinement. It was either that or face a full scale prison revolt by the other prisoners.

Ernst Karl was a stubborn man and convinced of his principles. It was going to be some very considerable time before he would even be allowed in the exercise yard with the other prisoners, and any man in the prison would have committed suicide rather than share a cell with him. In a way, it amounted to very much the same thing.

In the meantime, hindered in the performance of what he construed to be his duty as an ex-patrolman, his former colleagues who had placed him in this position were involved in equal, if not identical difficulties.

These stemmed from a case which had arisen long after Karl had left the service.

On the morning of May 10, 1973 an employee of the Municipal Waste Disposal Service, otherwise known as a garbage man, had opened a trash can belonging to a shop near the centre of the city and had found himself looking into the face of a young woman.

The head to which the face belonged had been severed just below the chin and one of the young woman's breasts was resting on top of it, something like a macabre skull cap.

The expression of the face was not peaceful and the garbage man, although not normally inclined to fainting spells, lost consciousness. By the time that the police party arrived at the scene he had recovered, but was still largely incoherent.

Dr Schminke, who had come out in the car with the inspector and Sergeant Schuhmacher, gave the garbage man a tranquillizing injection as it was thought that he might know something about the head in the garbage can.

As it turned out, he did not, nor did he have any idea who the woman might be.

A squad of technicians from the police laboratories had now arrived and the garbage can was carefully emptied out onto a large plastic sheet. Eventually, most of the woman was found in the garbage can and in other garbage cans nearby.

The body was taken to the police morgue where Dr Schminke arranged it in its proper order and cleaned the face and hair. After pictures had been taken for the purpose of identification, he conducted a thorough autopsy.

While the body was being removed to the morgue, the technicians had made an exhaustive investigation of the area and had found nothing which could possibly be construed as connected with the dismembered corpse.

'I didn't think they'd find anything,' remarked the inspector as the sergeant returned to the office with his report. 'She obviously wasn't killed there. Someone merely brought the body along and dumped it in the cans. It's astonishing that it wasn't merely set on the hoist and dumped into the truck. If it had been, we'd only have found it at the dump, or possibly not at all. How did the garbage man come to open it?'

'He said,' said the sergeant, 'in so far as I can remember, "I had a strange, eerie feeling as if my spine had turned to ice. An inner voice commanded, 'Open the can, Hannibal!' and so I opened it".'

'My own feeling is that he sees too many old movies on late television, but apparently he did have some sort of hunch. The can was unusually heavy, of course.'

'His name is Hannibal?' said the inspector. 'Hannibal what?'

'Gronk,' said the sergeant. 'We're checking him out now, but I think it's very doubtful that he has anything to do with the murder.'

'We don't know that it was murder until Igor reports,' observed the inspector. 'Could have been an accidental death with someone trying to dispose of the body in a panic or something like that.'

It had, however, been murder.

'Karate chops,' said Dr Schminke, settling into the chair beside the inspector's desk and accepting a cup of coffee from the sergeant and a cigarette from the inspector.

Being a very conscientious young medical officer, he had worked most of the night on the body and his blue eyes were slightly bloodshot.

'Time of death,' he continued, 'was late day before yesterday afternoon or evening. The body was cut up with what appears to be an ordinary butcher's knife and a small handsaw by someone who had no idea of anatomy, but who had plenty of time. He simply continued to hack or saw until he got through whatever section he was working on. He may have used a hatchet or a cleaver in some places.'

'Any attempt to conceal the identity?' asked the inspector.

'None,' said the doctor. 'The fingerprints are intact and the face was not disfigured. She didn't look too happy because I think she had been raped just before she was killed. There are traces of sperm in the vagina.'

'A small girl, I take it,' said the inspector, 'since she was inside a garbage can?'

'Not unusually,' said the doctor. 'Five feet two inches. A hundred and two pounds. Don't forget not all of the body was in the one can and, secondly, it's easier to get into the can when it's cut up in comparatively small pieces.'

'Did you find anything else?'

'Nothing,' said the doctor. 'No trace of clothing and I think the pieces were brought to the can in plastic sacks because there are no fibres of any kind clinging to the cut surfaces and they are, of course, very sticky.'

'The laboratory was able to establish that everything else in the can was from the shop it belonged to,' said the sergeant. 'We're checking the owner and the personnel of course.'

'Hardly likely they'd put the corpse in their own garbage can,' said the inspector. 'Missing Persons?'

'I was waiting for Igor's description and the picture,' said the sergeant. 'How old would you say she was, Igor?'

'Between eighteen and twenty-two,' said the doctor.

There were a number of girls between the ages of eighteen and twenty-two missing in the city of Vienna, but none of them corresponded to the description of the girl found in the garbage can.

'I've put out circulars,' said the sergeant. 'If she's from Vienna, somebody should recognize her.'

Somebody eventually did, but not for some time.

'The girl in that circular,' said the voice on the telephone to the communications central of the Vienna Police without preamble, 'I think that might be our Miss Morscher.'

'Your name and address?' said the communications officer, pressing the button for the monitor to come on the line and begin the trace.

There were a great many circulars out in Vienna and some of them were for very serious offences. Calls such as this had to be traced in so far as possible should the caller be unwilling to identify him or herself.

This was not the case here for the caller immediately replied that his name was Martin Katz and that he was calling from the Albo Manufacturing Company's stock control office. He was, he said, the manager of the office and until the preceding week there had been a girl working there who looked very much like the picture on the circular.

Katz had assumed that the girl had merely quit without notice. She had been with the firm little more than two months and had had a routine clerical job. After noticing the circular at the railway station, he had called Personnel and had been told that Miss Ilse Morscher had neither given notice nor had she drawn what money she had on the books.

He had then called the police.

A team was sent to the Personnel Department of the company and learned that the girl had come originally from Graz, had been twenty-one years old, unmarried and living locally in a small studio apartment.

The apartment was searched and produced nothing except some pictures of the dead girl and her relatives in Graz.

There were no pictures of men to whom she was not related and her parents, upon being contacted by the Graz police, stated that she had not had any steady male friend.

'There's no evidence of anything happening at the apartment,' said Sergeant Schuhmacher, 'and her personal identification papers weren't there so the assumption would be that she was accosted on the street, presumably by a total stranger, who took her somewhere and killed her. The motive was undoubtedly sex.'

'It's going to be difficult,' said the inspector, frowning. 'Do you have any leads at all?'

'We're working on the office staff, the girls she worked with,' said the sergeant. 'Since she had only been three months in Vienna, it's probable that these were the only persons that she knew. What I'm trying to do is get some idea of her personal habits, where she hung out when she wasn't working, her interests and so on. From that we might be able to determine where she was when she was picked up by the murderer.'

The results of the interrogation of Ilse Morscher's fellow workers at the office produced largely negative results. Ilse Morscher, it seemed, had been a shy, strait-laced girl who had never mentioned any contacts with men and who, if she had any special interests, had not mentioned them to her colleagues.

'She was like a tourist,' said the sergeant. 'It was her first time in Vienna, and when she wasn't working she went around looking at the sights of the city.'

'That's not much help,' remarked the inspector. 'Is that all?'

'Almost,' said the sergeant. 'If Igor is correct about the time of death, she was killed on Friday evening. Two of the girls at the office think they remember her saying that she was going to visit the Prater that weekend. They thought she meant Saturday, but she might have gone that same evening after work.'

'And?' said the inspector.

'I've marked out the route between her apartment and the Prater,' said the sergeant, 'and, given the distance and the current bus schedules, the most logical thing for her to have done is to have walked there. What I plan to do now is go over to the Prater myself and buy some samples of sausages and candy.'

The Prater is, of course, Vienna's huge amusement park, famous for the giant Ferris wheel which is often used as a symbol of the city.

'According to the analysis of the stomach contents in the autopsy report,' said the sergeant, 'sausages and candy were among the last things she ate. I want to know if it was sausages and candy from the Prater. If it was, she was either killed there or en route between there and her apartment.'

'Very sound reasoning, Karl,' said the inspector. 'I think you're on the right track and I suspect you'll find she was killed on the way home. There are usually too many people at the Prater for a girl to be picked up against her will, and the evidence seems to be that she was not a girl to allow herself to be picked up voluntarily.'

The lead, no thicker than a single thread, held true. The sausages and candy which Ilse Morscher had eaten on the last evening of her life did stem from the Prater and one of the sausage sellers was even able to identify the girl from her picture. She had been a pretty girl with a shy gentle manner who had seemed out of place amidst the boisterous surroundings of the amusement park.

'So now,' said the sergeant, 'we're conducting a door-to-door canvas along the route between her apartment and the Prater. I'm not really all that optimistic though. There are too many things that could have intervened. The girl may have met her murderer at the Prater and gone somewhere else with him or he could have picked her up along the route when there were no witnesses. It's mostly residential and we don't know with certainty how late it was when the contact was made.'

The sergeant could have afforded a little more optimism. Almost immediately, persons were found who had seen a girl resembling Ilse Morscher coming back from the Prater on the evening in question. It was not long before the search was narrowed down to an area of less than two blocks.

'Since he had to have some private place to rape her and cut her up,' said the sergeant, 'the assumption is that the murderer actually lives in this area. We're eliminating those families where such a thing would be impossible and searching the apartments of the rest. I think we're going to get him.'

And get him they did.

The search of the apartment of Johann Rogatsch, a forty-two-year-old house painter with a record of minor sex offences, contained traces of blood of the same group as that of the dead girl.

The plumbing in the bathroom was dismantled and tiny chips of bone and hair were recovered from the drains. Burned fragments of women's clothing were found in the furnace in the basement.

The police interrogators applied pressure, keeping up a relentless barrage of questions against the stubborn wall of the suspect's resistance.

The end was, of course, inevitable. Exhausted and conscious of the weight of the evidence against him, Rogatsch became entangled in contradictions and inconsistencies in his own statements, gave up and confessed.

He had, he said, wanted nothing more from the girl than a kiss, but she had resisted and he had given her a karate chop. He had only begun taking lessons in karate and he had chopped too hard. He was sorry. It had been an accident.

The court accepted that he was probably sorry, but not that it had been an accident or that all he had wanted was a kiss. On January 4, 1974 Johann Rogatsch was found guilty of first degree murder and rape and sentenced to life imprisonment.

It was the maximum sentence which the court could pronounce. There was, however, a higher instance and it was sitting in the pentitentiary at Stein to which Johann Rogatsch was now sent.

It was now some considerable time since Judge Karl had tried any cases in Stein prison, and he was therefore sitting in the exercise yard and not in solitary confinement, the warden having come to the conclusion that he had revised his ideas about the administration of self justice.

The other prisoners were less confident and Karl sat alone.

Presently he was joined by the new prisoner, Johann Rogatsch, who had never heard of Ernst Karl or his feelings on the subject of law and order.

Rogatsch had not been in the prison long and he did not intend to stay there much longer if he could help it. He had already approached several of the other prisoners with suggestions for a break-out and had been rebuffed. Not being a professional criminal, he knew none of the other prisoners personally and was not highly regarded by them either.

Rapist-murderers are not, as a rule, popular even in prison. There were undoubtedly many in the prison who thought that Rogatsch should have been executed for his crime, and perhaps for this reason no one warned him that the man with whom he was sitting was a sterner judge than any he was likely to find in the conventional law courts.

Johann Rogatsch was, however, not interested in backgrounds or past history. He was interested in getting out and for that he needed a partner.

'Hostages is what does it,' said Rogatsch. 'Everybody's taking hostages now and the cops can't do a thing. Now, the way I see it, all we have to do is grab the warden's kids. He's got two little kids. And then, maybe, we take one of the guards and we tell them, either we get turned loose, with a car and a head start, or the kids get it. They won't have no choice. What do you think?'

'I think your whole suggestion is illegal,' said Ernst Karl flatly.

'You just ain't kidding,' chuckled Rogatsch who thought that Karl was trying to be funny. 'Now, I know where I can get a table knife and we can sharpen it up in the workshop. The only chance we'll have at the kids is when they come over to their dad's office, but they do that every once in a while. We'll have to wait for the right time and then play it by ear.'

'The court is in session,' said Ernst Karl, gathering his legs under him and flexing his very large hands. 'Prisoner! How do you plead?'

'Guilty to everything,' answered Johann Rogatsch, taking his companion's actions for a game and finding him a remarkably witty person. 'And what I ain't did yet, I'll do as soon as I get a chance.'

'Johann Rogatsch,' intoned Karl in the same flat, solemn, toneless voice, 'you have pleaded guilty to the charges of intent to take hostage minor children and an employee of the prison service with the purpose of illegally escaping from Stein penitentiary. Do you have anything to say in your defence?'

'Only that I can't think of no better way to get out,' said Rogatsch, vastly amused. He had not noticed that the other prisoners in the yard had gradually drifted away and that he and Karl were sitting almost completely alone beside the wall.

'Your defence is rejected,' said Ernst Karl, moving slightly closer to the unsuspecting man. 'In the name of the state of Austria, I hereby sentence you to death by execution and may the Lord have mercy upon your soul.'

'I'll appeal against the sentence,' gasped Rogatsch, laughing so hard that the tears ran down his face. 'By God, Karl! You sure know the language! Anybody would think you were a . . .'

His last sentence was abruptly cut off as Ernst Karl's powerful fingers closed about his throat.

'The sentence will be carried out at once,' said Executioner Karl with just a touch of satisfaction in his voice.

None of the guards was close enough to intervene in time, and naturally none of the prisoners could recall having seen anything, but it was not difficult to solve the mystery of the murder of Johann Rogatsch in the exercise yard of Stein Prison. Ernst Karl not only confessed, but was extremely proud of his act.

'A dangerous criminal,' he said. 'It is fortunate that he could be eliminated before he caused any more harm. One of my best cases.'

The court before which he was tried on charges of unpremeditated murder thought it one of his worst cases and on December 2, 1974 sentenced him to life imprisonment. Incredibly, the court-appointed psychologists had found him sane and responsible for his actions.

Ernst Karl is now back in Stein prison and the prisoners are more nervous than ever. All of them know by heart Ernst Karl's reply to the judge when he was asked if he had anything to say before he was sentenced.

Karl had turned his back on the judge and had addressed the spectators in the crowded court room.

'Have no fear, good citizens of Austria,' he had said. 'Whether in prison or out, you can depend upon me to continue and even intensify my battle against the criminals and law breakers in our midst. I shall not rest so long as a single criminal remains unpunished.'

The inmates of Stein prison, convicted criminals to a man, are utterly convinced of the sincerity of his words.

10

THE PASSIONATE PARAMOURS OF PORTSMOUTH

It was three-twenty in the morning of November 5, 1971 when Police Constable Paul O'Donovan peered through the window of the parked car and saw the dead man with the cylindrical, wooden handle of the knife sticking out of his chest.

Normally, Constable O'Donovan would have paid little attention to a car standing in the car park on the Purbrook Heath Road, but this car was different from all the others. The windows were not steamed.

People in cars parked in such places and at such times are usually engaged in rather strenuous physical activity accompanied by a good deal of heavy breathing. It steams the windows.

This car was cold and silent and the dew lay thick on the roof. Whatever physical activity there might have been, it was over now and forever.

The activity for the police had, however, just begun and, as Detective Superintendent Harry Pilbeam, the forty-four-year-old Crime Co-ordinator for South-East Hampshire, stood shivering and waiting for the reports of his men on that cold morning of Guy Fawkes Day 1971, there was no way that he could know that he was embarking on a case which would prove to be the longest and the most complicated in the history of the Hampshire Police.

For, at this time, the investigation did not promise to be too difficult, the identity of the corpse having been immediately established and there appearing to be a number of possible clues.

Chief among these was the murder weapon itself, a slender, sharp-pointed Japanese paper knife. Thirty-five-year-old Peter Richard Stanswood had been stabbed seven times with it and, of great importance to the investigations, some of the blood on its handle as well as on the steering wheel of his car was not his, but of a totally different blood group which the police laboratory would later establish as being APGM 21 AK1.

Stanswood, one of the owners of a pedalo business on the Isle of Wight, had lived at 28 Ninian Park Road, Copnor, in Portsmouth, the naval port on the south coast of England. He was survived by his lovely thirty-two-year-old, red-haired wife, born Heather Pridham, and the couple's two children, Tina and Charles.

Even before dawn had broken on that grey November day, detectives working under Superintendent Pilbeam had called at the Stanswood home to inform Mrs Stanswood of the death of her husband and to determine whether she might possibly shed any light on the identity and motives of the murderer.

Stunned and nearly incoherent with the shock of the sudden news, she could only say that her husband's business associate in the pedalo business was a Mr Ken Thompson, but that they had got on well to the best of her knowledge. She suggested with apparent reluctance that the murder might have something to do with her husband's mistresses.

After a little urging, she provided the stupefied detectives with a list of names of over two dozen women with whom her husband had allegedly been intimate, including two who had borne him illegitimate children and one who was now pregnant with his child. She thought he might have been spending the preceding night with this last-named mistress, a Miss Wendy Charlton, who lived at 17 Taswell Road in Southsea. He had, in any case, not been home at all that night. Her statements were confirmed by the couple's children.

Although it had seemed impossible to the detectives that a man could have as many mistresses as Mrs Stanswood had said her husband had and still have time to devote to business, it turned out that she had actually been guilty of an understatement. Peter Stanswood had had far more mistresses than even his wife suspected and had still been a diligent worker who earned considerably more than an average income.

Mrs Stanswood's guess about her husband's whereabouts on the night of the murder was, however, accurate. Miss Charlton confirmed that he had been with her and had, during the course of the evening, telephoned a Miss Linda Reading, one of the mothers of his illegitimate children. When he left somewhat later, she had thought that he was going to Miss Reading or home.

With the exception of the murderer, Miss Charlton was, apparently, the last person to have seen Peter Stanswood alive, but the police were already beginning to realize that what had seemed a comparatively simple case was turning into a complex tangle of adulterous sex relations involving such numbers of people that it sometimes seemed half the population of Portsmouth had had reason to want to murder Peter Stanswood.

Before the case would end, more than 20,000 persons would be questioned and over 2640 statements taken, some of them several times when it became obvious that the previous statements were false.

And many were false, for, if Peter Stanswood had been astonishingly active in the pursuit of extra-marital adventures, his exploits had been largely dwarfed by a veritable army of housewives who enjoyed their lovers on what amounted to practically a production line basis.

There had been few complaints from their husbands. They were acting as lovers for the other housewives.

Under such circumstances, it was scarcely strange that many of the persons interviewed were, to say the least, something short of candid. In many cases the detectives, anxious to avoid domestic friction, were forced to interview the men separately at their place of work and their wives during their absence.

As in all cases where the murder victim is married, the widow had been considered the prime suspect although it was certain that she could not actually have been present at the murder. She could, however, be responsible with the actual killing carried out by one of her lovers.

For Heather Stanswood too had had lovers, some two dozen of them, according to her own statement to the police, and the most recent, and therefore most interesting to the police, was a thirty-nine-year-old gas conversion worker named Kenneth Joseph Fromant, married, the father of two daughters and resident at Hilary Drive, Crowthorne, in Berkshire.

Fromant had a police record, having been sentenced to five years' imprisonment in 1950 for shooting another man in the thigh. The incident had taken place during a confrontation between London street gangs and the victim had been attacking Fromant with a broken bottle at the time.

Although this prison record might indicate a tendency to violence on the part of Kenneth Fromant, it did not make him any better a suspect than Mrs Stanswood's other lovers or the husbands and lovers of Peter Stanswood's mistresses, and Fromant stated in his interview with the police that he had been in Berkshire on the night of the murder.

This could be neither proved nor disproved, but there was good reason to believe that Fromant had terminated his affair with Heather Stanswood at least two months before the murder. Moreover, neither he nor anyone else appeared to have taken the affairs very seriously.

Heather Stanswood had, it was true, once filed divorce proceedings against her husband when he became the father of his first illegitimate child in 1961, but there had been a reconciliation and the case had never come before the court. Since that time, he had had literally dozens of mistresses, many with Heather Stanswood's knowledge and some, apparently, with her approval.

One such case was represented by Elizabeth Thompson, the thirty-two-year-old wife of Stanswood's business partner and Heather Stanswood's oldest and best friend.

Mrs Thompson, at that time the mother of three children and living at Bell Crescent, Waterlooville, had formed a friendship with the then Heather Pridham at the age of sixteen when both girls were working as machine operators in a dress factory. The friendship had continued after Elizabeth Binning had married Ken Thompson in 1959. Heather had married Peter Stanswood one year later and the two men had also become friends, Thompson moving to the Isle of Wight in 1970 to join Stanswood in his pedalo boat business. The Thompsons had then gradually become estranged, but long before this, Peter Stanswood and Elizabeth Thompson had been engaged in sexual relations, certainly with the knowledge of Heather Stanswood and, possibly, with the knowledge of Ken Thompson who may have had sexual relations with Heather Stanswood as well.

It was in Elizabeth Thompson's statement to the police that the first mention of gas conversion workers other than Kenneth Fromant was made. She had, she said, entered into a relationship with one of the gas conversion men following a fire which had cost her her home and most of her possessions. She had also suffered a broken leg and the gas man had been helpful at a time when she sorely needed help. This was in 1970, not long after her husband had gone to the Isle of Wight.

Later that year, she had severed her connection with the gas conversion worker, whose name was not revealed to avoid domestic complications, and had taken up with another gas conversion worker named Arthur Gavin.

Mr Gavin was the brother-in-law of Kenneth Fromant who had been the lover of Heather Stanswood until September of 1971 when he left her for Elizabeth Thompson. There were no hard feelings and the two friends apparently exchanged confidences and lovers almost casually.

Such complicated histories involving adultery and illicit sexual relations between hundreds or, possibly, even thousands of persons in the Portsmouth area were the most striking characteristic of the case and also the most troublesome to the police in solving it. They were, however, of vital importance for, as the investigations progressed, it became increasingly certain that it was some facet of these intertwining relationships which had led to the murder of Peter Stanswood.

And with this certainty came the suspicion that one or more of the gas conversion workers, of whom there had been at times as many as a hundred in the city, were involved. Out of the hundreds of women interviewed, an enormous percentage admitted to having had adulterous relations with gas conversion men.

Aside from this, progress was slow. The source of the murder weapon had proved impossible to trace, there being many thousands of such Japanese paper knives which had been imported into the country. No fingerprints had been found on either the knife or the door handles of the car.

The autopsy had not been particularly helpful and had, actually, provided something of an additional mystery for it reported that traces of pheno-barbitone were present in the liver of the corpse. This could indicate that Stanswood had been, in some way, connected with the drug scene, but no evidence of this could be found.

There was also still no known motive. Stanswood had had no very serious enemies even among the men whose wives had granted him their sexual favours. No one had benefited by his death. In an atmosphere where casual, promiscuous sex was accepted as the normal pattern of life, it seemed hardly likely that anyone would have been so involved emotionally as to commit murder out of jealousy. Most of the husbands and wives appeared to know of the partner's extra-marital adventures and most of them seemed not to have cared.

If they had not cared before, they did now for, with the death of Peter Stanswood and the resulting publicity, it was no longer possible to gloss over such flagrant sexual activity. The people involved were not, for the most part, among the very young, usually thought of as liberal in their activities toward sex, but persons in their thirties, forties and even older. Open knowledge of adultery could be very damaging to such persons and, as one of the detectives put it, there were probably upward of a thousand persons in Portsmouth who did not sleep well as long as the investigations were going on.

And they went on for a very long time despite what seemed for a time a break almost at the beginning of the case.

The supposed break came less than a week after the murder and began with an incident in the Castle Tavern, Somers Road, Southsea. The occasion was a darts match with a team from the Royal Exchange Pub.

Peter Stanswood was well known in the Castle Tavern, where he had been a prominent member of the darts team. During the course of the evening, there was a drawing of tickets and, to the horror of all present, the name called out as winner by the girl behind the bar was Peter Stanswood.

An instant later, the horror was compounded when Peter Stanswood stepped calmly forward and claimed his prize!

It was, of course, not the murdered Peter Stanswood, but a roofing engineer from Purbrook by the same name who was on the darts team of the Royal Exchange Pub. Incredibly, although somewhat older, he looked very much like the dead man and had even frequented one of the same public houses, the Monckton Pub in Copnor Road not far from where the murdered Peter Stanswood had lived. For months afterwards, his wife was troubled by condolence calls from persons thinking him dead, and he found the whole experience extremely nerve-wracking.

Not a little of this nervous tension was produced by one of the police theories, i.e. that the murder of the other Peter Stanswood had been a case of mistaken identity. The murderer had really wanted to kill the roofing engineer and not the pedalo operator.

The theory was based largely on the fact that in the weeks preceding the murder, a number of anonymous calls had been received by the Peter Stanswood in Purbrook. Usually, the caller, a man, had asked for Peter Stanswood and had then said nothing more, but had remained on the line as the sound of his breathing could be heard. On other occasions, the caller had said nothing at all.

The roofing engineer had no idea who might have wanted

to harm him, but he accepted the police idea that, if the murder had been a case of mistaken identity, the murderer might attempt to correct his mistake, and for weeks he carried the telephone number of the police station in his pocket whenever he went out. He was also discreetly accompanied at a distance by one of Superintendent Pilbeam's men.

There was no attempt on the life of the surviving Peter Stanswood, but one significant thing did take place.

From the day that Peter Stanswood of Ninian Park Road was murdered, no further anonymous telephone calls were received by Peter Stanswood in Purbrook. To be on the safe side, the Post Office provided him with an unlisted number and the mystery of the anonymous caller was never solved.

One thing was, however, certain and that was that Peter Stanswood of Purbrook, a respectable father of three teenage children, was in no way connected with Peter Stanswood of Ninian Park Road or with the vast circle of subscribers to the joys of permissive, liberal sex in Portsmouth.

The gas conversion workers were, it seemed, almost to a man, and the investigations now led to one of the meeting places for gas men and adventurously-minded housewives in the Mecca Ballroom, Arundel Street, Landport.

Here, among the hundreds of women interviewed, was found the lead to the Scots housewife who, without realizing it, would provide one of the vital keys to the solution of the case.

It was July of 1972 and nearly nine months had passed since the murder of Peter Stanswood. On that afternoon the Scots woman, who asked that her name should not be revealed as her husband would not like it, was being interviewed by Detective Inspector Ernie Woolf and Detective Constable Roger Hurst. During the course of the interview she revealed, almost casually, that she had been visited on the night of the murder by her lover at the time, a gas conversion worker named Ian Dance.

This caused the detectives' ears to prick up for Dance had been interviewed and had denied being in Portsmouth that night. He was immediately brought back to police headquarters and, being confronted with the statement of his Scots mistress, he changed his story and admitted that he had been in Portsmouth on the evening of the murder. He had driven there, he said, in the company of another gas conversion worker, Mr Kenneth Fromant.

This was of great interest to the police, for the name of Kenneth Fromant had been on the list of friends, lovers and acquaintances with which Heather Stanswood had provided Inspector Woolf some two weeks after the crime.

Fromant had been interviewed at this time, but had denied being in Portsmouth, saying that he had been at his home in Berkshire.

Now, according to the statement of Ian Dance, he had been in Portsmouth after all and, although there appeared to be no connection between Dance and Stanswood, Fromant had allegedly been the lover of both his and his partner's wives.

On July 17, 1972, Fromant was brought to police headquarters in Cosham and interrogated for the second time. Confronted with the statement made by Ian Dance, he admitted that he had been in the Portsmouth area and that he had lied about this in his first statement.

He had, he said, spent the night with Elizabeth Thompson.

This was denied by Elizabeth Thompson, who was being interviewed in another room, but she did change her story also to admit that she had had sexual relations with Fromant on a number of occasions. Previously, she had admitted only to having had sex with him once.

Both Fromant and Thompson denied any connection with the murder of Peter Stanswood, but a sample of Fromant's blood, sent to the police laboratories, returned with the information that it belonged to Group APGM 21 AK1, the identical group to the blood found on the steering wheel of Stanswood's car and on the handle of the murder weapon.

Blood is, however, not like fingerprints and more than one person can have the same blood group. However, among all the persons tested so far, only Kenneth Fromant had Group APGM 21 AK1.

The police were, therefore, inclined to think that Fromant might very well be their man although they were still not in any position to prove it.

Their suspicions were strengthened a short time later by what Superintendent Pilbeam was to describe as a 'godsend' and a 'colossal piece of luck'. In spite of all the time which had elapsed, the car in which Dance and Fromant had come to Portsmouth was found standing in the yard of a garage at Bitterne, Southampton. Incredibly, it had not been driven since the night of the murder. It had failed its road test.

Samples of soil taken from the treads of its tyres were brought to the police laboratories where it was possible to determine that the samples were identical to the soil found at the scene of the crime.

Even with this, the case was far from complete. There was still no plausible motive and there was not the slightest evidence that Kenneth Fromant had ever even met Peter Stanswood while he was alive. In addition, although Heather Stanswood had listed Fromant as one of her lovers, he denied this and said he did not even know the woman.

Four months later, he was once again brought to police headquarters in Cosham and, this time, he changed his story again and admitted not only that he had known Heather Stanswood, but that he had had sexual relations with her over a period of time. He added, however, that he had had sexual relations with a good many Portsmouth housewives and that none of their husbands had been murdered. Why should he have chosen Peter Stanswood for a victim when he had never met him and his affair with Heather Stanswood had been so fleeting that he could scarcely remember it?

The police had no answer to this question, but they did have three major points in evidence against Kenneth Fromant. The car in which he had come to Portsmouth on the night of the murder had been at the parking area in the Purbrook Heath Road as shown by the soil on the tyres. The blood on the handle of the murder weapon and on the steering wheel of the victim's car were of the identical blood group to his. And he had engaged some two months prior to the murder in sexual relations with the wife of the victim.

The greatest difficulty was lack of a motive. If Kenneth Fromant was guilty of the murder, then it would appear that he had stabbed to death a total stranger for no reason at all.

Or had the killing really been a case of mistaken identity? Did Fromant think that the man he was murdering was the Peter Stanswood of Purbrook, the roofing engineer who had received the mysterious telephone calls?

The possibility was investigated as carefully as all of the other possibilities in the case. There was not the slightest evidence that Fromant had ever met or heard of the Peter Stanswood from Purbrook.

There had, it seemed, been no mistake. Someone had wanted to murder the Peter Stanswood who had been murdered and the person with the most plausible motive was still Heather Stanswood, his wife. Fromant, who had actually carried out the murder, had had no motive of his own, but had merely been acting at the instigation of his former mistress.

Early in 1975, the Director of Public Prosecutions came to the conclusion that the case against Fromant and Mrs Stanswood was sufficiently established and issued orders to the police to proceed against them.

On May 19, 1975, Superintendent Pilbeam went to the office of the manager of the North Thames Gas Board in London where Fromant was currently working and took him into custody.

'You are being placed under arrest,' he said, 'for the murder of Peter Stanswood.'

'What is there to say?' said Fromant stoically.

Oddly, although he had met the superintendent on several previous occasions, he appeared not to remember or recognize him at all.

He was taken back to Cosham where he and Heather Stanswood, who had resumed her maiden name of Pridham and who had also been taken into custody that same day, were formally charged with the murder of Peter Stanswood. Neither made any statement and they did not look at or speak to each other.

The committal proceedings against Kenneth Fromant and Heather Pridham were due to take place on July 12, 1975, but on the ninth, Mrs Pridham suddenly called for her solicitor and her barrister and, in their presence, made a startling confession to something which she said she had kept secret for nearly two years.

Elizabeth Thompson, she said, had confessed to her that she and Kenneth Fromant had murdered Peter Stanswood and had described exactly what had taken place that evening.

According to this statement, Elizabeth Thompson had called Peter Stanswood on the day of the murder and had made an appointment to meet him at the Purbrook Heath Road car park, presumably for the purpose of engaging in sexual intercourse.

Stanswood had accepted and when he arrived, she and Kenneth Fromant, who was her current lover, were waiting in the car in which he and Ian Dance had come to Portsmouth. Dance was not present, having been dropped off at the house of the Scots housewife with whom he was having an affair.

Elizabeth Thompson and Kenneth Fromant had then joined Peter Stanswood in his car, there had been an altercation and Fromant had received a cut in the arm from the Japanese paper knife which he had brought with him. Regaining control of the knife, he had then stabbed Stanswood to death.

Following the murder, Mrs Thompson and Fromant had driven to Mrs Fromant's home at 10 Philip Road in Waterlooville, where they had changed clothes and Mrs Thompson had stitched up the cut in Fromant's arm.

The motive for all this appeared to be that Elizabeth Thompson was in love with her friend's husband and resented his affairs with other women. Fromant seemed to have been drawn into the matter without being too clear as to what he was doing.

Elizabeth Thompson had, in the meantime, divorced her husband in 1973 and had acquired a new lover, a Mr Peter Jackson, to whom she bore a child early in 1974.

Brought to Cosham Police Headquarters and confronted

with the statement by Heather Pridham, she burst into tears, declared it nothing more than a pack of lies and was permitted to leave.

On July 12, 1975, the committal proceedings against Kenneth Fromant and Heather Pridham took place before the stipendiary magistrate Sir Ivo Rigby at Havant Magistrates Court and ended in committal for Fromant. Heather Pridham was ordered to be released as she was found to have no case to answer.

Checking of her statement concerning the confession of Elizabeth Thompson continued and, on August 5, 1975, Sergeant Cox went to Waterlooville where he arrested Elizabeth Thompson and brought her back to Cosham. She was charged by Superintendent Pilbeam with the murder that same evening and, on September 12, 1975, was committed to stand trial with Kenneth Fromant for the murder of Peter Stanswood.

The trial began on October 21, 1975 at Winchester Crown Court with Mr Justice Talbot presiding. The seventeen days that it lasted were so filled with testimony concerning the illicit sexual activities of a large segment of Portsmouth society that even the judge was moved to remark that Portsmouth was a city in which sexual promiscuity and adultery were rife within some social groups.

Much of the testimony was anonymous with names being suppressed by the police in order to avoid domestic quarrels and protect marriages, as far as possible. A very clear picture emerged, however, of the almost legendary exploits of the gas conversion men with the housewives of Portsmouth. Following the trial, these statements were destroyed.

The matter of the motive for the killing was never entirely made clear, but the indications were that Mrs Thompson had been more jealous of Stanswood than his own wife had been.

There were also suggestions that Kenneth Fromant had murdered Stanswood out of jealousy over his success with women. This theory was particularly popular with the foreign press which built up a sort of hypothetical competition between the two men based on the number of women with whom they had managed to commit adultery. Fromant had not been able to rack up as high a score as his rival and had, in a fit of jealous rage, murdered him.

This was, however, contradicted by the fact that Fromant had apparently never before in his life laid eyes on Stanswood up until the night of November 4, 1971 and, if he did not even know the identity of the man he was murdering, he could hardly have been jealous of his exploits.

Kenneth Fromant did not give any reason, his only comment on the murder being, 'that it was all for nothing'.

Called to the witness box to testify on his own behalf, he provided the court with one last sensation in a trial which was quite sensational enough to begin with.

'Yes,' said Kenneth Fromant. 'I was at the scene of the murder. I lied in my original statement. I was there and I was cut in the arm as Mrs Heather Pridham stated. However, I could not reveal the truth before because I wished to protect the true guilty party, Mrs Elizabeth Thompson! It was she who wielded the knife and not I!'

This 'confession' to his mistress's part in the murder did not impress the jury very much and on November 14, 1975, they found Kenneth Joseph Fromant and Elizabeth Thompson guilty of the murder of Peter Richard Stanswood. Oddly enough, the jury apparently found more evidence of Mrs Thompson's guilt than of Fromant's, for the verdict in her case was unanimous while Fromant was convicted with only a majority decision of ten to two.

Both were sentenced to life imprisonment by Mr Justice Talbot, who remarked that he did not think that the court had even yet heard all of the truth concerning the case.

And well he might, for there were a number of questions which were never answered.

The motive was, of course, one of the most important, but there was also the matter of the murder weapon which could not be traced and the origin of which remained unknown. It had also not been possible to ascertain when and where Peter Stanswood had received his invitation to drive to the Purbrook Heath Road rendezvous.

There was the question of the knife wound which Kenneth

Fromant had admittedly received in the arm. Had it been in the course of a struggle with Stanswood and, if so, how had Fromant managed to regain control of the knife and kill his adversary with it?

Then, there were the traces of pheno-barbitone found in the liver of the corpse. Had Stanswood been connected with the drug scene? There was not the slightest evidence that he was.

Perhaps Elizabeth Thompson and Kenneth Fromant know the answers to these questions, but, if they do, they did not reveal them at the trial or after. Instead, they sat engrossed in their own affairs and not even looking at each other until the trial was over.

Fromant received his sentence impassively and without changing expression. Mrs Thompson showed scarcely more emotion, but appeared to be on the verge of tears as she was led away to begin serving her sentence.

11

TO LOVE IS TO KILL

On the northern edge of central Germany, where the strangely formed hedges of the ancient kingdom of Muenster give way to the moors and low-lying plains of the north, lies the historic Teutoburger Forest, swinging in a great curve from Rheine in the west, through Bielefeld to Paderborn in the south-east.

To the north-east of Bielefeld lies Herford and, beyond that, Rehme. Rehme is not a very large town, not nearly as large as Herford or Bielefeld, but in the spring of 1961 an event took place there which was to put fear into the hearts of women and girls for many miles around.

Not immediately, though. When Oscar Riedel, a middle-aged foreman in a shoe factory, walking to the Rehme railway station to go to work, came upon the corpse of the girl lying in the ditch, it was taken as an isolated incident. That is, the public took it as an isolated incident. The police were not so sure.

April 8, 1961 was a Saturday, but the shoe factory where Riedel was employed was working. The German economic wonder was in full swing and some plants were working straight through the week.

Oscar Riedel did not mind. He liked his work and he was making money. Moreover, the spring was not as rainy as it often is in central Europe and this particular Saturday was bright and sunny enough to be in June.

Half-way to the railway station, Riedel came upon a figure lying in the ditch beside the road, a figure which he could not see clearly because of the rank growth of grass and weeds along the edge. Assuming that some drunk had fallen into the ditch and had passed out or even injured himself there, Riedel started to clamber down with a view to offering help.

He had only progressed far enough to get a clear look at the figure when he froze. This was no drunk. It was a girl, a girl standing almost on her head, her skirts up over her face and her legs widespread to display obscenely the naked lower torso. There was blood on her white thighs and belly and what looked like the shreds of torn underwear lay around her.

The conclusion that the girl had been raped was inescapable and Riedel promptly tumbled down into the bottom of the ditch to offer help. However, the hand which he seized was cold and stiff and there was no pulse in the slender wrist.

The girl had not only been raped, she had been murdered!

Shaking with horror, Riedel scrabbled out of the ditch and ran wildly off in the direction of town. Five minutes later the local constable knew that Rehme had had its first murder case in at least two generations.

Not, of course, that the constable could do much about it. Rehme is too small to have its own Criminal Investigations Department and such matters are handled out of the city of Minden, six miles to the north-east.

The constable, therefore, came out to the scene of the discovery, verified Oscar Riedel's report and immediately called Minden. Forty minutes later Inspector Gerhard Heidel and his assistant, Detective-Sergeant Leopold Eisenbach, arrived bringing with them the department's medical expert, Dr Herbert Krause.

The doctor immediately proceeded to an on-the-spot examination of the corpse while the sergeant began staking off the area in one metre squares.

'Are we going to need the lab squad, Leo?' said the inspector.

'Doubt it,' said the sergeant. 'If there's anything, it's right around the body. I can take care of it.'

The doctor had by now turned the dead girl's skirts back from her face and the inspector asked the local police if they were able to identify her.

They were. She was a twenty-three-year-old local girl who lived with her parents and worked as a salesgirl in one of the shops. Her name was Ingrid Kanike. Being a small town, they also knew that she had been neither engaged nor going steady.

'She was a nice girl, but a little plump,' said the chief constable. 'Worried about her weight a lot.'

'We'll go over and talk to the parents,' said the inspector. 'They have to be notified and they may be able to give us some idea of where she was last night and what she was doing, assuming, of course, that this happened last night.'

'It did,' said the doctor, 'around midnight.'

The inspector and the constable left and when they returned an hour later, the sergeant and the doctor had both completed their work.

'Nothing,' said the sergeant. 'I found her handbag. It hadn't been opened. Usual stuff a woman carries around with her. Small amount of money. From the marks on the ground, he simply grabbed her, dragged her into the ditch, tore off her underwear and raped her. Whether he strangled her before or after, I don't know.'

'After,' said the doctor. 'Or at least death took place after. He was probably holding her throat while he was raping her, but he only shut off her breath after he had finished.'

'Fully consummated, I take it?' said the inspector.

The doctor nodded shortly. 'Fully,' he said. 'The girl was a virgin which is where the blood on the thighs and belly comes from.'

'You think he may have known her?' said the inspector.

'Doubtful,' said the doctor. 'This is an almost classic sex crime. The man is a sadist who can, very probably, only achieve sexual satisfaction by killing or at least severely injuring his partner.

'He has a compulsion and the first available female is the one taken. This girl merely had bad luck. She probably never set eyes on him before in her life.'

'Well, I didn't get very much from the parents either,' said the inspector. 'They didn't even know she was missing. She went to a movie in Minden last night and should have come back on the train which arrives here at seven minutes past twelve.'

'And the murderer jumped her as she was walking home,' said the doctor. 'A clear picture.'

'Not quite,' said the inspector. 'Her parents said she often went to the movies in Minden and that then she got back after they had gone to bed. On a Saturday morning like this, the parents still weren't up when she went off to work so they wouldn't normally see her until evening. That's why they didn't know she was missing. They thought she'd gone to work.'

'That doesn't alter anything,' said the sergeant.

'No,' said the inspector, 'but they also said that she never walked home from the railway station at night. She was afraid and she took a cab.'

'We'd better take a good, hard look at the cab drivers here,' said the sergeant.

'Exactly,' said the inspector. 'So, if you would like to start with that, I'll send for the ambulance and get the body moved down to the morgue. You're sure there aren't any further clues?'

'There aren't any clues at all,' said the sergeant.

There were no clues at the railway station either. Although nearly all of the some fifteen or twenty persons who had been on the 12.07 train from Minden to Rehme were located, none of them could remember seeing Ingrid Kanike.

'She may not even have been on the train,' said the sergeant, reporting on the results of the investigation. 'The fact is, the girl was rather retiring and not at all conspicuous. Add to that the late hour and the half empty train and it's quite possible that she escaped notice. But we can't be sure.'

'What about the cab drivers?' said the inspector.

'Six of them at the railway station stand,' said the sergeant. 'All local men. All middle-aged. All married. Not one of them has been driving a cab for less than eight years. Herb says they don't fit the pattern.'

'Herb also says that we haven't heard the last of this,' said the inspector quietly. 'He thinks there'll be more.'

'Not in our district, I hope,' said the sergeant. 'Because

I can tell you right now, I don't think we're going to solve this one.'

Nor did they.

There were no clues. No leads. Nothing to investigate. Pictures and identification data was assembled on all the persons who had been on the 12.07 train from Minden as well as the Rehme cab drivers, but there was no reason to suspect any of them. No explanation was ever found as to why Ingrid Kanike had chosen just on that one night not to take a cab, but to walk home and into the arms of her murderous lover.

The case eventually ended up in the unsolved section of the Minden police records and no similar cases were reported anywhere in the area. Dr Krause had, it seemed, been wrong. The rapist was not a deviate who could find satisfaction only in the death of his partner.

Or was it that he did not have a very active sex life?

Four years passed and then, once again, there was the murder of another woman under, to say the least, mysterious circumstances. This time, the crime took place indoors and there were almost too many clues.

The victim was a twenty-six-year-old secretary named Ursula Fritz. She had failed to report for work on May 17, 1965 and, when she had still not appeared by Friday of that week, the firm had simply sacked her and had sent her final cheque by mail to her home address. No one had bothered to check on her personally.

Eventually, on May 25th, her landlady had come to the conclusion that she had skipped without paying her final rent, due on May 20th. She therefore used her pass key to open the door and enter the woman's one-room apartment.

Ursula Fritz had not skipped and, no sooner was the door opened, than the unfortunate landlady was struck in the face by such an unbelievable stench that she fainted and fell on the floor, receiving a nasty cut over the left eye as her head struck the edge of the door.

Recovering her senses after some little time, she crawled, dizzy and covered with blood, down the stairs and telephoned the police. She still had no idea what had happened in Ursula Fritz's room, but she was quite certain that anything that smelled that way must be illegal.

All this took place not in Rehme, but in the city of Herford, eight miles to the south-west, and Herford has its own department of criminal investigations. It was an Inspector Anton Jech, a Detective-Sergeant Dieter Schmidt and a Dr Juergen Schoenauer who eventually arrived at the scene. They found that Mrs Schroeder, the injured landlady, had been quite right. What had transpired in Ursula Fritz' apartment was definitely illegal.

'She's been dead for over a week and it was warm in here,' said the doctor. 'I don't think that any kind of an examination is possible until we get her down to the morgue.'

'Then let's do it,' said the inspector. 'This had better be a crime or I'll have those patrolcar cops walking a beat in the factory district until they go on retirement.'

The two patrol car officers who had answered Mrs Schroeder's summons had simply reported a woman murdered in her bed to the station. This had brought out the homicide squad, but there was no real reason to believe that Ursula Fritz had died from anything other than natural causes. Fortunately for the patrolmen, it was soon established that Miss Fritz had not died of natural causes. She had been raped and strangled in her own bed.

'You're quite sure of that, Juergen?' said the inspector, 'with the body in such a state of decomposition? When was she killed?'

'The evening of May fifteenth,' said the doctor. 'I wouldn't have put these things in the autopsy report if I wasn't certain.'

'How can you tell she was raped?' asked Sergeant Schmidt.

'He ejaculated inside her,' said the doctor simply. 'Maximum penetration. She wasn't co-operating. She was struggling so hard to keep her legs together that she strained several of the muscles in her upper thighs.'

'Cause of death?' grunted the inspector.

'Manual strangulation,' said the doctor. 'He crushed her throat. The larynx was fractured.'

'A nasty business,' said the inspector. 'Our investigations

show that the woman was something of an old maid, didn't have any male friends and certainly none who would have been visiting her in her room.'

'And yet someone was,' said the sergeant. 'And he didn't break in. There were two glasses. One with her fingerprints and one with a man's. There were seven cigarette butts in the ashtray and only four burned matches. There were fibres of grey serge of a type used in men's suiting on the bedclothes. There was a man there and she didn't expect him to do her any harm.'

'The trouble is,' said the inspector, 'we can't find any man she knew that well.'

'If I were you, I would concentrate on persons with a record of sex crimes,' said the doctor. 'This has all the signs of a compulsive sex crime, a sadist who can obtain satisfaction only through the suffering of his sex partner. I would be willing to bet that this is not the first time he's done this.'

'Well, if it isn't, he wasn't caught the other times or he'd be in jail now,' said the inspector. 'Send a circular to all stations, nation-wide, Dieter. Give the circumstances and ask if anybody has anything similar in the unsolveds.'

Minden, of course, did.

'The circumstances of your case in the circular are almost identical to the case of Ingrid Kanike in Rehme in April of nineteen sixty-one,' said Inspector Heidel speaking to Inspector Jech over the telephone. 'We investigated it, but we never solved it. Do you have any leads in your case?'

'Clues yes, leads no,' said the inspector in Herford. 'Would you send me down copies of everything you have in the file? With Rehme only eight miles from here, I think there's a good chance the cases are connected. Maybe between the two of us, we can do something.'

It was essential that something be done, for the newspapers had recalled the case of Ingrid Kanike in Rehme four years earlier and were billing the new killing as part of a series. Many women and girls in the district were refusing to go out unaccompanied after dark and there was some criticism of the police.

'Never mind the criticism,' said Inspector Jech. 'It's

worth it if it keeps the women off the streets at night. The newspapers may just be right.'

The file on the Kanike case proved to be of no value in the Fritz investigation and it appeared that that too would end up in the unsolveds. Once again, there was nothing to investigate.

And then, a month after the discovery of the body of Ursula Fritz in Herford, an arrest was made in Rehme. A thirty-four-year-old unemployed butcher named Gerd Simmon was arrested near the Rehme railway station as he attempted to rape a fourteen-year-old girl.

Simmon was not a local man and the residents of Rehme, assuming that he was the mysterious rapist-murderer of Ingrid Kanike and Ursula Fritz, quickly formed a crowd and would possibly have lynched him had not Sergeant Eisenbach come rushing down in response to the local constable's urgent call and whisked him off to Minden.

Inspector Jech in Herford was immediately notified and, upon his arrival, Simmon was subjected to severe interrogation by Inspector Jech and Inspector Heidel.

Simmon did not deny the attempted rape of the fourteen-year-old nor did he make any effort to conceal his police record. He had been charged four times with attempted rape and child molestation and convicted twice, serving one sentence of two years and six months and one of three and eight. But he denied that he had had anything to do with the death of Ingrid Kanike and stated that he had never been in Herford in his life.

A strange-looking man with a great deal of carroty-red hair on his head and his entire body as well, he had exceedingly long arms and huge hands.

He appeared also to be totally lacking in nerves.

Nothing that the two inspectors could say shook him in the slightest. He was, he calmly admitted, a sex criminal. He could not help himself. He had never killed anyone.

After a long session of questioning which was actually more tiring to the police than the suspect, Simmon was removed to the detention cells, charged with the attempted rape in Rehme and held for further questioning.

The police withdrew to Inspector Heidel's office for much needed cups of coffee.

'Any comment or suggestions?' said Inspector Heidel.

'I think we're wasting our time with the questioning,' said Inspector Jech. 'We could put Simmon through a sausage machine and the pieces would come out saying, I am a sex criminal, but I have not killed anybody.'

'I think we're wasting our time with Simmon altogether,' said Dr Krause quietly.

'I would agree with that,' said Dr Schoenauer. 'Simmon is a fumbler. He probably doesn't even want to rape the girls or maybe he's incapable. In any case, there's nothing in his record about his actually raping anyone. It's all attempted, but never with success.'

'Exactly,' said Dr Krause. 'And the murderer of Ingrid Kanike and Ursula Fritz was as deadly as a steel trap. Once he got his hands on the woman, it was maximum penetration and death. Simmon bears the same relationship to him that a grass snake does to a king cobra.'

'Well, you gentlemen are the medical experts,' said Inspector Heidel, 'so we have to accept your opinion. However, I think that we might go over the people who were in that train the night that Ingrid Kanike was killed, in so far as they can still be located and see if any of them can recognize a picture of Simmon. He's not a man you'd be likely to forget.'

'We could also try the cab drivers,' said Sergeant Eisenbach.

'And we'll show his picture to Ursula Fritz's landlady and the people she worked with,' said Inspector Jech. 'As you say, he's a man you'd remember.'

No one did. Not a soul in Rehme or in Herford could be found who could recall ever having seen anyone who looked like Gerd Simmon.

He was eventually brought to trial for the attempted rape and sentenced to two years imprisonment.

'Do we give up now?' said Sergeant Schmidt. 'There isn't anything left to investigate, is there?'

'Give the material the routine cross check and send it to

the unsolveds,' said the inspector shortly. 'We'll have to wait for his next one.'

The routine check, carried out before a case is finally sent to the unsolved files, did produce something of interest this time.

'When Minden interviewed those cab drivers at the Rehme railway station the second time, one of them told a different story to the one he did at the time of the Kanike murder,' said Sergeant Schmidt, handing the inspector two typed statements.

The inspector took the statements and compared them.

'You're right,' he said. 'Call Minden and tell them about this. Rehme's their responsibility, but I'd like to hear what this fellow has to say. Wouldn't hurt to put a little pressure on him.'

The cab driver's name was August Fennel, he was fifty-four years old, married, born and raised in Rehme and a cab driver for close to twenty years. Inspector Heidel put pressure on him.

'Whatever the case,' he said, 'we have positive evidence here that you issued a false statement to the police. One of these versions has to be false. Now, I can charge you on that or I can hold you on suspicion of the murder of Ingrid Kanike. What I would prefer is that you tell me instead what really happened on the night of April seventh, nineteen sixty-one. It may then not be necessary to charge you at all.'

Fennel shuffled his feet. He was a watery-eyed man with the shoulders of a bull and the stomach of a dedicated beer drinker. When he spoke, his voice was startlingly high.

'I didn't want to get mixed up,' he whined. 'I ain't never had no trouble and I didn't want to get mixed up. I was afraid I'd get blamed for it.'

'You will get blamed for it,' said the inspector, 'unless you tell me exactly what happened.'

'I was at the station when the 12.07 came in,' said Fennel. 'The Kanike girl got into my cab. I knew who she was. I'd drove her before and I knew her address. Didn't know her name until after she got murdered though.

'Any time I'd drove her before, she'd been alone but that

night she had a man with her. They got into the cab together.'

'What did he look like, this man?' interrupted the inspector. 'Did you know him? Have you ever seen him before or since?'

'No, I don't think so,' said Fennel. 'To tell the truth, I didn't get too good a look at him. He was a young fellow, thirty maybe. Nice looking. About my height, I guess. He wasn't from Rehme.'

'All right,' said the inspector. 'I'll want you to look at some pictures later on and see if you can identify this man again. So, what happened then? You drove the girl and this strange man to her home?'

'No,' said the cab driver, looking extremely apprehensive. 'When we got just to that spot where they found her body later, the man told me to stop the cab, that they'd walk the rest of the way. I stopped the cab, he paid me the full fare and they got out. And that's all I know about it.'

'Did the girl appear frightened?' said the inspector. 'Did she get out of the cab willingly?'

'As far as I could see, she did,' said the cab driver. 'They were talking together in the back and they seemed friendly enough. She didn't say "Du" to him though.'

'Du' is the intimate form of address in German, used with relatives, children, and close friends.

Fennel was not charged, but given a severe talking to and released.

'If he'd told us the truth at the time,' said Inspector Heidel bitterly, 'we might have solved the case and Ursula Fritz might still be alive. So much time has passed now though, that the testimony is close to worthless.'

'I take it he wasn't able to make a positive identification from any of the pictures you took at the time,' said Inspector Jech who had come up to Minden to learn the results of the questioning of Fennel.

Inspector Heidel shook his head. 'He might have at the time,' he said, 'but it's been over four years now and whatever impression he did have, has faded.'

'Still, the fact that she got into the cab with this man

would seem to indicate that he was not a total stranger to her,' said Jech thoughtfully. 'You've checked out her male acquaintances? People she came into contact with at work?'

'We've practically reconstructed her life,' said Heidel. 'It wasn't hard. She lived at home. She only worked at the one place. She had the same girl friends from the time she was in school. We could account for practically all her time for long periods. She wasn't having an affair of any kind, if that's what you're thinking.'

'Not exactly,' said Jech. 'I was thinking more of a casual acquaintance, someone whom she knew well enough to share a cab with, but not well enough to use the intimate form of address.'

'Rehme is a small place,' said Heidel. 'A cab driver like Fennel knows almost everyone in town, by sight at least. He didn't know this man and we have every reason to believe that Ingrid Kanike never knew any casual male acquaintances from out of town. Don't forget, if she did know him, even casually, she'd know that he wasn't from Rehme and why would he be getting off the train there at midnight then?'

'You think he was on the 12.07 from Minden then?' said Jech.

'My own theory is that she met him on the train,' said Heidel. 'She was a plump girl who hadn't had too much luck with the boys and she ran into a handsome, well-spoken man on the train. He probably told her that he came from Rehme, suggested they take a cab together and then, once away from the station, persuaded her to walk the rest of the way to her house with him. She, no doubt, thought it was her big romance, poor girl.'

'Sad,' agreed Jech. 'But Fennel couldn't identify any of the pictures of the men who were on the train?'

'There are only four who come in question,' said the inspector. 'The others were too old, too young or we were able to establish definite alibis so close to midnight that it would have been almost impossible for them to have done it.'

'Two of them, Otto Johanns and Emil Bach, are from

Rehme. One, Karl Mueller, is from Minden and the other is from Bielefeld. His name is Dieter Beck. Oddly enough, all of them work in Rehme, three of them in the machine tool plant over by the river.'

'You're thinking of Croiset, I presume?' said Jech.

Hiedel nodded. 'You can't convict people on the statements of a clairvoyant, of course,' he said, 'but still, it is remarkable the accuracy he's shown with such things.'

Croiset was the famous Dutch clairvoyant, Gerard Croiset, who had been successful in solving many criminal cases throughout Europe. He had been called in by the family of Ingrid Kanike after the murder and had stated that the murderer worked in a machine factory near Rehme. There were, however, several machine factories and they employed a large number of men.

'Well, I guess that's the end of that then,' said Jech getting to his feet. 'I wonder when he'll kill the next one?'

'Four years from now, if he runs true to form,' said Heidel. 'By the way, I'm sending my sergeant down to you. I'd like him to get the exact time and circumstances of the Fritz murder and then we'll see if we can establish an alibi for any of the four men on the train with Kanike. Maybe we could eliminate one or two of them.'

'If we knew that it was the same man in both cases,' said Jech. 'I'm afraid your sergeant is going to have a tough time with the alibis. Our medical man wasn't able to establish the time of death precisely. She'd been dead too long when we found her.'

Nonetheless, Sergeant Eisenbach was able to eliminate one of the four suspects. Otto Johanns had been in the hospital for the entire week in which Ursula was raped and murdered. At this point the investigations came, once again, to an end, there being nothing further to investigate.

'A very unusual pattern,' commented Dr Krause. 'As a rule, a sex criminal of this type strikes more often and the intervals between his attacks become increasingly shorter. The fellow must be obtaining sexual relief in some manner, but it seems impossible that it could be by non-violent means considering what we know of his previous activities.'

'Well, if he's been raping anyone, it hasn't been reported,' said the inspector. 'Granted that far more rapes go unreported than otherwise, the area is sufficiently aroused by now that I think any woman undergoing an attack of this sort would report. You still think it was the same man in the Kanike and Fritz cases?'

The doctor nodded. 'And so does Schoenauer down in Herford,' he said. 'However, we disagree on when he'll strike again. Schoenauer says this year yet. I say not for another four years, the same interval as the last time.'

As it turned out, both the medical experts were wrong. It was the night of February 28, 1968 when the murdering rapist claimed his next victim. The body was found on the morning of the twenty-ninth by a railway track walker named Leopold Beisel.

Beisel had set out from Bielefeld that morning on an inspection tour of the ten mile stretch of track between that city and the village of Werther in the Teutoburger Forest to the west. Although February is normally one of the coldest months of the central European winter, the day was sunny and the temperature above freezing. It was ten o'clock and he had covered approximately half the distance when he came upon the body of the girl lying beside the tracks.

Beisel's first thought was an accident. There were passenger trains running over the line and, in Europe, a surprising number of people either mistake the exit between coaches for the toilet door or lean carelessly against a not properly locked door and fall out. This despite the fact that the doors on all trains are carefully and conspicuously marked in several languages. Depending upon how fast the train is moving and the manner in which they fall, a person may very well survive this. Beisel therefore ran forward with the intention of offering first aid or whatever else could be done, but stopped dead in his tracks as he came close enough to get a clear view of the corpse.

For corpse it was. The face was black, the eyes protruded horribly from their sockets and the tongue, black and swollen, hung so far out of the mouth that Beisel did not realize what it was. There were other indications as well.

The girl's skirt had been pushed up around her waist, her torn underwear lay in shreds around her and there were blue bruises on the widespread thighs.

Leopold Beisel read the newspapers and he instantly thought of the murdering rapist who had killed Ingrid Kanike and Ursula Fritz. There was little doubt in his mind that this was the third victim.

There was also little doubt in his mind that the woman was dead, but he went forward, knelt and laid his fingers on the artery in the throat. There was no pulse and the flesh was cold and hard to the touch.

Although he was not a Catholic, for reasons about which he himself was not clear he made the sign of the cross over the body and muttered a short prayer. He then got rather heavily to his feet and set off at a trot down the tracks. The nearest telephone was nearly a mile distant.

This time it was the team of Inspector Ludwig Pfeiffer, Detective-Sergeant Max Kramer and Dr Hans Fuchs of the Bielefeld Department of Criminal Investigations who arrived at the scene.

Beissel had given them a very good indication of what to expect in his report over the telephone, and in Minden and Herford Inspectors Heidel and Jech, Sergeants Eisenbach and Schmidt and Drs Krause and Schoenauer were also heading south for what was eventually to be a general meeting of Criminal Investigations Department personnel at the scene of the latest rape and murder of the series. On the question of whether the Kanike, Fritz and the present case were all parts of a series carried out by the same man the medical opinion was unanimous. It was.

On what to do about it, there was less unanimity. Inspector Pfeiffer was of the opinion that every sex criminal with a police record in the entire area should be brought in and screened for alibis. Inspector Jech thought that there should be wide-spread appeals to the public for information. And there was no way of knowing what Inspector Heidel thought for he said nothing. His unsolved murder was, of course, the oldest.

In the meantime, a large number of technicians from the

police laboratory in Bielefeld had arrived and were going over the area literally by the square inch. All they were able to find was the girl's handbag. It had not been opened and contained, among other things, her personal identity card. From this it was learned that the girl's name was Anneliese Herschel, that she had been twenty-one years old, unmarried and a resident of Werther.

'The only prints on the bag are hers,' said the chief technician. 'Apart from the bag, there was only this in the side pocket of her coat.'

'This' was an ordinary book of paper matches with advertising printed on it. The advertising read: Igloo Bar, Kon Street 4, Bielefeld.

'Check it out, Max,' said Inspector Pfeiffer, handing the book of matches to the sergeant.

The investigations at the scene of the crime now being completed, the body was sent to the morgue and the police party returned to police headquarters in Bielefeld. It was only after they had arrived that Inspector Jech remembered Gert Simmon.

'Wasn't he sentenced to two years and wasn't that just about two years ago?' he demanded.

No one was sure of the dates, but the penitentiary was telephoned and they confirmed that Gerd Simmon had been released on February 16th, twelve days before the murder.

'That,' said Inspector Jech, 'is too much of a coincidence to be one.'

There was no disagreement on this score and within a matter of minutes the telephone and telex wires were humming as the police forces throughout north Germany were alerted to be on the look-out for Gerd Simmon, thought to be the rapist-murderer who had been sought for so long.

While this was going on, Sergeant Kramer returned to headquarters with the news that Anneliese Herschel had, indeed, been in the Igloo Bar the night of her death and that she had left with a man. He wanted pictures of all possible suspects to show to the witnesses of whom there were several.

Pictures of Simmon, Fennel and the three remaining

suspects who had been on the train to Rehme on the night that Ingrid Kanike was killed were rushed down and the sergeant returned to the Igloo Bar.

At four that afternoon there was a great cheer as the desk sergeant on duty in Minden called to report to Inspector Heidel that Gerd Simmon was in custody.

'Splendid!' exclaimed the inspector. 'Where did they pick him up?'

'Right here,' said the desk sergeant. 'He's been in the detention cells for the past four days. He celebrated his release from jail a little too enthusiastically and just about wrecked a bar over on the east side. You want to talk to him?'

'No,' said the inspector despondently and hung up the telephone.

The search for Gerd Simmon was called off and it was to a decidedly gloomy conference of criminal police officers that Sergeant Kramer returned at nearly six o'clock.

The sergeant was not gloomy.

'Well, it looks like we've finally got him,' he announced. 'I have a positive, independent identification from three different persons, including the bartender.'

'Identification of whom, Max?' said Inspector Pfeiffer. 'We've just learned that Simmon was in jail at the time of the crime.'

'Not Simmon, chief,' said Max. 'Beck. Dieter Beck. The boy from Bielefeld who was on the train the night Kanike was killed.'

And Dieter Beck it was. Picked up at his home in Bielefeld, he made no effort whatsoever to deny the Kanike, Fritz and Herschel murders.

'I knew that you'd get me sooner or later,' he said apathetically as the Criminal Investigations officers from three cities clustered around. 'I'm glad it's over. I didn't want to kill those girls. It's just something that comes over me and then I can't help myself. I'll confess to the murders, but I don't want to talk about it.'

Beck did eventually talk enough to establish with certainty that he was the murderer of Ingrid Kanike, Ursula Fritz and Anneliese Herschel. He had, it seemed, chosen them quite deliberately because they were types who would not be very popular with men and who were thus very susceptible to the attentions of a handsome, well-spoken man which Beck definitely was.

Contrary to the medical opinion, Beck had been quite capable of normal sexual relations and had had a number of girl friends all of whom described him as a completely satisfactory lover. Several reported that he had had a habit of caressing their throats with his large, powerful hands while making love.

They had found it rather touching.

During the trial which lasted from June 22 to June 26, 1969 the court found Dieter Beck's conduct more dangerous and inexcusable than touching and handed down a verdict of premeditated murder on all three counts. He was sentenced to three terms of life imprisonment.

12

THE INSATIABLE WIFE

Tortuous and twisting as a dream in the mind of a murderer, the Ems river rises near the ancient city of Muenster and weaves its way northward through the heart of the great German moors.

Klein Hesper, Gross Hesper, Gross Fullen, Niederlang, Sustrum and Bourtang, the silent, lonely, water-logged plains of Emsland stretch out along the Dutch border to Emden and the chill, grey waters of the North Sea.

A strange place to live, beautiful at times, sinister at others, and yet men have lived among the moors since the dawn of time. There is security in a place where the single false step of the stranger may lead to the deadly quicksand traps along the unmarked path.

Roughly in the centre of this great expanse of moors lies the little town of Meppen, with 30,000 souls, little more than a village, but still the largest community in its district. With the exception of Lingen, seventeen miles to the south, none of the villages have as much as 10,000 inhabitants and many are too small to appear on any map. In some of these smaller villages all the inhabitants have the same surname.

There are not so many villages, in any case, and between them lie the swamps, the reeds, the low bush, the occasional bit of higher, forested ground and the black, sullen lakes and ponds, some of which have a discernible bottom and some of which do not.

On May 30, 1972, a small, somewhat scrawny and very tough man named Georg Richter disappeared. He was twenty-six years old, married and the father of four daughters, Anja, six, Kathi, four, Alexandra, two, and Petra, one. He was very attached to these daughters.

On Monday, June 6th, Mrs Ursula Richter came into Meppen from the little community of Emslage-Ruehlerfeld where the family lived to report this disappearance.

As is customary in such matters, she gave her name, age, address and number of dependent children, causing Detective-Sergeant Dieter Schwarz, who was taking down the report, to start slightly and drop his pencil.

Mrs Richter, it seemed, was the mother of a six-year-old daughter, but only twenty years old herself. What was more, she looked it, being dark-haired, dark-eyed, astonishingly built and very lovely – so lovely, in fact, that the sergeant found it hard to believe that any man in his right mind would have voluntarily left her.

Mrs Richter was, apparently, not totally unaware of her attractions. Her mini-skirt was scarcely wider than a respectable belt and the looks which she bestowed upon the bedazzled sergeant were of a temperature to nearly explode the ammunition in his service pistol.

'My God! What was that?' exclaimed his superior, Inspector Horst-Dieter Geiger, after Mrs Richter's delightful hips had swayed out through the office door.

'Eh . . . uh . . . a missing person report,' said the sergeant. 'Her husband's been gone for a week. Goerg Richter, aged twenty-six. Didn't mention what he does for a living. Not much, I guess.'

'I should think not,' said the inspector. 'Too busy otherwise.'

'Well . . . uh . . .,' said the sergeant, still bemused.

'Hold it!' cried the inspector. 'Richter. Richter. I have the feeling we have something pending on a Richter. Take a look in the current files, will you?'

The sergeant took a look.

'You're right,' he said. 'Georg Richter. Emslage-Ruehlerfeld. Two charges of burglary and one of theft. Released on own recognizance and awaiting trial on all three.'

'Only he's not awaiting,' said the inspector. 'See how easy it is to solve cases? The lady has barely left the office and we have been able to determine that her husband has disappeared in order to avoid trial and, no doubt, a subsequent jail sentence.'

'Brilliant!' said the sergeant in near sincere admiration, '—but Mrs Richter didn't want to know why he left, she wanted to know where he went to.'

'And, I suppose, when he was coming back,' said the inspector, reaching for the next report in his In-tray. 'Tell her when the statute of limitations expires.'

'I can't file it without an investigation,' said the sergeant.

'Then investigate,' said the inspector.

The sergeant investigated.

This signified mainly that he went to Emslage-Ruehlerfeld and talked to the neighbours, following which he had a beer in the local tavern and spoke at some length with the bar tender, in this case the owner.

'I'm not quite so dazzled by your solution of the Richter case as I was,' he remarked upon his return to the office. 'The Richters have a boarder. Nice young man. Nineteen years old. Muscles of a draft horse. Quite handsome too. His name is Kurt Adomeit.'

'Oh?' said the inspector, putting down the file that he was working on and reaching for his cigarettes. 'That does put rather a different light on the matter, doesn't it?'

'I fear for Mr Richter's safety,' said the sergeant, peering gloomily into the office coffee pot which was cold and empty.

'I fear that they've been a little too sly for us,' said the inspector. 'Has he really been missing a week?'

The sergeant nodded. 'At least,' he said. 'The gossip is bad. They say that Mr Richter was a boxer and that he used Mrs Richter as a punching bag. They also say that Mr Adomeit put her to other uses.'

'Put or puts?' said the inspector.

'He's off driving his truck at the moment,' said the sergeant. 'It's what he does for a living. I assume that he will take up his boarder's duties again once he returns.'

'But he wasn't out driving his truck a week ago when Mr Richter disappeared, right?' said the inspector.

'No,' said the sergeant. 'He apparently doesn't drive it

very often. Any idea as to where we should look for the body?'

'Certainly,' said the inspector. 'In the moors. There are about five hundred square miles of them and Mrs Richter and Mr Adomeit have had a whole week in which to select the most ideal resting place for the late lamented Mr Georg Richter. If they actually have done him in, we'll never find the body. I'm not even a local man and I know six pools within a half mile of here that you could lose an elephant in.'

'So it goes in the unsolved murder file,' said the sergeant.

'Not on your life it doesn't,' said the inspector. 'It's not a murder case. It's a Missing Person report. You and I may have some nasty suspicions, but there's no evidence of any kind that Mr Richter didn't leave simply to avoid trial. In fact, I still think that's the most likely explanation. Was Richter insured?'

The sergeant shrugged. 'I'll find out,' he said.

Georg Richter, it turned out, was not insured and further samples of the gossip in Emslage-Ruehlerfeld brought out the widely held opinion that Mr Richter had not objected too strongly to Kurt Adomeit's alleged attentions to his wife.

'The situation seems to be that he was crazy about the children, but he wasn't really all that keen on Mrs Richter,' said the sergeant. 'He got her pregnant when she was only thirteen and I guess he had the choice of marrying her or going to jail so he married her, but the consensus of opinion in Emslage-Ruehlerfeld is that the lady is too much for any one man.

'It was Richter who brought Adomeit into the house and some say that he was looking for help.'

'Just what I said!' said the inspector. 'The heat was on here, so he cut out. Our boy is undoubtedly living happily somewhere in Holland by now with a new name and, probably, a new wife.'

Two days later, the inspector's theory was confirmed.

A telephone call was received from the village constable of Neuringe on the Dutch border. He reported that there was a car with a Meppen licence plate standing on the bottom of a deep, but clear pool near his village. If Meppen was interested in having it, they could come and get it.

The sergeant noted down the licence number, which the constable had been able to read easily through the water, and did a little checking with the local automobile licensing office.

'Odd,' he said after he had put down the telephone. 'Mrs Richter didn't mention that Mr Richter took the family car with him. As a matter of fact, she didn't mention that he owned a car.'

'And he does?' said the inspector.

The sergeant nodded. 'It's sitting at the bottom of a pond over by Neuringe,' he said. 'They say, if we want it, we'll have to come and fish it out ourselves.'

'Well, tell Sam to take the tow truck,' said the inspector. 'You probably better go along too. For all we know, Richter may be in it.'

Georg Richter was not in his car nor was anything else.

'Stripped,' said the sergeant. 'There's not so much as a chewing gum wrapper in it and there are no prints either. I went over the thing by the square centimetre.'

'Why?' said the inspector. 'Do you still think that Mrs Richter and Adomeit murdered poor Georg?'

'More than ever,' said the sergeant. 'What does that car over there on the Dutch border in fourteen feet of crystal clear water do? It points like a neon sign to Holland. Somebody is supposed to believe that Richter went over the border and that somebody is us.'

The inspector looked thoughtful. 'Maybe he was just lazy,' he said. 'He drove the car to the border and then got rid of it in the most convenient manner. He couldn't take it with him into Holland because the foreign licence plate would have been easy to trace.

'Doesn't hold up,' said the sergeant. 'It wasn't convenient. He'd have had to walk a couple of miles from where he left the car to a border crossing point. It would have been a lot simpler to take the train out of Meppen.'

'You convince me,' said the inspector. 'All right. What happened then? Mrs Richter and Mr Adomeit murdered Mr

Richter and, having disposed of the body, drove the car to the pond near Neuringe knowing full well that somebody would spot it sooner or later and that the assumption then would be that Mr Richter had gone into Holland, never to return. Is that what you have in mind?'

'Something like that,' said the sergeant. 'If Richter had really wanted to get rid of the car, there are enough ponds around there where it would never have been seen again. This pond had a hard bottom.'

The inspector sighed and got up to go and stand in front of the window. It was a beautiful, warm, early summer day and a gentle breeze was blowing in from across the moors, laden with the scent of flowers and green, growing things.

The inspector sighed again, more heavily, and turned back to his desk.

'All right,' he said. 'Assuming that it was murder, what can we do? You know yourself that the examining judge would never issue an indictment on nothing but suspicion. Where are we to get the evidence that a crime has even been committed?'

'There could be something in the house,' said the sergeant.

'After all this time?' said the inspector. 'If they took the trouble to drive the car over to the Dutch border and push it into a pond, they took the trouble to clean up the house before she ever reported him missing.'

'What you're saying is that this is a perfect crime,' said the sergeant. 'We know a man was murdered, but we can't prove it.'

'Maybe you know it,' said the inspector, 'but I don't. I agree that it's possible, probable even, but I don't admit that it's a perfect crime either. Not that there aren't perfect crimes and even in this district, but they'll have to get away with it longer than a couple of weeks before I call it a perfect crime.'

Ursula Richter and Kurt Adomeit got away with it, if, indeed, they were getting away with anything, for a good deal longer than a couple of weeks.

In June of 1973, one year after the disappearance of Georg Richter and following receipt by the Meppen Police of a report from the Dutch authorities that no trace of the man had been found in Holland, Ursula Richter filed suit for divorce on the grounds of desertion. It was, of course, granted without delay.

'Very circumspect,' observed the inspector. 'She waited a whole year and, as I understand it, her conduct toward Mr Adomeit, at least in public, has been beyond reproach.'

'Makes it all the more suspicious,' grumbled the sergeant. 'He's still boarding there and the children have practically accepted him as their father, but he and Mrs Richter are the souls of propriety. There isn't even any gossip any more.'

'Well, if there is, it won't last much longer,' said the inspector. 'I imagine that our love birds will be getting married shortly, now that Mrs Richter is a free woman again.'

With which statement he demonstrated that even inspectors of police can be very badly mistaken at times. An entire year passed again and it was only on June 16, 1974 that Mr Kurt Adomeit led the former Mrs Ursula Richter to the altar. The bridesmaids were Anja, Kathi, Alexandra and Petra Richter, now nine, seven, five and four respectively.

'All right,' said the sergeant. 'I admit it. It was a perfect murder. We'll never find the body. There'll never be any evidence. We suspected it was murder from the start, but we couldn't do a thing about it. They pulled it off right under our noses.'

The inspector scowled unhappily. 'I wouldn't mind so much if we just knew for certain,' he said. 'Is Georg Richter living under an assumed name in Holland or some other country or is he rotting at the bottom of some quicksand on the moor?'

'We'll never know,' said the sergeant, thus democratically demonstrating that police sergeants can be just as wrong as inspectors.

It was going to be almost another year before anything new was learned in connection with the Georg Richter case and then it was not directly.

'Mrs Richter . . . er, that is, Mrs Adomeit seems to have an unfortunate effect on her husbands,' remarked the inspector as the sergeant came into the office one morning early in June of 1975. 'Here. Take a look at this.'

He shoved a sheet of form paper across the desk.

'Osnabrueck police?' said the sergeant. 'What do they want with Adomeit?'

'They're not too precise,' said the inspector. 'They want to talk to him in connection with some kind of swindle. I get the impression that they're not ready to bring a charge yet, but they want us to pick him up, presumably to throw a scare into him.'

'Should I go get him?' said the sergeant, dropping the form back onto the desk. 'Could be that he's not here. The last time I checked I was told that he spent a lot more time driving the truck than he used to.'

'You're insinuating something,' said the inspector.

'The gossip in Emslage-Ruehlerfeld is that Adomeit can't take care of his wife any more than her first husband could,' said the sergeant. 'I don't mean financially.'

'And I suppose knowing the fate of the first husband, he's reluctant to bring in help,' said the inspector. 'You've never completely given up on that business, have you?'

'I check out the gossip every once in a while,' admitted the sergeant. 'You never know. There could be some kind of a break. Richter's father doesn't believe that his son simply ran off. Says he'd never have left the children.

'As for Adomeit bringing in help, as you put it, he wouldn't think of it. He's jealous as hell. Punched a couple of the local boys in the nose for just talking to his wife in the tavern.'

'Should I go see if he's there now?'

'In a minute,' said the inspector, picking up the telephone. 'I'm going to call Osnabrueck and see just what they have in mind. Could be that we can take advantage of this in some way if they have enough to hold him for any length of time.'

The inspector was on the telephone for some time, during which the sergeant went off to check on the progress of several other matters. When he returned the inspector was just putting down the instrument.

'Good thing that you didn't go out to pick him up,' he

said. 'They don't want him picked up. They want him shadowed the next time he comes to Osnabrueck. They think he's peddling phony drugs down there. A nice racket. The buyers can't very well complain to the police.'

'Shadow him?' yelped the sergeant. 'How're we supposed to do that? That truck driver drives a BMW 2002 and it's eighty miles down to Osnabrueck. The fastest thing we've got is a Volkswagen. He'd be out of sight before we left the city limits.'

The inspector pushed the chair back from the desk, clasped his hands behind his neck and gazed thoughtfully at the somewhat dingy ceiling.

'I'd like to have him in custody,' he mused. 'I don't know what we could get out of him, but I have the feeling that this is a sort of break, if we know how to exploit it. Say the man's a murderer, being in the detention cells should make him a little nervous, particularly if we hint that he's being investigated for something other than drug trafficking.'

'If the drugs are phony, they can't get him on drug trafficking,' said the sergeant. 'All they could charge him with is obtaining money under false pretences. And then they'd have to get one of the users to swear out a complaint.'

'No problem,' said the inspector. 'They've got some users on the payroll down there, but they haven't been able to pick up his trail when he hits the city. That's why they want him shadowed down.'

He sat forward in the chair and began patting his pockets for his cigarettes.

'You're right, of course,' he said. 'The BMW's too fast for us. We'll have to think of something else.'

'Well, he almost surely comes down State Road seventy through Lingen to Rheine and then takes the E8 into Osnabrueck,' said the sergeant. 'If you think it's important enough, I could go down and sit on the edge of the city limits and pick him up as he goes past, but I might have to sit there a week. Why can't Osnabrueck do the same thing?'

'I'll ask them,' said the inspector.

Osnabrueck could, provided that the Meppen police furnished them with a picture of Adomeit and the licence number of his car. The only information which they had was his name and the fact that he lived somewhere near Meppen.

'We can take care of that,' said the inspector, speaking to his opposite number in Osnabrueck over the telephone, 'but I'd like a favour in return. Will you see if you can get anything out of him that we could use to hold him up here for a week or so?'

'Nobody's that innocent,' said the inspector in Osnabrueck. 'We'll get you something.'

What they eventually got, after Kurt Adomeit had been picked up at the city limits and trailed to the small hotel and, later, the park where he transacted his business, was an admission that he had pulled the same swindle in several other cities in the area. This meant that he could be taken to his place of residence for trial rather than be tried on separate charges in a half dozen towns and cities.

'None of the other places are anxious to take jurisdiction anyway,' said the inspector. 'As you say, the only charge possible is obtaining money under false pretences and it'll be a wonder if he gets more than a fine.'

'Thought for a minute that we might be able to sustain an attempted murder charge. Some of the people peddling phony drugs use stuff that will kill you. But he didn't. It was completely harmless stuff. An addict could shoot a wheelbarrow load and get nothing more than frustrated.'

The sergeant was sent down to bring back the prisoner, which he did with some enthusiasm. He too was becoming convinced that there was, at least, a chance of a break in what he had always considered to be the Richter murder.

He was to be disappointed. The Osnabrueck police had leaned rather heavily on Kurt Adomeit and he looked a bit shaken, but he was by no means broken or ready to admit to anything. He was perfectly aware that the affair with the drugs was a minor matter and that, as a first time offender, there was little likelihood of his receiving anything more serious than a fine. No sooner had he arrived in Meppen than he began to demand his release.

The inspector stalled.

'Why doesn't he yell for a lawyer?' said the sergeant. 'He'd have him out of here in five minutes.'

'Doesn't want to pay him,' said the inspector. 'He's so sure of himself that he thinks he can save the lawyer's fee. He will too, unless we think of something quick.'

'I don't know what we could think of,' said the sergeant. 'He admits everything on the phony drugs charges, but if you ask him anything about Richter, he simply says he doesn't know anything about it and that he understood that he ran off to Holland. We can't get through his guard with anything.'

The inspector paced rapidly up and down the office.

'This Adomeit isn't sharp,' he muttered. 'He's just stubborn. He knows we can't break his story and he sticks to it. If there was a murder, the woman was the brains behind it . . .'

He turned suddenly to the sergeant. 'What's she been doing while Adomeit was in custody down in Osnabrueck?' he demanded. 'It's been over a week since he was picked up.'

'How do I know?' said the sergeant. 'I don't check her out twice a day.'

'Then do it now,' said the inspector. 'Go over there immediately. Find out what the gossip is. Has she been faithful to Adomeit while he was in jail in Osnabrueck?'

The sergeant's face lit up in abrupt comprehension.

'I get it!' he explained. 'Adomeit is jealous as hell! If he were to learn that his wife was two-timing him while he was in detention, he might get mad enough to lose his head and say something indiscreet.'

'Right,' said the inspector. 'Adomeit's a pretty straightforward character and he's got a bad temper. If he loses it, he could say anything. So pray that Mrs Richter hasn't been able to control her passionate nature.'

'Couldn't we fake it?' asked the sergeant.

'If we don't mind changing professions afterwards,' said the inspector. 'We tell her husband something like that and it isn't true, the lady could sue us down to our underwear.'

'But say that she has been playing around,' said the

sergeant, 'how are we going to tell Adomeit that? He wouldn't believe us.'

'I don't know,' said the inspector, 'but I'll think of something. In the meantime, go and find out what's happening with Mrs Adomeit's love life.'

Not entirely to the sergeant's surprise, a good deal was happening in the love life of Mrs Ursula Adomeit. She had not only been unable to control her passions, but she had not even made a serious attempt. The first night after she had learned that her husband had been arrested in Osnabrueck, she had shared her bed with a lover. Since then, she had had at least four others.

'No question about it,' said the sergeant. 'Emslage-Ruehlerfeld is so small that everybody knows when you sleep with your own wife, let alone somebody else's. Mrs Adomeit has been up to her old tricks. Have you figured out how we're to slip the news to Mr Adomeit?'

'The old loud-mouth drunk act, I suppose,' said the inspector. 'We'll have to be sure that we get somebody Adomeit doesn't know.'

'I've got a cousin with the force in Lingen,' said the sergeant. 'He doesn't actually drink, but he can put on the best act you ever saw. He even looks drunk when he's cold sober.'

'Get him,' said the inspector.

Two hours later Kurt Adomeit, until then alone in the detention cells, acquired company as a seedy-looking man reeking of alcohol was pushed into the neighbouring cell.

'Lemme out! Lemme out! I'm innoshent!' bawled the man, falling against the bars which separated his cell from Adomeit's and clutching them for support. 'Hi Jack! You in for shtealin' the mayor's watch or his wife?'

'I'm in for being drunk – the same as you,' said Adomeit. 'Where'd you take on the load at this time of day?'

'The Black Lamb,' said the drunk. 'An' I ain't drunk. You're drunk!'

'You don't mean the Black Lamb in Emslage-Ruehlerfeld?' said Adomeit.

'Thash the one!' slobbered the drunk.

'I know some people over that way,' said Adomeit. 'What's the news in Emslage-Ruehlerfeld?'

'They got the hottest woman in Europe over there,' said the fake drunk. 'She's finished off two husbands and now she's takin' on every man in the village. There ain't enough of them to handle it. They're callin' out the army! They're . . .'

Adomeit had gone suddenly tense and pale.

'What's her name?' he snapped.

'Urshula, Urshula somethin' or other,' mumbled the drunk and fell over backwards as Kurt Adomeit's arm came straight between the bars like a piston rod, the hooked finger tips just grazing his throat.

'I'll kill you! You bastard!' hissed Kurt Adomeit. 'And I'll kill that bitch!'

The fake drunk began to scream in terror.

'Help! Help! He's crazy! He's tryin' to kill me!'

The uniform sergeant in charge of the detention cells came down the corridor.

'What's going on here?' he demanded.

'I want out!' snarled Adomeit. 'You're holding me illegally! I want a lawyer.'

'You'll have to talk to the inspector,' said the sergeant, unlocking the cell door.

Adomeit was still livid and trembling with rage when he was ushered into the inspector's office. It was obvious that what he had heard from his neighbour in the cells was only something which he had already expected and feared.

The inspector was friendly but firm.

'No,' he said, 'I'm not going to let you out of here right now, even if you get fifty lawyers. Look at the state you're in! That drunken fool apparently told you something about your wife's activities over in Emslage-Ruehlerfeld and, if I let you out now, you're going over there to do her an injury of some kind. You'll get in all kinds of trouble. And maybe there's nothing to the stories anyway.'

'The hell there isn't!' snarled Adomeit. 'I know that bitch! She'd stop at nothing! How many times did she come over to me minutes after Georg had climbed off her! She couldn't get enough! And if anybody stood in her way, why then . . .'

He paused abruptly.

'She got rid of them,' finished the inspector. 'Didn't she, Kurt? And one day, she'll get rid of you too. Or can you take care of her? Is that why she's going with every able-bodied man in the village?'

Adomeit looked as if he were on the verge of apoplexy. His face was as white as marble, but there were angry red flecks around his eyes and at the corners of his jaws. He seemed to be struggling for breath and he opened his mouth, but no words came out.

'You can kid yourself, if you want to, Kurt,' said the inspector, 'but don't kid me. We know that you and Ursula got rid of Georg and sooner or later we're going to be able to prove it. Get it over with now and save yourself a lot of trouble.'

This was all nothing but the purest bluff. All that Adomeit needed to say was what he had been saying for the past three years, that he knew nothing of what had happened to Georg Richter, and the inspector would be forced to let him go. There was no evidence. There was no body. There was no plausible motive.

Perhaps Adomeit did not realize this or perhaps he was simply too angry and torn by jealousy to think clearly, or perhaps he was simply tired of trying to cope with a woman whose sexual appetites were so much stronger than his own or any man's, but suddenly he let his breath out in a great whoosh and slumped down in the chair.

'I'll show you where the body's buried,' he said in a low voice.

Behind the desk, the inspector had also slumped with the release of the almost unbearable tension. He was sweating profusely and he was as exhausted as if he had carried out a physical struggle with the prisoner.

'Very sensible,' he said. 'We'll go immediately.'

The body of Georg Richter was buried five feet deep in the Esterfeld Forest, a scant mile from the Meppen Police headquarters. Since it was now July 1, 1975 and he had lain there since May 30, 1972, nothing remained but a skeleton with the skull smashed in.

'I did that,' said Adomeit, almost modestly. 'We had to because the rat poison just wouldn't work.'

Later at police headquarters, Kurt Adomeit made a full confession to the murder of what must have been one of the toughest little men in North Germany. Georg Richter had been a hard man to kill.

'Ursula and I became intimate at the end of 1971,' said Adomeit. 'She was completely insatiable and I think that Georg would have been grateful if he'd known we were having an affair. Maybe he did know.

'He wasn't jealous, but he was bad-tempered and he used to beat her up pretty badly sometimes.

'Finally, she said to me that he was going to have to go and she bought a tube of sleeping tablets. They were supposed to be very strong and she put the whole tube in his tea. It didn't even make him sleepy.

'She got some more sleeping tablets and she tried it again. She tried it three or four times and it never had the slightest effect on Georg. He didn't notice a thing.

'After a while, she got discouraged with the sleeping tablets and she bought a can of rat poison. It was supposed to be deadly. She put it in almost everything Georg ate, spoonfuls at a time.

'It didn't even give him an upset stomach.

'Then she tried mouse poison, which was supposed to be even stronger. I think Georg liked the taste. He mentioned several times that he thought her cooking was improving.

'I didn't like it. I thought it was sort of weird and I said maybe it would be better if she just asked Georg for a divorce, but she said no, he'd just beat her up and he wouldn't give her a divorce because he'd have nobody to look after the children.

'On the evening of May 13, 1972, Georg went to bed around ten o'clock. The girls had already been put to bed at eight and there was just me and Ursula still awake.

'After a while, she came in with the hatchet we used for chopping kindling all wrapped up with adhesive tape. She gave it to me and said, "Now is the time to do it. He's asleep."

'I went into the bedroom and Georg was sleeping with his mouth open. I took the hatchet and hit him on the head with the blunt end as hard as I could. His head just sort of exploded and splashed blood and brains all over the wall.

'We cleaned everything up and took him over to the Esterfeld Forest and buried him. Then Ursula got all the bed clothes and put them in the washing machine to get the blood off while I drove the car over to the Dutch border. We figured that if it was found there, people would think he'd gone to Holland.

'By the time I got rid of it, it was past midnight and I had to wait until morning to catch a bus back to Meppen. When I got back Ursula had cleaned everything up so good that there wasn't a trace of what had happened to Georg. In a way, I'm sort of glad we got caught. It's been bothering me for a long time.'

Confronted with this statement, Ursula Adomeit at first denied all knowledge of the crime, but, under persistent questioning, changed her mind and confirmed it in nearly all details.

Both she and Adomeit pleaded extenuating circumstances and were able to produce evidence that the dead man had frequently beaten his wife and had otherwise neglected her. This apparently made an impression on the court for it ruled that they were to be tried under the more lenient juvenile code and on November 12, 1975 handed down the maximum sentences under that code of ten years imprisonment for each.

13

LADYKILLER

With the approach of spring in Germany, Germans are much given to repeating the folk saying, *'Der April weiss nicht was er will'*, meaning that April doesn't know what it wants to do with respect to the weather.

This is usually a fairly accurate observation, but on April 19, 1967, which happened to be a Wednesday, April knew very well what it wanted to do in the little town of Darmstadt, West Germany.

It wanted to pour down golden sunshine from a cloudless blue sky and it wanted to raise temperatures to where unsuspecting birds would think it May and burst into their spring mating songs, and it wanted to stimulate the trees to put out the first, tender green leaves which was, of course, a very dangerous thing to do as April in central Europe is quite capable of producing a hard, killing frost out of its sleeve, so to speak.

None of these considerations bothered Ingrid Riedel in the least. As far as she was concerned, it was spring, the weather was beautiful, she was sixteen, her mirror told her she was pretty and, most important of all, it was twelve-thirty, school was out and Mummy and Heidrun would have lunch ready at home.

Ingrid had an excellent appetite and, despite her new-found dignity as an almost grown-up young lady, she could not resist a few skips as she trotted up the front walk to the door of the really quite nice villa at 9, Leo-Tolstoy Street.

To her astonishment, the door was locked.

'The ninnies!' said Ingrid, pressing the doorbell.

There was no reply.

'How strange!' murmured Ingrid. 'They've gone off somewhere and left me without lunch.'

She could not imagine where her mother and sister might have gone that they would not be back by this time, but it was obvious that they were not. The thing to do then was to go in and get her lunch ready herself. There would be plenty of things in the refrigerator.

Getting in was no problem. The lock on the kitchen window at the back of the house was defective and if you jiggled it right you could push the window up and climb in. Ingrid had done it before and she did it now.

Once inside the kitchen she was assailed by a weird feeling of loneliness. The house in which she had been born and in which she had lived all her life suddenly seemed much too quiet. It was, she thought, as if something had stopped, something like the ticking of a clock to which one has become so accustomed that it is only noticed when it stops.

'Mummy!' called Ingrid in a little, hesitant voice. 'Heidrun?'

The only reply was the same silence of the stopped clock, only now it was stronger. Ingrid squared her shoulders. She was a girl of very considerable personal courage and she had been taught to face problems rather than avoid them.

'There is something wrong with this house,' she said aloud in a clear, firm voice. 'And I shall see what it is.'

The words seemed to echo in the empty hall where the stairs led to the second floor and she felt the little hairs on her forearms and the nape of her neck rise. Nonetheless, she went out of the kitchen and down the hall to the stairs. Before ascending them she stopped at the front door, unlocked it and opened it a crack. The sight of the spring sunlight outside was somehow reassuring.

Upstairs, her parents' bedroom was tidy and the beds were made, meaning that her mother and sister had finished the housework before going wherever they had gone. So too was her own room where she had half expected to find a note explaining the strange absence. There was none, and she turned back to the stairs and then stopped in front of her sister's room. The door was closed, but there was nothing unusual about that. The Riedels were a tidy family and doors were normally kept closed.

'Heidrun?' whispered Ingrid, resting her fingers on the panel of the door.

Suddenly, she snatched at the handle and, in a sort of panic, pushed the door wide open. Heidrun was lying in bed with the bed covers drawn up over her face!

An immense feeling of relief swept over her. It was a joke! A silly joke! Mummy and Heidrun had hidden in their beds just to scare her. Everything was all right.

In two bounds, she crossed the room, caught hold of the top of the bed cover and jerked it completely away.

'You silly . . .,' she began and then the words died in her throat. The bed cover still clenched in her fist, Ingrid Riedel put back her head and screamed and screamed and screamed.

Lying on the bed was the naked body of her sister Heidrun. She lay spreadeagled on her back and her long blonde hair was fanned like a halo about her head. Only it was no longer blonde. It was a dark sullen red, the red of fresh blood, and all around her the sheets were soaked with what seemed an absolutely incredible amount of the same substance. Her mouth had fallen slightly open and her large blue eyes stared sightlessly at the ceiling.

Later, Ingrid was to have no recollection of stumbling down the stairs or of calling the police, but she did so for there was a record of a call being received at the Darmstadt police headquarters and five minutes later a patrol car arrived with two officers in it.

Ingrid was lying on the front steps in the spring sunshine and she was only able to speak in a whisper because she had screamed her vocal cords raw. No one had come to help her. The Leo-Tolstoy Street district is expensive and the houses are not close together.

While one of the officers remained with Ingrid, the other drew his gun and went up to the second floor of the house. The gun was there because Ingrid was not entirely coherent and he was not sure what he was going to find inside.

A few moments later he came back down with the gun holstered and a shocked look on his face. Heidrun Riedel had been twenty years old and the officer was only two years older. It was the first time that he had had to verify death in a corpse.

'Homicide,' he said in a low voice, turning his face away from the crying girl. 'I'll call the station and tell them.'

'Ask them if we can take this girl to hospital,' said his partner. 'She ought to be under a doctor's care.'

The station said that it was all right to take the girl to the hospital, but that one officer should remain at the scene to see that nothing was tampered with until the squad from the Criminal Investigations Department arrived.

'You're certain the girl is dead?' said the dispatcher. 'I shouldn't send the ambulance?'

'There's no pulse or heart beat or signs of respiration,' said the officer. 'She's dead.'

'Multiple skull fractures,' said Dr Philipp Frenzl, the department's medical expert, looking at Inspector Ludwig Eberling through his horn-rimmed glasses. 'Something very heavy like a hammer or the back of a hatchet. She hasn't been dead more than two hours.'

'Sex crime?' asked the inspector.

The doctor probed delicately with rubber-gloved fingers.

'Sex motive perhaps,' he said. 'She wasn't raped. The girl is still a virgin.'

'Perhaps she slept naked,' suggested Detective Sergeant Guenther Weber who was down on his knees looking under the bed. 'Ah-ha! Here's something!'

'What?' said the inspector, lowering himself to one knee and trying unsuccessfully to bring his head lower than the bottom of the bed.

'A hammer,' said the sergeant, 'a heavy hammer. Looks like there's blood on it.'

'Leave it where it is,' said the inspector. 'We'll move the bed later and photograph it in place. Probably the murder weapon.'

'You want the complete lab crew out?' the sergeant asked.

The inspector nodded. 'Tell them on the double,' he said. 'The body's barely cold. If we can get any kind of a lead, we may be able to get him before he goes too far. In the meantime, I'll take a look around the house.'

The sergeant went out to the police car parked at the kerb and called the station. He had heard about Ingrid Riedel from the patrol car officer who had remained at the scene and, after having ordered the laboratory crew out, he called the hospital to ask if the girl was in a state to be questioned.

She was not, as the doctor at the hospital had immediately placed her under heavy sedation and put her to bed.

'She was in deep shock,' he said in response to the sergeant's question. 'You're going to have to be very careful about questioning even after she comes out of it. An experience like this could have permanent effects.'

'An experience like what?' said the sergeant who knew nothing of the circumstances and who thought that Ingrid might have been attacked as well.

'The patrolman said he thought she'd discovered her sister's murdered body,' said the doctor. 'She didn't say anything herself.'

'He saw both of them so he may have noted a family likeness,' said the sergeant. 'We don't know yet who the victim is.'

As the sergeant returned to the house, the inspector was just coming up the stairs.

'There's another one in the basement,' he rumbled. 'Tell Philipp and then give me a hand to go over this house. God knows how many more corpses there are in here.'

The one in the basement was in fact the only other corpse.

'The mother of the girl upstairs, I would judge,' said the doctor. 'The family resemblance is strong. The circumstances are almost identical.'

Forty-eight-year-old Erna Riedel lay flat on her back on the concrete floor of the basement with the plastic sheet which had covered her body beside her.

Like her daughter, she was completely naked and, like her, she had died of multiple skull fractures, the blood soaking her blonde hair and spreading in a shallow pool around her head. Her eyes and mouth were closed.

'No indication of rape here either,' said the doctor,

probing again. 'Of course, she's a mature woman who's had children and there could have been penetration without violence. However, I can't detect any ejaculate inside the vagina and she was not in a state of sexual excitement herself at the time she was killed.'

'Which was when?' said the inspector.

The doctor shrugged. 'Roughly the same time as the girl upstairs,' he said. 'I can't give you a closer estimate until I get them over to the morgue for the autopsy.'

'Would you say the same hammer?' said the inspector.

'I should think so,' said the doctor, parting the blood-soaked hair to examine the wounds.

'Then this woman was presumably killed first here in the basement and the murderer then went upstairs, killed the girl there and left the hammer lying under the bed,' muttered the inspector. 'But what was the girl doing lying naked in bed at ten o'clock in the morning and what was her mother doing down here in the basement naked. Could this have been a family of nudists?'

The laboratory technicians, who had by now arrived, were able to answer the question. The Riedels had not been nudists and neither mother nor daughter had been naked at the time of their deaths.

'In both cases,' said the technician in charge of the squad, the women's skulls were smashed with the hammer and they were stripped immediately thereafter. We know it was immediately because there is only a relatively small amount of blood on the clothing. Oddly, he seems to have tried to conceal it.'

'Oddly is right,' said the inspector. 'What did he do it for in the first place? The doctor says he didn't rape them.'

'Sex,' said the technician shortly. 'He masturbated over the bodies after he'd killed and stripped them. There are traces of semen on the floor and on the body of the older woman.'

'In short, a sex freak,' said the inspector. 'Would this be a normal pattern of behaviour for him?'

'Probably,' said the technician. 'Not, of course, that he's necessarily killed someone before. His thing may merely be masturbating over a naked woman and he wouldn't have too much trouble finding willing partners for that.'

Dr Frenzl did not agree.

'Considering the violence of the acts,' he said, 'I cannot believe that this was a simple matter of wanting to masturbate over a naked woman. The violence itself was a part of the pattern of sexual behaviour and it would not be surprising if he has a record of attacks on women. Not rape, mind you. He may well be incapable of conventional rape. But a violent assault on a woman and the removal of her clothing.'

It was seven o'clock in the evening of the day of the murders and the doctor had come to the inspector's office to report on the initial findings of the autopsy which was not entirely completed. It was far enough along, however, to determine that there would be no surprises. The Riedels, mother and daughter, had died within a half hour of each other and at approximately nine-thirty in the morning. There were no other indications.

'Well, maybe he's got a record,' said the inspector, 'but not with us. Guenther is still checking with records in Frankfurt and Mannheim, but I have the feeling he's not going to come up with anything.'

'What were the lab's conclusions on the hammer?' asked the doctor. 'They were over to take the fingerprints and some casts of the wounds for comparison.'

'Positive,' said the inspector. 'It was the murder weapon in both cases. The weird thing is that the only prints on it are Mrs Riedel's and they're on the head. The lab's conclusion was that the hammer belongs to the house and that Mrs Riedel handed it to her murderer. Possible, of course, if she didn't know that he was going to murder her.'

'What about the husband?' said the doctor. 'Has he been located?'

The inspector nodded. 'He was on a business trip in Austria,' he said. 'I talked to him on the telephone. He's coming back tonight, but he won't be able to help us. Didn't have any idea of who might have done it. Thought it must be a madman.'

'In a way it was, no doubt,' said the doctor thoughtfully.

'So there are no clues, no leads, nothing? What are you going to do?'

'There's a possible lead,' said the inspector. 'Mrs Riedel kept an address book and in it, among her friends and relatives, are the names of a number of hand workmen, gardeners, plumbers and so on. She noted beside each name what they did and where to get hold of them.

'Now, certain things we can deduce. There's no evidence of any kind of a struggle in the house so the murderer was admitted peacefully. He was someone they knew and someone who had some business there.

'Secondly, if Mrs Riedel actually handed the hammer to her murderer as the lab thinks, then it was not for him to kill her with, but for some kind of a job that he was supposed to do. *Ergo*, the man was presumably a hand workman of some kind and, possibly, one who had worked for her before.'

'Shrewd,' said the doctor. 'And what luck are you having?'

'I'll know in a few minutes,' said the inspector. 'Fritz is checking the list for possible criminal records and I've got four men trying to trace the whereabouts of the people this forenoon.'

'Then I'll wait,' said the doctor. 'You don't happen to have a cup of coffee around here anywhere I suppose?'

There was, of course, as in all self-respecting criminal investigations offices, a pot of hot coffee discreetly concealed behind a screen in one corner, but the doctor had barely had time to pour a cup and return to his chair when the reports began to come in.

'Mostly negative,' grunted the inspector sourly, checking off the names on the master list on his desk. 'They were practically all working this morning. There are only two left. One we can't locate and the other's out of the country.'

'I should think he'd be the top suspect,' observed the doctor. 'When did he leave?'

'Yesterday, according to his wife,' said the inspector. 'So, if she's not lying and if he really did leave the country yesterday, he's eliminated too.'

The telephone rang. 'Eberling,' growled the inspector,

picking it up. 'Yeah Fritz. Good boy. Nothing on the others? Okay. Bring it on over.'

He put the telephone back into the cradle and his thick, black cigar back into the corner of his mouth.

'One of the hand workmen has a record,' he said. 'Robbery. Breaking and entering. Fellow named Klaus Schmidt. Forty-two years old. Plumber by trade.'

'I thought they could all be accounted for this morning except two,' said the doctor. 'Is this one of the two?'

'This is the one we couldn't locate,' said the inspector. 'The other one's a thirty-three-year-old house painter named Hans Schuetz. He's the one that's married and told his wife he was going to France to look for work.'

'A married man would be a less likely suspect,' said the doctor, frowning, 'but this Schmidt doesn't sound so likely either. His record isn't over sex crimes. It's over robbery. This was a sex crime.'

'Or are we merely supposed to think that?' said the inspector.

'A faked sex crime?' said the doctor. 'Well, I suppose it could be . . . Was anything taken from the house?'

'Not insofar as we've been able to determine,' said the inspector. 'We'll only know for certain tonight when Riedel gets in from Austria. Personally, I doubt that anything was taken. There were plenty of objects of value in the house and even quite an amount of money.'

'But how so robbery then?' said the doctor in bewilderment.

The inspector shrugged like a water buffalo heaving out of a mud wallow. 'Who knows?' he said. 'Maybe the robbery went wrong. Maybe Mrs Riedel or the daughter caught him red-handed and he killed them. Then in order to avoid suspicion, he deliberately didn't take anything and rigged it to look like a sex crime. Don't forget, unless Guenther finds something with the other towns, we don't have any record of a sex criminal with a similar *modus operandi*. There's more reason to believe that the murderer is a hand worker rather than a sex criminal.'

As the inspector had anticipated, Sergeant Weber was

unable to find any record of any similar sex crime either in Darmstadt or in any of the neighbouring towns. Nor could any trace of Klaus Schmidt, the plumber-burglar, be found.

'He left his room without notice and without even using up all the rent he'd paid in advance,' said the sergeant. 'It would be almost an admission of guilt, but unfortunately he left before the crimes took place.'

'Could still be construed as an admission of guilt,' observed the inspector. 'He may not have planned on killing the women, but he may have planned on burglarizing the house and, since he knew he'd be a suspect, he was all set to cut out in any case.'

'Could be,' said the sergeant. 'That's much the manner in which he went about it in the case where he was convicted. Arranged to get work as a handyman in a big house and then filed the catches on the locks so that he could get in at night. Mrs Riedel may have caught him doing something like that. There was nothing wrong with the locks though. I checked them.'

'We'll find out, if I can get him into an interrogation room,' said the inspector grimly. 'All we need is to know where he is.'

And twenty-four hours later, he had his wish. Klaus Schmidt was, it seemed, right in Darmstadt. A police informer reported that he was seen on most evenings in the Tip-Top Bar.

'I'll take the stake-out myself,' said Sergeant Weber. 'That's a rough place and if we put more than one man in there, it's going to get around. By the same token, I wouldn't like to leave this to one of the junior men. If Schmidt's guilty, he'd have nothing to lose by adding a cop to his score.'

'Go ahead,' grunted the inspector. 'It's your funeral.'

It nearly was. Two evenings later, Klaus Schmidt walked into the Tip-Top Bar and was confronted by Sergeant Weber who had been drinking a beer at the bar.

'Criminal Police,' said the sergeant, flashing his credentials. 'You are to accompany me quietly.'

The squat, black-haired man took one look and, with

startling agility, leaped a good six feet sideways, landed running and was within a yard of the door leading to the toilets and the alley behind the building when Sergeant Weber snapped the slide of his service automatic, fired a warning shot into the wall over his head and called in a dangerously level voice, 'Don't move!'

Schmidt whirled, crouched and produced a gun of his own from the waistband of his trousers.

For a long minute there was stalemate.

'Drop the gun and put your hands up,' said the sergeant, moving forward and turning to present a smaller target.

Whether Schmidt would have dropped the gun or would have fired was a question which remained unanswered for, at that moment, a beer bottle sailed out of the crowd of customers, apparently aimed at the sergeant's head. The sergeant was moving and the aim was bad. Instead of striking him in the back of the head, it sailed past his ear and struck Schmidt squarely in the face, throwing him off balance.

An instant later, the sergeant's gun was rammed into his stomach and the wrist of the hand holding his gun was seized and twisted.

'I said, "Drop it!",' said the sergeant.

Schmidt dropped the gun and the sergeant, taking no chances, put handcuffs on him.

Leading his prisoner to the bar, he took a bill from his pocket and handed it to the bartender.

'A free beer for the boy who threw the bottle,' he said. 'The police appreciate your assistance.' And then led Schmidt out of the door to the accompaniment of some very picturesque cursing.

At police headquarters Klaus Schmidt was booked for resisting arrest and illegal possession of a deadly weapon, following which he was sent to the detention cells to ponder on the waiting interrogation room and the inspector in the morning.

Rather than ponder, however, he fell promptly and soundly asleep. Klaus Schmidt had excellent nerves and he was to prove it in the days to come. Nothing that the inspector could do or say would bring anything out of him other than the bare statement that he had not killed anyone and that he did not remember where he had been on the forenoon of the nineteenth, but he thought very probably that he had been sleeping somewhere.

The inspector was much irritated by this stubborn resistance, but he was also impressed.

'He's too confident,' he said. 'He knows he's got nothing to worry about. I don't think he's guilty.'

'Then the only other possibility we have is Schuetz,' said the sergeant. 'But he's not a possibility because his wife says he was in France at the time.'

'She says,' repeated the inspector. 'But was he? Get her down here and let's see how well she sticks to that statement. I'm going to let somebody else lean on Schmidt for a while. He's beginning to get on my nerves.'

Mrs Marta Schuetz was able to demonstrate the truth of her statements with written evidence.

'Here,' she said. 'This is the letter that Hans sent me the day he left. It's dated the seventeenth.'

The inspector examined the letter which was no more than a note.

'Please forgive me, Marta,' it read, 'but you will not be seeing me again until things get straightened out. I have taken fifty marks from our joint savings account.'

The letter was dated April 17, 1967 and signed Hans.

'Do you have the envelope in which this came?' asked the inspector.

Mrs Schuetz had thrown the envelope away.

'Satisfied?' said the sergeant, after the woman had left.

'Not by a long sight,' said the inspector. 'If we had the envelope, there'd be a postmark on it with the date. As it is, he could have written the letter last July . . . or on the afternoon of April Nineteenth.'

'The content was ambiguous to say the least,' said the sergeant. 'What did he mean, "please forgive me"? Forgive him for what? And, "until things get straightened out". What things?'

'You heard her,' said the inspector. 'She thought he meant

she was to forgive him for taking off like that and he wanted to get their financial affairs straightened out. They only got here from East Germany four months ago and I guess they've been having a hard time. Maybe he meant to forgive him for taking the fifty marks out of their . . .'

His voice trailed away and he sat staring at the sergeant with an expression of such fierce concentration that the sergeant involuntarily flinched.

'Get over to the Savings Bank!' he barked suddenly. 'If the withdrawal of that fifty marks took place on the seventeenth, we'll forget about Schuetz. If it was any other date, we'll call Interpol.'

The withdrawal slip was dated April 19, 1967.

'Aside from that slight slip, very clever, Mr Schuetz,' said the inspector. 'He knew that his wife wouldn't check the postmark on the envelope and he may have known that anything mailed at the main post office gets carried out locally the same day. She simply thought he mailed it on the seventeenth and she only got it two days later. In actual fact, he mailed at noon. What does Interpol say?'

'They're looking,' said the sergeant. 'They don't think they'll have too much trouble in locating him.'

Interpol is the European International Police Organization which attempts to co-ordinate police work between various countries. Their agents are rather good at finding people and, as they had predicted, they did not have very much trouble finding Hans Schuetz.

The house painter was living in Paris and working at his trade. As a foreigner he was, of course, registered with the police in his local *arrondissement*. It was merely a matter of finding out which one.

Schuetz was returned to Germany on a charge of suspicion of murder and, upon his arrival in Darmstadt, made a statement in which he neither confessed to nor denied the crime.

'I cannot recall having killed the Riedels,' said Schuetz.

During the months in detention which followed, however, the inspector was able to stimulate his memory to a remarkable extent.

A search of Schuetz's apartment turned up blood-stained work clothing which he had apparently hidden there while his wife was out shopping. Although he never admitted it, it seemed also probable that he had simply left the letter in the mail box at that time and had never mailed it at all.

Schuetz and his wife had not been on good terms and she had actually not seen him since the seventeenth, a fact of which he had taken advantage.

According to Schuetz, his troubles with his wife had also been one of the causes of the murders.

'We had not had sexual relations for a long time,' he said, 'and I could not afford to pay a prostitute. On the morning that it happened I had the feeling that Mrs Riedel had no objection to our becoming more intimately acquainted and, as I passed her in the cellar door, she brushed her hips against me. I think I must have lost my head then.'

It was practically the only confession that Schuetz ever made and he resolutely refused to discuss the details of the murders or his motives in carrying them out.

Despite the predictions of the laboratory technician and Dr Frenzl, Schuetz seemed to be fully normal sexually and had no record of sex offences or, indeed, any offences in either East or West Germany. His wife reported that they had led, up to the time of their estrangement, a normal sex life.

On October 13, 1968, a year and a half after the day when Ingrid Riedel had come so gaily home to find the greatest horror of her life awaiting her in blood-drenched silence, Hans Schuetz was brought to trial, pleaded guilty to two charges of unpremeditated homicide and was sentenced to life imprisonment. It was the maximum sentence which the court could impose.

14

HATCHET WORK

When Ingeburg Grunwald failed to return home from work on the evening of June 19, 1974, Mrs Elizabeth Hermann immediately called the police. Mrs Hermann was Ingeburg's mother and, although her daughter was twenty-two years old and a married woman, she was still inclined to be somewhat protective of her.

In Mrs Hermann's opinion, Ingeburg had not been very lucky, even though her problems were of her own making. The Hermanns had moved heaven and earth to prevent their then nineteen-year-old daughter from marrying the only one year older Wolfgang Grunwald, but it had all been in vain. Ingeburg had simply allowed herself to become pregnant and that, of course, was the end of the parental opposition to the marriage.

Looking back now, Mrs Hermann sometimes wondered if it would not have been preferable to have an illegitimate grandchild. After all, the marriage had lasted only two years until Ingeburg had come home with her baby and filed divorce proceedings against Wolfgang. Still, she thought, she could be thankful that there had been no unpleasantness. Wolfgang had not opposed the divorce. He had probably welcomed it. It was easier to project an image of a suave, sophisticated man-about-town without a wife and child.

But that did not alter the fact that Ingeburg was not home nor was she at the filling station where she worked. Mrs Hermann had called and the attendant had said that she had left at four o'clock, the usual time. It was now six and there was no reason in the world why she should not be home. Ingeburg was not the sort of girl to go off somewhere without telling her mother.

Mrs Hermann had an uneasy feeling that Wolfgang Grunwald might have something to do with this disappearance. Could it be possible that he was attempting a reconciliation? She did not mention this possibility to the Officer-in-Charge of the Missing Persons Section at police headquarters, but merely contented herself with the information that her daughter was missing and that she was estranged from her husband.

'We'll look into it and call you back,' promised the officer. 'If she does contact you in the meantime, please let us know. I'm sure everything will be all right.'

The last sentence was routine and did not in any way reflect the true opinion of the officer. Munich, one of Germany's largest cities, is as dangerous for pretty young girls as large cities are anywhere and Mrs Hermann had stressed that her daughter was very pretty indeed.

The Missing Person Section's files were full of reports of missing pretty young girls and it could safely be assumed that a certain number of them were now leading exciting, if not necessarily pleasant, lives in the harems and brothels of North Africa and the Middle East.

The officer therefore handed the F.I.R., as the First Information Report form is called, to a young plainclothesman lounging in a chair beside his desk and instructed him to see what Wolfgang Grunwald might have to say about the disappearance of his estranged wife.

The plainclothesman was back in less than an hour.

'Negative,' he said, dropping the F.I.R. onto the desk and himself back into the chair. 'The husband's watching television with the grounds for the estrangement: Turkish woman named Bahar Kandlbinder. Looks pretty rough. She's at least ten years older than he is.'

'Kandlbinder?' said the officer. 'That's a Turkish name? It's German as Schultz.'

'Maybe she's married,' said the plainclothesman. 'I didn't ask, but she's Turkish all right. I recognized the accent.'

'You check at the filling station?' said the officer.

'Yeah,' said the detective. 'Girl left at the usual time. Nobody noticed nothing.'

'Well, maybe she's gone to the movies,' said the officer optimistically. 'She'll probably turn up by herself.'

Mrs Hermann called at nine. Her daughter was still not home. She wanted to know what the police were doing.

She called again at eleven. She was very worried.

Then she called at one, at three, at four-thirty and at six. At the six o'clock call she was slightly hysterical which was hardly strange considering that she had not had a wink of sleep all night. There was not much that the night duty man could do for her. The F.I.R. had been checked and any further checking would have to be done by the Criminal Investigations Department. Missing Persons did not have the personnel.

She did achieve one thing. She created a strong desire in the Missing Persons Section to get rid of the case. At eight-thirty the following morning, Detective-Sergeant Sepp Meier found the F.I.R. in his In-tray.

The sergeant read it thoughtfully. When he had finished, he marked a question mark on it with blue pencil and dropped it into the In-tray of his superior at the desk opposite.

Inspector Josef Biedermann, ploughing into the day's work with his usual energy and sending up little puffs of smoke from the first of the day's short black cigars like a miniature steam engine, snatched it up, glared at it and gave a violent snort.

'What in hell do these question marks mean, Sepp?' he demanded. 'You're always putting question marks on things and dropping them in my box.'

'Means I want to know what you plan to do about it,' said the sergeant. 'You're the one who makes the decisions.'

The inspector scanned the report more carefully.

'Well,' he said. 'One thing is clear. Missing Persons wants to get rid of it and I can see why. Look at the calls here. Six, nine, eleven, one, three, four-thirty, six. The woman's driving them up the wall. What's your opinion?'

The sergeant shrugged. 'Not enough information to have one,' he said. 'I can pull Ferdy off the Bockwiller case for a while this afternoon if you want it checked out some more.'

The inspector tossed the F.I.R. back across the desk. 'Have him check it out,' he said and plunged back into the paperwork.

By that afternoon there was a break in the Bockwiller case and Ferdy could not be taken off it, so the sergeant left his paperwork and went out and checked it himself.

'Don't know what to make of this Grunwald business,' he remarked that evening as he and the inspector were preparing to leave the office.

'Grunwald?' said the inspector.

'The F.I.R. Missing Persons sent over this morning,' said the sergeant. 'Ferdy was busy. I took it.'

'And?' said the inspector.

'A little weird,' said the sergeant. 'The woman just left her place of work and disappeared. No reason. The husband didn't have any reason to do anything to her. He's all in favour of the divorce so that he can get married to his Turkish masseuse.'

'What in the devil is a Turkish masseuse?' said the inspector, stretching out a hand for the F.I.R. which the sergeant was holding.

'In this case, the daughter of a former Turkish military attaché,' said the sergeant. 'Name is Bahar Kandlbinder, age thirty, formerly married to a German named Kandlbinder, but now divorced, profession, masseuse specialized in only one part of the body. She's Grunwald's girl friend.'

'Specialized in only one part of the body?' said the inspector, getting red in the face. 'What the hell . . .?'

'Sex massage,' said the sergeant briefly. 'It's the in-thing.'

'Don't we have a vice squad?' said the inspector.

'Yes, but a liberal government,' said the sergeant. 'It's more or less legal.'

'God Almighty!' said the inspector. 'Well, it's not our department. What about the girl?'

'Not a trace,' said the sergeant. 'According to my information, she's not the type to run off and live in a commune so I suppose it's either the Middle East trade or maybe she ran into some kind of a nut.'

'Very possible,' said the inspector. 'Pick up a picture of

her and have some circulars distributed tomorrow. We'll have to see if anything turns up.'

Two days later something did.

A very broad man with one leg, who was a retired wrestler, was draining a lock on the River Isar which runs through Munich. At the bottom of the lock, Locktender Otto Bickel found a woman's handbag. The bag contained money and identification papers in the name of Ingeburg Grunwald and Bickel immediately brought it to the police.

'Bad,' said the sergeant, coming back into the office from the police laboratory where the technicians were examining the bag. 'It's been in the water since the day she disappeared and it doesn't seem to have been opened at all. Usual junk that a woman carries around with her and quite a bit of money.'

'Not slavers then,' said the inspector. 'They'd have kept both the money and the papers. I'm afraid all we can do now is wait for somebody to find the body. You're having the river dragged, of course?'

'Of course,' said the sergeant.

No body was found in the Isar and on Sunday, June 23rd, a young, rather noble-looking man with clear, blue eyes, wavy blond hair and a prominent chin, went off for a walk in the Hofoldinger Forest ten miles to the south of the city and solved the mystery of what had happened to Ingeburg Grunwald.

The body lay at the foot of a steep slope on its back, the limbs extended like a starfish, and the head was no more than a shattered mass of splintered bone, torn flesh, extruded brain and black, dried blood from which one dull, sightless and socketless eye glared hideously. There was a good deal of dried blood on the rest of the body as well and the girl's clothing was badly torn and disordered with the exception of her nylon stockings and black, high-heeled shoes which were, incongruously, in perfect order. Since the body had been lying there for four days, it had attracted a large number of insects and even some small animals.

Hans-Dieter Hofstein, the young walker, was violently

ill, wept, nearly fainted and then made off as fast as his legs could carry him, muttering, 'Oh God! Oh God! Oh God!'

It took him twenty minutes to reach the nearest telephone and, it being a Sunday, it took the station over an hour to collect the personnel and the vehicles and bring the entire police homicide party to where Hofstein was waiting.

The young man told them exactly where the body could be found, but refused to accompany them, stating quite simply that he would rather spend the rest of his life in jail than have to view the corpse again.

He was, of course, not taken to jail, but his identification papers were carefully checked. There have been cases where a murderer 'discovered' the body of his own victim.

That this particular victim was the missing Ingeburg Grunwald was quickly established, the sergeant having brought out a set of the girl's fingerprints taken from personal possessions in her home earlier. While the sergeant was rolling the prints for comparison off the dead fingertips, Dr Guenther Brockmuehle, the department's medical expert, was making a quick examination of the body as found.

The examination was quick because, although required by regulations, it was not very useful under such conditions where clouds of insects rose with every manipulation of the corpse.

'All right, all right,' said the doctor, getting back to his feet and looking around for the stretcher bearers. 'Let's get her into the box. Bring one of those towels and beat off the flies as well as you can. I'll deal with the rest when we get her down to the morgue.'

The stretcher bearers came forward with the metal coffin used for transporting corpses to the police morgue, Ingeburg Grunwald was loaded into it and the coffin was placed in the low, flat trailer known as a corpse transporter, which had been brought out behind the police car.

'Was she raped?' asked the inspector, standing to one side and emotionlessly puffing on his cigar. He was not a man without feeling, but this was his job. He had seen a great many corpses in his time and some had been in worse shape than this one.

'No,' said the doctor. 'Her underwear is in place and there's no laceration of the external genitals. Looking for a motive?'

The inspector nodded. 'Weapon? Time?' he said.

'Hatchet or small axe,' said the doctor. 'Her head was split like a pumpkin. Several blows. Probably from behind. There are no defence marks on the hands or forearms. Time, I can't tell you until I've done the autopsy. Three or four days at least.'

'She disappeared on the afternoon of the nineteenth,' said the inspector.

'Probably then,' said the doctor. 'Can I take her down to the morgue now? Even if I don't start the autopsy until tomorrow, I'm going to have to do something about the bugs immediately.'

'Go ahead,' said the inspector. 'I'm going to stay out here with Sepp for a while. I want to see what the lab boys turn up.'

The laboratory technicians who had come out with the party had staked off the area in one metre squares and had been going over it square by square, any finds being spotted and noted on a sheet of squared paper.

Although it was Sunday and overtime pay in the Criminal Investigations Department was no more than a fond dream, they worked methodically and rather slowly so that the inspector had to wait for some time.

Finally, the technician in charge of the group came over and said, 'Well, that's it. I don't believe that we'll find anything else. Want to hear it?'

'I'm not standing out here because I love nature,' said the inspector shortly.

'She wasn't killed where the body was lying,' said the technician. 'She was killed up above the slope there and the body was then thrown over.

'There's a logging trail up there and the marks of a car's tyres. We have casts. There are three sets of footprints leading away from the car tracks, one set of which are the dead woman's. We have casts of the other two. A man and a woman or a teenage boy. The small ones are sports shoes.

'Twenty-six yards from where the car was parked the woman was hit so hard over the head that her heels sank a half inch into the ground. It's fairly soft.

'Good bit of blood at that point and then carry and drag marks to the top of the slope here. They couldn't have been very strong. There were two of them and the woman wasn't that heavy, but they dragged her more than they carried her.'

'Here's the description of the clothing she was wearing when she disappeared,' said the inspector, handing him the F.I.R. 'Does it check?'

The technician checked the clothing against his own notes.

'Everything checks except this red velvet jacket on the F.I.R.,' he said. 'It wasn't on the corpse.'

'She must have left it in the car,' said the inspector. 'Tell me, would a woman in her right mind come out here for a walk in the woods with her estranged husband and his mistress?'

'How would I know?' said the technician. 'I only find and assess what's there. You boys are the deduction experts.'

'There's no sign of a struggle or that she was dragged out of the car?' asked Sergeant Meier, who had been listening silently to the report.

'Nope,' said the technician. 'Everyone was walking normally except for the little one. He or she seems to have been running over the stretch between the car and the scene of the murder.'

'Strange,' said the sergeant. 'The little one was running, but it was Grunwald who was murdered. What would that mean?'

'The only thing any of this means to me,' said the inspector, 'is that these three people must have all known each other and they must have had a reason for coming out here to the woods. With two of them the reason was, no doubt, murder, but that certainly wasn't the reason that Mrs Grunwald had. It might help us if we could determine what her reason was.'

'Logically, the other two persons would be Grunwald and

his Turkish girl friend,' said the sergeant. 'They could have made some kind of a pretext, discussing the divorce or something, to get her out here, but the problem is: Why? They were in agreement on the divorce and there was no question of a property settlement. None of them had anything, not even insurance.'

'Well, there was a motive,' said the inspector. 'This wasn't something done on the spur of the moment. It was planned. And if Grunwald and his friend did it, then they were goddamnably cold-blooded about it. The detective from Missing Persons checked them out at six-thirty and they could barely have finished killing the girl then.'

'Still, they didn't think of everything,' observed the sergeant. 'If these tyre tracks match the tyres on Grunwald's car and if these footprints match his and Kandlbinder's shoes, we've got them.'

Wolfgang Grunwald and Bahar Kandlbinder were taken into custody an hour later and brought to the headquarters of the Criminal Police where they were subjected to intense interrogation. Both denied all knowledge of the crime and stated that they had spent the entire afternoon and evening of the nineteenth together.

In the meantime, the laboratory technicians were busy with Grunwald's green Opel Kadet and the contents of the apartment which he shared with Bahar Kandlbinder. Casts of the car's tyres were taken and all of the shoes and clothing belonging to the couple were brought to the police laboratory. By eight o'clock that evening, the laboratory was ready with a report.

'The tyre tracks do not match,' said the chief of the laboratory section. 'The shoe prints are the right size for Grunwald and Kandlbinder, but they do not match any shoes found in the apartment. None of the clothing shows any signs of blood stains or places where blood stains were removed.

'We did not find any trace of a hatchet or small axe.'

'Perfect score,' remarked the inspector whose secretary had just brought him in some sandwiches from across the street and who was making his dinner at his desk. 'Go home,

Gerda. There was no reason for you to come in in the first place.'

The secretary left reluctantly. She was a large, blonde woman who did not think that the inspector could do anything without her and who, consequently, bribed the dispatchers to inform her when he was called in during off-duty periods.

'Shall I tell the Interrogation Room to turn them loose?' asked the sergeant, getting to his feet.

'No,' mumbled the inspector, his mouth full. 'They've had plenty of time to get rid of the shoes and the clothing and even to change the tyres on the car. They're not innocent. They're just smarter than we thought they were.'

'We can't hold them very long without material evidence,' said the sergeant. 'We aren't even able to suggest a motive.'

'You'll get the material evidence tomorrow,' said the inspector. 'We'll start by checking the dry cleaning shops to see if Grunwald or Kandlbinder turned in any bloody clothing on the afternoon of the nineteenth or the morning of the twentieth. Then we'll check the places that sell tyres and see if we can determine whether Grunwald bought a new set recently. And, finally, we'll check out the hardware stores and see if we can find a clerk who can recognize Grunwald or Kandlbinder as the purchaser of a hatchet during the week preceding the nineteenth. Also, you can have all the ashes pulled out of the furnace at the apartment house to see if there's any trace of that red velvet jacket. The heating's off now, but they could have burned it up in the furnace anyway. It's coal. If there's nothing in the firebox of the furnace, get an exact description of the jacket and put out circulars all over town. I want action on this case.'

'I gathered that,' said the sergeant dryly.

Action there was, and results too. First of all, the store where Wolfgang Grunwald had bought a heavy hatchet of the trademark 'Bear' on June 13th, less than a week before the murder, was located. Grunwald had been careless. The store was only four blocks from the apartment house where he lived and some of the clerks knew him by sight. Then, the tyre store where Grunwald had bought a new set of tyres two days before the murder was found. Finally, the red velvet jacket which had belonged to Ingeburg Grunwald was found hidden under a bush on the Theresien Wiese, the meadow-like fairgrounds along the Isar. It had been drenched with blood.

Confronted with this evidence, Wolfgang Grunwald promptly broke down and confessed to a knowledge of the murder which he said had been committed by his mistress, Bahar Kandlbinder.

'Ingeburg was going to have her put into an insane asylum,' he said. 'So Bahar asked me to buy the hatchet and get her to come out to the woods with us to talk over the divorce. While I waited at the car, Bahar and Ingeburg went on into the woods and then I heard a sound like someone splitting open a hollow log. A minute later, Bahar came back and said that she'd killed Ingeburg and that I was to help her get rid of the body. We threw it down the slope and then went back to town where I took our shoes and the hatchet and threw them in the Isar. The following morning, I changed the tyres on the car. I was afraid of being caught because I knew that I should have reported Bahar to the police for killing my wife, but by then it was too late.'

Bahar Kandlbinder had a different version.

'Wolfgang hated Ingeburg because, after they had separated, she was angry and she told his company about a lot of things that he'd stolen there and money that he'd taken and he got into a lot of trouble.

'Then, in the first part of June, I told him I didn't want to continue with him any longer and he became very angry. He boxed my ears and then he took my head and hit it against the bed post. I started to scream for help and he wrapped me up very tightly in a blanket. His face was like a crazy man's and I stopped calling and stayed very quiet. Then he seemed to get over it and everything was all right. I didn't say anything more about leaving him.

'When we went out to the woods with Ingeburg I still didn't think he'd really do it and I stayed in the car with the hatchet while he and Ingeburg went into the woods. All at once, he yelled, "Bring it to me!" and I knew he meant the hatchet. I ran after them and Ingeburg was standing with her back to us. I don't think she suspected anything. I handed Wolfgang the hatchet and then I saw he really was going to do it and I turned around and put my hands over my face.

'There was a terrible sound as if something had chopped into a big cabbage or a water melon and then more chopping sounds. I can never forget those sounds as long as I live. I will confess to anything, but I don't want to talk any more about what happened there in the woods.'

'So who is telling the truth?' asked the sergeant as he and the inspector returned to their office following the interrogation of the two suspects.

'She is,' said the inspector, 'but we're going to have to be a little tricky. Only the two of them were present so it's his unsupported word against hers. He's German and she's a Turk and a sex masseuse to boot. I'm afraid if we leave it the way it is, the jury will convict the wrong person.'

'So what do we do?' said the sergeant.

'We charge Kandlbinder with the murder and Grunwald with being an accessory after the fact,' said the inspector. 'Announce that to the press.'

'But . . .?' said the sergeant.

'We want Grunwald to think he's in the clear,' said the inspector. 'He'll go right up to the trial thinking that the most he can get is two or three years as an accessory. Then we'll hit him with the murder charge and provide the prosecutor with everything we can to sustain it. It'll be close to a year before this comes to trial so we'll have plenty of time to work on it. What we want to show is that Grunwald not only carried out the murder, but also carefully planned it in advance.'

'Are you sure we can?' said the sergeant dubiously.

'Absolutely,' said the inspector. 'Because he did. The hatchet and the tyres were bought well in advance. He knew just what to do with the bloody clothing and the hatchet after it had been used. He realized that there would be shoe prints and tyre marks. The whole thing shows the effects of careful thought over a period of some time. Do you think that a Turkish sex masseuse is capable of that?'

The sergeant shook his head. 'No,' he said. 'She isn't and, as a matter of fact, I believe her when she says she wanted to break off with Grunwald. After all, he wasn't much of a catch. No money. Nothing in the way of prospects. And probably not even much of a lover by her standards. I agree with you that the woman is innocent of the actual murder, but are you going to tell her what you're trying to do?'

'No,' said the inspector. 'There are only two of us who know so, if it gets out, it was either you or me who leaked it. I'd hate to break in a new assistant, but . . .'

'You won't have to,' said the sergeant. 'But it's going to be a rough year for Mrs Kandlbinder.'

On the face of things, Bahar Kandlbinder did not appear to suffer as greatly under the murder charge as the sergeant had anticipated, but resigned herself with oriental patience to her apparent fate. She was, however, extremely reluctant to discuss the murder and, in what seemed to be an effort to avoid further questioning on the subject, made a full confession to having killed Ingeburg Grunwald herself!

'I'm sorry that I didn't confess before,' she said. 'It happened just the way Wolfgang said it did.'

She had in fact only been informed that Wolfgang Grunwald had accused her of the murder and not of any of the details of his account. Subsequent questioning showed that she had no idea of what he had told the police.

'Which,' said the inspector, 'merely confirms my opinion that the woman is innocent. She thinks that she's going to be railroaded by a German court for a murder she didn't commit so she's being as co-operative as possible. All she wants is to get it over with.'

In the meantime, things had been going well with the search for evidence of Wolfgang Grunwald's guilt. Tests carried out in the police laboratory showed that the first blow which had split Ingeburg Grunwald's head nearly in half could not have been delivered by a person as short as Bahar Kandlbinder unless she was standing on something.

Nothing had been found at the scene on which she could have stood nor was any mention made in either of the confessions of her standing on something to strike the first blow.

The report which Ingeburg had made to her husband's company concerning his thefts and embezzlements was verified and a number of witnesses were found who stated that Grunwald had said on several occasions that he would 'get even' with her for it.

Finally, the clue of the footprints found at the scene tended to support Bahar Kandlbinder's version of the events. The Grunwalds had walked ahead into the forest and she had come running after them with the hatchet when Grunwald called her.

One month before the trial was due to take place the indictments were altered and Wolfgang Grunwald was charged with the murder of his wife. However, the shock did not provoke him to a confession, as the inspector had hoped, and he clung stubbornly to his original statement that he had only been a helpless witness to the murder carried out by Bahar Kandlbinder.

The court did not think so. The police had done their homework too well and on May 22, 1975, less than a year after the murder of Ingeburg Grunwald, Wolfgang Grunwald was found guilty of premeditated murder with no extenuating circumstances and sentenced to life imprisonment.

Bahar Kandlbinder was found guilty of acting as an accessory after the fact to murder and was sentenced to two and a half years. Even though the verdicts were not appealed, Wolfgang Grunwald never acknowledged his guilt and steadfastly maintains that Bahar Kandlbinder and not he is the true murderer of his wife.

15

GHOULISH PRACTICES

Vampire. A reanimated corpse which sucks the blood of living victims.

Ghoul. An evil demon which feeds on the flesh of corpses.

Necrophile. One who seeks to engage in sexual relations with the dead.

Strange creatures, but not at all uncommon. They can be seen on television almost any night of the week and only very small children are frightened. Everyone else finds them amusing for they know that there are, of course, no such beings.

Well, perhaps not, but what was it then that was in the mortuary of the great cemetery of Hamburg-Ohlsdorf, West Germany, on the night of April 14, 1971?

Something was there and it left clear traces of why it had come and what it had sought. The only thing not clear was what it was.

Curiously, the night of April 14, 1971 was well suited to such terrible activities. The weather was cold and wet with black, low-hanging clouds driving across the face of a sickly pale, waning moon. As midnight drew near, the wind rose, wailing and sobbing among the tombstones and sending sharp, startling rattles of rain against the tall gothic windows of the darkened mortuary.

In the hall where the corpses lay, awaiting the final ceremony of their burial, there was neither light nor heat. The dead have no need of either. Nor was the hall locked or guarded. No one would ever escape from that hall and no one but a madman would ever seek to enter.

And yet, as midnight passed and the church tower bell boomed slowly out its solemn twelve strokes, there was movement in the chill darkness of the hall of corpses; quick, furtive movement where there should have been no movement at all.

There was the scrape of a match and the tiny, yellow leaf of a candle flame sprang into being. Crooked, grotesque shadows danced along the wall and there were the sounds of coffin covers being drawn back and the rustle of paper. The corpses were all clad in paper shrouds until it would be time for them to put on their finery for the funeral.

With some, of course, it would make little difference what they wore, for the coffin would not be opened during the ceremony. Such was the case with little Käthe Bauer who had died at the age of twelve when struck by a car as she crossed the street on her way home from school. Käthe had been a pretty little girl, but the rear wheel of the car had gone directly over her face. At the funeral on Sunday, the coffin would remain closed.

It was open now and Käthe, who had died a virgin, was taking part in a sort of wedding feast where she was not only the bride, but also the dinner!

In the morning, when Mortuary Attendant Gerd Fröhlich came in to work at a quarter past eight, she was still seated at the festive board, her naked little-girl's body leaning against her coffin, the bloody marks of the bridegroom's passionate kisses and caresses on her budding breasts and lightly haired genitals and a deep cut across the veins of her left wrist.

On either side of the coffin were the stumps of burned down candles from the mortuary's own supply and some of the other corpses had been raised in their coffins to serve as guests at the wedding.

For a wedding and a feast it had definitely been. The thick, semi-congealed blood of the corpse had been sucked out of the veins in places, there were bite marks in the white flesh of the thighs and throat and a determined attempt had been made to consummate the marriage, an attempt which had been foiled only by the stiffness of the corpse. Across the cut on the left wrist was the imprint of another wound, but this in the fresh, red blood of the living and not the gummy, brown ichor of the dead.

Had Gerd Fröhlich been a man with a weak stomach, he would not have chosen to work in a mortuary, but this was something considerably beyond anything that could be expected in the way of normal mortuary work. Fröhlich barely made it to the lavatory where he lost his breakfast and, as it seemed to him, everything that he had eaten for several years. He then wiped his mouth and staggered, still retching, to the office where he dialled the number of the police.

His description of what had happened was so vivid that Inspector Frank Luders of the Hamburg Department of Criminal Investigations came out personally to have a look.

He was accompanied by his assistant, Detective-Sergeant Max Peters, and the department's medical expert, Dr Ludwig Strauss, who carried out an immediate examination of the body of Käthe Bauer.

While the inspector, looking not unlike a funeral director himself, stood glumly watching the doctor at his work, the sergeant went out to the police car and returned with a finger print kit.

'A lot of prints here,' he remarked, dusting the edges of the open coffins. 'What do you think he had in mind? Grave robbing?'

The inspector did not reply, but the doctor said, 'Hardly. These people weren't laid out for their funerals yet. There's nothing to rob.'

'He may not have known that,' said the inspector.

'He wasn't interested,' said the doctor, stepping back and stripping off his rubber gloves. 'What we have here is a ghoul and a necrophile. He wanted food and sex from the corpse. From the looks of the cut on her wrist, I would judge that he also wanted to exchange blood with her. He seems to have succeeded in everything but the sex. She was not dead long enough or too long, however you look at it, for that.'

The inspector was, necessarily, a man with strong nerves, but there was almost a shrill edge to his voice now as he snapped, 'That's nonsense, Ludwig! There's no such thing as a ghoul!'

'Very well then,' said the doctor. 'If you insist, it was a perfectly ordinary, well-balanced person who came in here last night, tried to have sex with this little girl's corpse and sucked quite a bit of blood out of her. He also bit off a few small pieces and apparently swallowed them as I don't see them here. By my definition this is a ghoul, but if you are convinced that it was just a casual visitor . . .'

'Point taken,' interrupted the inspector. 'I suppose you would agree that this is a dangerous psychopath?'

'Definitely,' said the doctor without hesitation.

'Then spare no efforts, Max,' said the inspector. 'I'd like to get him before he tries this on someone alive.'

No efforts were spared, but the police were unable to find the slightest clue as to the identity of the mortuary's strange visitor. The Hamburg police also circulated a description of the incident to all police stations in Germany, but the little village of Bisselmark, forty miles to the east of Hamburg, did not receive the circular for the simple reason that Bisselmark is too small to have a police force.

Had there been one, however, it would have been presented with the most incredible case on the morning of April 17, 1971 when the local undertaker entered his place of business to find his latest and, at the moment, only client sitting upright in her coffin with her knees hooked over the sides.

A woman in her forties who had died of cancer two days earlier: her eyes were propped open with match sticks and the crotch of her underwear had been cut away.

Standing in a circle around the coffin were a number of burned down candles and, since it had been raining the night before, the marks of muddy shoes in a strange pattern as if someone had been performing some sort of ritual dance.

The undertaker was shocked and frightened, but he hurriedly replaced the corpse in its coffin and cleaned up all traces of what had transpired the night before. As he feared that the family might hold him responsible for the desecration of the corpse, he said nothing to anyone and it was only much later that he reported the incident to the police.

Following the incident in Bisselmark, the ghoul moved west, so far west in fact, that he left the mainland altogether and landed on the North Sea island of Sylt.

Sylt enjoys an interesting reputation in Europe because it is the site of the largest concentrations of nudists in Germany and, possibly, in the world.

Every summer brings thousands of sun-worshipping Germans, Danes, Swedes and Norwegians to splash in naked ecstasy in the chill waters of the North Sea or to frolic along the white sand beaches in temperatures which bring visions of ear muffs and parkas to less hardy races.

However, even for the Nordics, May 4th is a trifle early in the year for nude bathing and there were therefore only token numbers of visitors in Westerland, the main town on Sylt, when Pastor Harold Segen entered the antechamber of his church at approximately eight o'clock in the morning to find the lid of the coffin which was there removed.

Inside the coffin was Mrs Gertraud Frankle, who had died two days previously of circulatory disorders at the age of fifty-two. She was still lying peacefully on her back with her eyes closed, but, to the pastor's astonishment, the hilt of what looked to be a hunting knife projected from her chest.

Pastor Segen immediately notified the police and the body was examined by the medical adviser attached to the Department of Criminal Investigations.

His findings were that the knife, an ordinary souvenir hunting dagger with a chrome plated blade sharp on one side only and an imitation stag horn handle in the form of a deer's head bearing the inscription 'Souvenir of Sylt', had been thrust with considerable force directly through the woman's heart and then given a single half-turn.

The police did not suspect a ghoul because they knew that there was no such thing. Rather, they suspected an enemy of the family, but although the investigation continued for some months, no clue as to the identity of the culprit was discovered. The attack on the corpse in the church in Westerland was an isolated incident and nothing further of such nature took place in the town or anywhere on the island.

If ghouls take vacations, this one had taken his early for by May 30, 1971 he was back at work on the mainland and in a city with even more erotic associations than the nudists of Sylt. The city was Flensburg on the German side of the border with Denmark and its claim to fame was merely that it was the headquarters of the world's largest mail-order sex shop, founded by the equally famous Beate Uhse.

'Merely' is perhaps not entirely the right term in this case. There are statistics to the effect that one German in every five is a Beate Uhse customer which could mean that the Germans are very active in sexual matters, or precisely the opposite as many of the Uhse products are intended to make possible that which no longer comes naturally.

The scene was, as usual, a cemetery. In this case, the Mühlen Cemetery and on the night of May 30th there was nearly a full moon. Not that this had anything to do with it, of course. The ghoul was as active during the dark of the moon as at any other time, but perhaps he had need of light for the special operation which he had in mind and it would hardly have done to bring along a lighted lantern or even a flashlight. There are houses quite near the cemetery.

It was fortunate that there were houses because it is hard to say what might have happened to Marion Steiger on the morning of May 31st if a housewife living in one of them had not looked out and seen her run wildly into the street and collapse in the middle of the pavement.

Being a level-headed woman, the housewife first called the police and the ambulance and then went to see if she could do anything to help the young woman who was now trying to sit up and seemed to be suffering from a severe shock.

This impression was confirmed by the intern who arrived with the emergency ambulance, but the police could make no sense of what she was saying and finally set off in the direction from which the housewife had seen her come.

Only the cemetery lay in this direction and just inside the gate to it lay a woman's purse. Inside the purse was the personal identity card of Marion Steiger and a number of other personal items.

A little further on, the patrolcar officers came upon first one shoe and then the other and finally a veritable trail of flowers from what had obviously been a large bouquet.

'Look for a tombstone with the name Steiger on it,' said the senior of the two officers. 'There must have been something wrong with the grave. Maybe an animal got at it.'

A few moments later they found the grave of Helga Steiger who was Marion's mother. The grave was in perfect condition. The two officers came to a halt, puzzled, and then both saw simultaneously the scattered earth in the next row of graves. It looked as if a demonic grave-digger had been at work.

'Grave-robbers!' exclaimed the senior man, running around the gravestones to the other path.

But it was not grave-robbers and the sight which met his eyes gave him such a start that he automatically and unthinkingly drew his service pistol. The coffin had been buried deep, nearly six feet deep as the regulations required, but it had been dug completely free. One end was smashed to kindling and the corpse had been dragged to a sitting position with the hands resting stiffly on top of the unbroken lower end.

It was a man for it was dressed in a man's suit, but where the head should have been there was nothing but a ragged stump of neck.

'No wonder she was in shock!' whispered the second patrolman. 'What in God's name has happened here?'

His partner was, of course, unable to answer the question, but Dr Theodore Fichtenbauer, the medical expert attached to the Flensburg Police Department of Criminal Investigations, thought that he could.

'Somebody needed a skull,' he said matter-of-factly, letting himself down into the grave to squat on the top of the splintered coffin. 'Could be satanists or somebody who thinks he's a witch, or even a medical student.'

He probed casually with naked fingers in the already somewhat putrid flesh of the mangled neck, causing Detective-Sergeant Lutz Iggel to turn faintly green and gag slightly.

'If he was a medical student, it was his first year,' he remarked. 'Simply hacked it off with a butcher's knife or something similar.'

Inspector Richard Brinkmann, who had taken charge of the affair, decided that it had probably been satanists. As in other parts of the world, the decline in influence of the established religions had brought with it a rise in satanism, witchcraft, various Eastern religions and a number of home-grown sects.

A very large, very patient and very stubborn man, he pursued his investigations of the supposed satanists for over a year and a half without finding the slightest trace that any such group had ever existed in Flensburg.

It did not occur to him that this might be the work of a ghoul or vampire for he knew that there were no such things.

Perhaps the inspector might not have continued with the search for so long had he not found evidence of what had happened to the missing head. Two days after the desecration of the grave in Mühlen Cemetery, a middle-aged veterinarian named Karl Konzemius had opened the door to the small garden house in the garden which he leased on the edge of the city, to find a human nose and two ears lying on the floor.

The bits of flesh had begun to decompose badly and had attracted a number of flies and other insects so that, even though a veterinarian and accustomed to unpleasant sights, Konzemius was nearly overcome by nausea. When he had recovered from this, he carefully closed the door of the garden house and went to notify the police.

The inspector, his assistant and Dr Fichtenbauer came out together and a search of the garden house produced quite a few more parts of the head.

'Ah yes,' said the unshakable doctor, holding up the corpse's tongue. 'Here is the tongue and these were the eyes. He dug them out with the point of a knife.'

At this point, Sergeant Iggel left the garden house and

refused to return. In addition to the ghastly sight, the parts were beginning to smell quite strongly.

'This is presumably the scalp,' remarked the inspector, who was made of somewhat stronger stuff. 'At least, it's got hair on it.'

'Cut off everything he could,' said the doctor. 'All he wanted was the skull. What's that bottle there?'

'According to the label, it was burning alcohol,' said the inspector. 'It's empty now.'

'That explains these spots on the floor,' said the doctor. 'After he'd cut off everything that he could, he poured the alcohol over it and set it on fire to burn off the rest of the flesh. Wouldn't work of course. He'd need a lot more alcohol and, in any case, he obviously didn't get the brain out. However, it will eventually rot away and run out if he keeps it long enough.'

The inspector did not leave the garden house, but he did not look very much at his ease either.

The nose, scalp, eyes and ears of the dead man were placed in a small jar and buried with him for the second time. The skull remained missing, although by now most of the police forces in Germany were looking for it.

Like the Hamburg police, Inspector Brinkmann had sent out a circular to all police stations in Germany and, since there had now been several more incidents, there had been a considerable response.

There was, to begin with, the violation of the corpse of Käthe Bauer in Hamburg. Then the Westerland police reported the stabbing of the corpse of Mrs Gertraud Frankle. And finally, even the undertaker in Bisselmark came forward to recount the strange happenings in his establishment. He had read of the other cases in the newspapers and asked that the identity of the Bisselmark corpse be kept secret in order to spare the feelings of the family.

Inspector Brinkmann was still convinced that the deeds were the work of a sect of devil worshippers and he thought that it must be an entire gang to be ranging over such widely separated places as Hamburg, Sylt and Flensburg.

His assistant did not agree. Although a rather stylish

young man who wore his black hair nearly down to his shoulders and who displayed a distressing tendency to tie-dyed jeans and brilliant shirts, he had had an excellent training at the police school and he was, perhaps, slightly more open-minded than the inspector.

'There isn't any common pattern,' he argued. 'Flensburg is the only place where any part of the body was actually taken away and the only place where it was a man. In Hamburg, it was a little girl and there were definite sexual indications. In Bisselmark, there were indications that he'd examined her genitals, but not that he'd tried to have intercourse. And in Westerland, he didn't even disturb the corpse. Either these incidents are not connected or we're dealing with someone who's not following a rational pattern. I think it's the latter.'

'I don't know what to think any more,' said the inspector. 'Hamburg refers to the fellow as a ghoul, but there aren't any ghouls.'

'There aren't any satanists either,' said the sergeant. 'Not serious enough ones to go around beheading corpses. We've been following up this satanist theory for so long now that I've picked up a good deal of information on it. All that are known here in Germany are harmless.'

'Harmless!' said the inspector, a regular churchgoer and comparatively devout man, in a shocked voice.

'Physically harmless,' said the sergeant, who never went to church at all. 'Theology aside, these are mostly sex clubs with costumes. They get together and celebrate the Black Mass with a naked girl for an altar. Then they all have a nice little orgy and go home feeling wonderfully wicked and sweat it out in the shop or the office until the next meeting of the coven. It's about on the level of a bowling club. If one of those people came across a severed head, they'd die of fear.'

'I can see that you've gone into the thing thoroughly,' said the inspector, looking thoughtfully at his assistant as if he were wondering whether his investigations might not have led him further than was suitable for a police officer.

'All right. Supposing that we accept that the fellow is a ghoul. Where does that leave us?'

'With not quite so urgent a problem,' said the sergeant. 'We've been operating on the assumption that this is a group of satanists who could very well transfer their interest to living persons: a baby for the purposes of sacrifice or a young girl for the Black Mass. Right?'

'Right,' said the inspector.

'Well, if the fellow really is a ghoul or, at least, thinks he is, he's no danger to a living person,' said the sergeant. 'He's only interested in corpses. Granted, it's not pleasant to have bodies dug up and mortuaries raided, but at least there's no danger to human life.'

'Not too much different to Theodore's theory,' observed the inspector. 'He says that the fellow is a necrophile, a lover of corpses. Says its a recognized mental aberration. I say, if he loves corpses so much, why does he stick knives in them and cut off their heads?'

'Still,' said the sergeant, 'if this is the same fellow in all cases, he's never been known to harm a living person.'

'I was waiting for you to say that,' said the inspector. He dug through the mass of papers in his 'in progress' box and brought out a double-page, typed circular. 'Listen to this.'

He cleared his throat, leaned back in his chair and began to read.

'On the afternoon of June 27, 1971 a group consisting of Anton Berbach, aged forty-seven, insurance inspector, Ingeborg Thomas, aged thirty-four, housewife, and Heinz-Martin Thomas, aged thirty-nine, office employee, all resident in Feucht, were walking in the forest approximately three point five kilometres south-west of that city. At approximately three-forty-seven o'clock, they . . .'

'Where's Feucht?' interrupted the sergeant.

'Five miles south-east of Nürnberg,' said the inspector, 'on the highway to Regensberg. This is a circular from the Nürnberg Police.'

'But that's clear in the south of Germany,' said the sergeant.

'Right,' said the inspector. 'Your ghoul has gone south.'

He rustled the paper and resumed, '. . . they came upon the body of a woman lying near the path in a small clearing. The woman, later identified as Martha Krüger, aged thirty-six, housewife and resident in Feucht, had died as the result of one twenty-two calibre, long-rifle bullet which entered the left temple and remained embedded in the brain.

'In addition, the body showed fourteen knife wounds of varying sizes and depths. Several of the knife wounds displayed tooth marks and the imprint of human lips in blood. The assumption is that the murderer bit and drank the blood of his victim.'

'But that's a vampire, not a ghoul!' exclaimed the sergeant. 'It couldn't be the same man!'

'Just a minute,' said the inspector. 'I'm not finished yet.'

'Lying on top of the corpse of her mother was Lydia Krüger, aged three. The child was crying bitterly and was covered with her mother's blood. She was uninjured. The child's statement, made to the Thomases and Anton Berbach and later to the investigating officer of the Nürnberg Department of Criminal Investigations, was: "Mummy fell over and the man came and hit her with a knife. Then, he tried to eat her up. I was scared." '

'A madman who thinks he's a vampire,' said the sergeant. 'Do they have any leads?'

'Not a thing,' said the inspector. 'But then, ghouls and vampires don't leave any traces. They merely crawl back into their graves or fly away or whatever. Nürnberg thinks that it was the same man who broke into the mortuary in Hamburg. They've asked for photographs of the teeth marks.'

'It's impossible,' said the sergeant. 'How could you have a combination of ghoul-vampire? Vampires suck blood. You can't suck the blood of a corpse.'

'Oh yes you can,' said the inspector. 'At least, if it hasn't been dead too long. Theodore says that it's gummy and sticky at first and then it turns to a yellowish, stinking liquid which might not seem very appetizing to you or me, but which can be drunk. On the other hand, it would . . .'

But at this point the conversation was terminated as the

sergeant clapped his hand over his mouth and ran wildly out of the office.

'He's going to need a stronger stomach than that, if this case continues,' said the inspector, shaking his head.

Whether the case continued or not was a moot question. It did not, in any case, continue in Flensburg where no further reports of ghoulish or vampirish activities were received by the police. But the inspector continued his dogged investigation of possible satanist organizations.

In Nürnberg things were more active and, for the first time, the ghoul, vampire, necrophile or simply madman seemed to have struck twice in the same place. On November 3, 1971 forty-year-old George Weichert was riding in a car with his fifteen-year-old daughter, Steffi, when the driver lost control of the vehicle. Leaving the road, the car turned over a half dozen times and ended up in a forest fifty yards from the road. The driver escaped with no more than cuts and bruises, but George Weichert was killed instantly and Steffi died in hospital the next day. She and her father were buried side by side in Nürnberg's south cemetery on November 6th.

Oddly enough in view of later developments, the accident had taken place at the crossroads to Feucht and less than a mile from the point where a vampire had sucked the blood of Martha Krüger before the terrified eyes of her little daughter.

On the morning of November 7, 1971 a young man named Horst Weber came to visit the grave of a relative at the South Cemetery and at approximately nine-fifteen, rounded a high hedge to come upon the most horrifying sight of his life.

Steffi Weichert had been dug up from her grave and removed from her coffin. Completely naked, she sat stiffly on a mound of earth beside the open grave, her forearms resting on her wide-spread knees. Her head was tipped backward and the dull, sightless eyes were wide open and seemed to be staring almost greedily at the petrified young man.

She had been a pretty girl when alive, but the accident had badly damaged the upper part of her face and head so that the eyes stared out of a hideous mass of swollen flesh which had turned blue, black, green, purple and yellow.

Against these more sombre colours, the red trickle of fresh blood which ran from between her lips, over her chin and down between her young breasts, made a bright contrast.

As Weber stood transfixed, a light breeze lifted the fine blonde hair of the dead girl, lending the terrible face a grisly semblance of life.

Horst Weber did not believe in vampires except for those appearing in the movies, but here, before his very eyes and less than ten feet away, was a vampire which had during the night clambered from its grave to feast on some unfortunate victim and had been caught by the rising sun before it could get back.

Not, of course, that the sun had actually risen. It was a typical November day, overcast and cold, and the vicious little wind which whined about the cypresses and shook the hedges, seemed filled with eerie, wailing voices.

As far as he knew, he was completely alone in the cemetery.

Horst Weber followed the rules for dealing with vampires. He turned and ran like hell. Being a man mindful of his responsibilities as a citizen, he did not only run, but ran directly for the nearest police station, some six blocks away.

As chance would have it, he had gone less than two blocks when he nearly collided with a patrolman coming from that same station whose duty it was to maintain law and order in the district.

'There is vamp . . .!' gasped Horst Weber, skidding to a stop. 'That is, there's something wrong in the cemetery.'

He had caught himself in the last instant before telling a police officer that there was a vampire sitting in the cemetery, a remark which he felt certain would have gained him a free interview with the police psychiatrist.

To his horror and astonishment, the police officer seemed to grasp very well what he had intended to say.

'My God!' he gulped. 'It's the vampire! Run to the station and tell them I need help. I'm going after him.'

Whereupon the officer drew his service pistol, snapped the slide to put a round in the chamber and ran off in the direction of the cemetery, leaving Weber with the impression that he had somehow wandered onto the set of a B grade movie.

No German would disregard an order from a person in authority and he resumed his dash to the police station where he told what he had seen and what the patrolman had said with considerable trepidation.

Once again, his word was accepted without question and a party immediately roared away in the squad car while the desk sergeant called headquarters to alert Inspector Julius Misner, the investigations officer who had been assigned to the Krüger case and who had left instructions that he was to be notified of anything of a similar nature.

It being Sunday, the inspector was at home and by the time he had been contacted and picked up by his assistant, Detective-Sergeant Hans Bohm, and the sergeant had stopped again to pick up the department's medical expert, Dr Jürgen Platt, it was past ten before the party arrived at the cemetery.

As it turned out, there was no great hurry in any case.

'This happened hours ago,' said the doctor. 'Sometime during the middle of the night. And this isn't a vampire. It's a young girl who's been in some kind of violent accident, motor car, I should think.'

'I can see that,' said the inspector. He was a quiet inconspicuous-appearing man with a very matter-of-fact manner of speaking. 'The person who found her was frightened and reported her as a vampire. You're familiar with the ghoul-vampire cases in northern Germany and you examined the body of Martha Krüger. What I want to know is whether this is the same type of case.'

The doctor nodded and began a careful examination of the corpse.

'The blood on the mouth isn't hers,' he observed. 'He kissed her when his own mouth was full of blood.'

'Whose blood?' said the inspector.

'His presumably,' said the doctor. 'It wasn't hers. There's

a cut here under the left breast and he was sucking and chewing on it, but the blood isn't fresh. She's been dead three or four days.'

'In the Hamburg case,' said the inspector. 'He cut himself and pressed the wound to a cut on the girl's wrist.'

'Same principle here,' said the doctor. 'And, as in the case in Hamburg, he's tried to have sexual intercourse with her. Unsuccessful of course. The body is much too stiff.'

'But you would say then that it resembles the Hamburg case?' interrupted the inspector. 'What about the Krüger murder?'

'Hamburg, yes, definitely,' said the doctor. 'It was almost certainly the same man. It's highly unlikely that there would be two persons suffering from the same fixation running around here in Germany at the same time. It's not at all a common disorder.'

'But not unheard of either?' said the inspector.

'No, not unheard of,' said the doctor, 'but we don't know with certainty what is troubling our friend. Is he merely a necrophile, a person who is enamoured of the dead? Or does he really believe that he is a ghoul or, as the case may be, a vampire?'

'Does it matter?' said the inspector.

'Oh definitely,' said the doctor. 'If he's a necrophile or if he thinks he's a ghoul, then he's going to bother no one but dead people. If he thinks he's a vampire, then you're going to get cases like Martha Krüger. He may only be trying to drink the blood of corpses because he doesn't have access to the blood of living persons.'

'You keep saying "Thinks he's a ghoul",' interjected the sergeant. 'As I understand it, a ghoul is a person who eats the flesh of corpses and this one certainly does just that. It would seem to me that he's about as well qualified to be a real ghoul as you can get.'

'There is no such thing as a ghoul,' said the inspector firmly, putting an end to the conversation.

For the remainder of the day the detection experts from the police laboratory went over not only the area immediately around the grave of Steffi Weichert, but the entire cemetery.

No effort was spared because, unlike the other cases in the north of Germany, there was a possibility here that the ghoul who had dug up and mutilated the corpse of Steffi Weichert was also the vampire who had murdered and sucked the blood of Mrs Martha Krüger.

'I'm not an expert in abnormal psychology,' said the inspector, 'but I have had a good deal of experience with sex criminals and in such cases the offender frequently starts out with relatively harmless acts, he exposes himself to women or he attempts sexual contacts with minors. A proportion of these people never go any further than that, but some enter into a sort of constant progression from bad to worse. They begin, let us say, by exposing themselves to children, go on to actually engaging in sexual play, finally end by raping a child and then, if they're not taken out of circulation, killing one. One step leads to another.'

'But do they go back down the scale?' said the sergeant. 'If your theory is correct, the ghoul began his activities in north Germany where he sucked the blood of corpses and attempted sexual intercourse with them. Eventually, he came down here to us, but he did not carry out any acts against dead bodies. Instead, he began immediately with a murder. Then he went back to desecrating corpses. Is that possible?'

'I don't know,' admitted the inspector. 'We're dealing with a madman here. I don't think anyone can predict his actions or decide what he is capable of.'

Madman or ghoul he might be, but he was either a very sly or a very lucky madman. Not a single clue as to his identity had ever been found at the scenes of his supposed crimes and it was to be no different in Nürnberg.

'He didn't leave a trace,' said the technician in charge of the group. 'At least, he didn't leave a trace that can be connected with the desecration of the corpse. There are foot prints here in the cemetery, hundreds of them, and one set may be those of the ghoul, but there's no way to tell which set.

'We've recovered enough of his blood from the corpse to

identify the blood group, but you can't identify a man by his blood group. You can only say who it wasn't.

'He apparently wore gloves when he was digging up the body. He used one of the cemetery's own spades, but there are no prints on it.

'The only thing we have is photographs of the bite marks on the corpse. However, they're not very clear and, although they seem about the same size and shape as those on Mrs Krüger's body and the ones sent down from Hamburg, it's not an identification that would stand up in court.

'In any case, it doesn't help us because the identity of the ghoul or vampire or whatever he is isn't known in those cases either.'

'You've overlooked one thing,' said the inspector.

The technician looked startled.

'The ghoul reads the newspapers,' said the inspector.

The technician looked even more startled.

'He didn't disturb any other grave,' said the inspector. 'He went directly to that one and only that one. He knew she had just been buried.'

The inspector's logic was impeccable, but it did not help in solving the case for, although the death notices were read every day and no funeral of a young girl took place without a plainclothes officer unobtrusively present, no suspect was arrested. The persons present at the funerals were always friends or relatives of the deceased.

If attending funerals of young girls was an undemanding, if mournful, duty for the detectives of the Criminal Investigations Department, the watch on the cemeteries was not. It was now winter and the winters in southern Germany are cold, overcast, dismal and depressing even for persons not lying hidden behind tombstones in a cemetery in the middle of the night.

Understandably, these night watches in the cemeteries were done almost exclusively by the most junior men on the force and, although there must have been many times when other professions appeared infinitely more attractive, it is a tribute to the morale of the Nürnberg police that not a single rookie turned in his badge or reported himself sick.

The job was, however, without risk. Although the watch was maintained throughout the winter, the ghoul made no further appearances.

'Probably gone back to north Germany,' remarked the inspector. 'Or maybe out of the country altogether. He seems to move around a good bit. I think we can suspend the cemetery watch.'

'It's not popular with the men,' said the sergeant in what may well have been the understatement of all time.

The watch at the cemeteries and at funerals of young women was consequently dropped, but the inspector was mistaken about the ghoul's departure. He was still right there in Nürnberg and he was still active.

He had merely become somewhat more careful about hiding the traces of his activity. But not careful enough.

'You know, Ellie,' said George Warmuth to his wife one morning early in May of 1972, 'I don't know how it's possible, but I have the feeling that somebody's been fooling around with the bodies.'

'My heavens!' exclaimed Ellie Warmuth. 'Who'd want to do a thing like that?'

George Warmuth was the Mortuary Attendant at Nürnberg's West Cemetery, but he had never heard anything about a ghoul nor about the desecration of the corpse of Steffi Weichert.

Very few people not attached to the police had, and this was because Inspector Misner had made every effort to keep the matter secret. The German police are as a rule reluctant to divulge anything concerning a case until at least some progress has been made toward solving it. The advantage of this is that a suspect under questioning cannot say that he read an account of the matter in the newspapers to explain how he came into information concerning the case.

Warmuth did not even know that his mortuary had been under surveillance for the past five months, as had all mortuaries in the city, and he would have been very surprised indeed to learn that he and all his fellow mortuary attendants had actually been considered prime suspects, by Sergeant Bohm at least.

As the sergeant had put it, 'They're used to them as customers. It would be only one more step to become friends.'

Whether the ghoul could be considered a friend of his victims was dubious, but in any case the suspicion proved without foundation, although the inspector had considered it possible because of the ease and familiarity with which the ghoul seemed to move about cemeteries, mortuaries and other places with which the ordinary person would scarcely be familiar.

This was exactly the same conclusion reached by George Warmuth.

'I think,' he told his wife, Ellie, 'that it has to be one of the employees. Grave-digger probably. Nobody likes the job and we always have a big turn-over.'

'But what could they possibly want of the dead people?' said Mrs Warmuth. 'I haven't noticed anything.'

Mrs Warmuth was as familiar with the corpse hall and the other rooms of the mortuary as her husband as she was responsible for the cleaning. She did not as a rule have any contact with the bodies themselves.

'Well, it's hard to say,' said Warmuth. 'Any jewellery they're going to wear isn't put on until just before the funeral. Could be he's after gold teeth or it might be some kind of a pervert that's fooling around with the women's sex organs. I'm going to start waiting for him in the office tonight and see if I can't catch him red-handed.'

Red-handed was an excellent description of the condition of a ghoul taken in the act, but George Warmuth did not know that there was a ghoul about in Nürnberg.

Nor would it probably have bothered him much. A husky six-footer who had fought in some of the hardest battles of the Second World War, he often said that there was nothing left that could surprise him and that he doubted there was anything that could kill him after what he had lived through.

He was to discover very shortly that he was wrong on both counts. That evening after dinner he renounced his favourite television programme and slipped quietly over to the office of the mortuary where he sat waiting patiently and quietly in the dark. It was May 5, 1972 and a pleasant early spring night outside.

The ghoul was punctual. At shortly before ten o'clock there came the faint sound of the door leading to the room where the bodies were displayed before the funeral opening and closing.

Warmuth got silently to his feet. He had recognized the sound instantly and he knew in exactly which direction the intruder would be heading: the vaulted corpse hall in the basement.

It was his plan to descend to the hall before the stranger and wait for him in one of the alcoves along the wall and he moved swiftly to the stairway which was closer to him than it was to the corpse display room.

Arriving at the foot of the stairs, he was astonished to see that the lights were on, and for a moment he thought that the other had in some mysterious fashion managed to arrive before him.

Then he remembered that his wife had been down there earlier that afternoon for cleaning materials which were kept in a closet at the far end. Any time that Mrs Warmuth came down for cleaning materials, the lights were left burning.

This was because the light switch was not on the stairs, but half way down the hall. Although she had been the wife of a mortuary attendant for a good many years now, Ellie Warmuth still did not like to turn out that light and walk half the length of the corpse hall in the dark to the stairs.

Warmuth did not mind and he quickly switched off the light and slipped into the nearest alcove. If it were burning, the corpse robber or whatever he was might be frightened away before Warmuth could lay his great hands on him.

Almost immediately there was the sound of footsteps on the stairs and along the hall as the stranger advanced confidently to the light switch and turned it on. He obviously knew his way around the mortuary, but when Warmuth peered around the corner of the alcove, he saw, to his astonishment, that the man was not an employee nor ever had been in the time that he had been there.

He would have been even more astonished had he known

that he was looking at the ghoul which had kept Nürnberg's police lying out in the freezing cemeteries throughout the winter.

The truth was, the man did not look like a ghoul. He was short, almost slightly built, with dark wavy hair and a blunt nose, and he wore steel-rimmed glasses of the type paid for by the national health insurance.

Despite this sorry appearance, he was a very real ghoul and he promptly proved it by moving matter-of-factly to the nearest coffin and pushing back the lid. Inside the coffin, Warmuth knew, was the body of a thirty-seven-year-old woman who had only arrived at the mortuary the day before.

Warmuth was expecting that the man would now probe the woman's mouth for gold teeth or draw up the paper shroud to examine the genitals, but instead he leaned over, placed his hands on the woman's cheeks and kissed the corpse square on the mouth!

The action was so unexpected and startling that Warmuth gave an involuntary jump and started out of the alcove. As he did, the cuff of his trouser leg caught on one of the trestles standing there and dragged it along the cement floor with a loud scraping sound.

'Damn!' exclaimed Warmuth, expecting to see the little man race off in the direction of the stairs.

Amazingly, he did no such thing but remained where he was with his lips pressed to the mouth of the corpse.

Recovering himself, Warmuth ran forward and seized the little man by his shoulder.

'Here!' he shouted. 'What do you think you're doing?'

The man turned from the coffin, drew a black automatic pistol from his inside jacket pocket and shot George Warmuth in the stomach.

As the big man fell to the floor, the ghoul calmly holstered his weapon and ran off up the stairs.

'All through the war without a scratch,' grunted the severely wounded mortuary attendant. 'I'll be damned if I'll be killed by a midget.'

He then crawled up the stairs to the office, knocked the telephone off the desk, dialled the number of the emergency ambulance and said, 'Man with a bad gunshot wound in the stomach. West Cemetery Mortuary. Make it fast, will you?' Following which, he lost consciousness.

The ambulance made it fast and this was fortunate for the 7.65 mm slug had pierced his large intestine, his small intestine and his bladder and he was well on the way to bleeding to death.

He did not die and, forty-eight hours later, he was already feeling well enough to describe his strange visitor to Inspector Misner. The inspector was not surprised because he had no preconceptions of what a ghoul should look like and it could as well be a little man with glasses as anyone else.

Forty-eight hours after the shooting was, of course, May 6th and a Saturday. The inspector's interview with George Warmuth had taken place at the hospital immediately after lunch and, although he had not been surprised then, he was soon going to be.

He had barely regained his office where the police artist was waiting to attempt a composite drawing from Warmuth's description as taken down on the inspector's tape recorder, when there was a call from the village of Lindelburg, twelve miles to the east of Nürnberg. A government game warden named Werner Beranek was on the telephone.

Beranek was almost incoherent with excitement.

'Just kids!' he yammered. 'They're just kids and both dead! He must have shot them. I should have cut down on him with the shotgun, but I didn't know. He's riding a red motorbike, the man you want. A red motorbike!'

'Calm yourself,' said the inspector. The switchboard had transferred the call directly to him upon learning that it was a homicide report. 'Who do you think shot who?'

Beranek pulled himself together with an effort. He had just run nearly two miles to reach the telephone and he was still badly out of breath.

'It's a young couple,' he said. 'They're in a grey Mercedes parked about a hundred yards from the turn-off to Wolkersdorf. I was coming down the Lindelburg road about half an hour ago and I saw the car. The doors were open and there was a little man with glasses and a leather hat fussing around it and doing something. As soon as he saw me, he ran and got onto a red motorbike and drove off down the Wolkersdorf road as fast as the machine would go.

'I thought then that there was something funny so I ran up to the car and there was a couple in it, the boy in the front seat and the girl in the back seat. They were both covered with car rugs and when I pulled them back, I saw they were both covered with blood and dead. I immediately fired three shots into the air as an alarm, but nobody heard me so I had to run into Lindelburg to reach a telephone.'

'Stay where you are,' said the inspector. 'We're on our way.'

He dropped the telephone into the cradle and turned to the sergeant. 'Get every car in the area out to Lindelburg. We'll be looking for a little man on a red motorbike and I think that we can use Warmuth's description. Unless I'm greatly mistaken, our ghoul has come out in the open.'

The inspector's suspicions were confirmed that same evening when Dr Platt recovered the bullets from the corpses of twenty-four-year-old Marcus Adler and eighteen-year-old Ruth Lissy. They matched exactly the bullet taken from the body of George Warmuth.

Adler, who owned a transport business in Bruchsal, fifty miles to the north-west of Nürnberg, had come down to visit Miss Lissy, to whom he was engaged. According to the reconstruction of the crime, they had driven that afternoon to the solitary country road and had there engaged in sexual intercourse in the car. They had then decided to take a nap and Adler had lain down in the front seat while Miss Lissy had lain in the back.

While they were asleep, the ghoul had crept up and had shot both of them through the head, killing them instantly. He had then shot the girl a second time under the left breast, presumably to provide a flow of blood for drinking.

That he had drunk of the fresh blood there was no doubt. His lip marks were on Adler's head wound and on the wound beneath the left breast of the girl.

He had only begun with an examination of the girl's sex organs when he was surprised by Beranek for, although the body was found with the underpants removed and the thighs wide-spread, it was possible to show that she had not been entered by any person other than her fiancé. She had also been wearing her underwear at the time that she was killed for it was soaked with urine from her relaxing bladder.

'A terribly dangerous man,' said the inspector. 'He must have merely been riding past, saw the car and, after parking the bike, circled back on foot. He couldn't have known that they were coming there. It was just a chance opportunity and if he gets another, he'll take that too.'

The policy of secrecy had now been totally abandoned, partially because the ghoul was no longer merely a threat to the dead, but to the living as well, and partially because it had become impossible to maintain.

One of the most massive police efforts in the history of the Nürnberg police had gone into operation with patrolcars and road blocks halting and taking into custody every person found riding a red motorbike, drawings of the ghoul made from the descriptions posted in every public place and appeals to the general public for assistance being broadcast over the radio and television stations at frequent intervals.

'If he's here, I think we'll flush him out,' said the inspector. 'Warmuth says that the drawings are a good likeness and so does Beranek. The only thing I'm afraid of is that he's cleared out altogether.'

Four days had passed since the distribution of the posters and the publicity in the newspapers and radio stations and there had been no reports from the public. However, unknown to the inspector or anyone else, a heavy-set, middle-aged transport company worker named Helmut Kostan had thought of reporting his suspicions a half dozen times during that period.

The reason that he had not was the very nature of the crimes which seemed to him so awful that he simply could not believe one of his fellow workers capable of them. He had read the newspaper accounts carefully and the descriptions corresponded on every count. Beranek had said that the murderer of Marcus Adler and Ruth Lissy wore a leather hat and rode a red motorbike.

Kuno Hofmann, the little man with dark, wavy hair, with a blunt nose, with steel-rimmed health insurance glasses, who worked beside him loading trucks, sometimes wore a leather hat and he rode a red motorbike to work.

George Warmuth had said that the ghoul in the mortuary was wearing a grey and brown striped jacket, a black or dark-blue V-neck sweater under it, brown, creaseless trousers and black shoes with bright, metal buckles.

Helmut Kostan had seen Kuno Hofmann wearing just such a costume less than a month earlier.

And finally, what seemed like proof positive, the ghoul had not been startled when Warmuth had accidentally made a noise nor had he said so much as a single word himself.

Kuno Hofmann was a deaf-mute.

And yet, Kostan hesitated. He was a simple man and a slow thinker, but he was certain of one thing, he did not want to get anyone in trouble with false accusations. Kuno Hofmann might be a deaf-mute, but he was a good worker and well-liked at the Demerag Transport Company, not least of all because of his habit of bringing pornographic films for showing during the lunch hour. No one had ever had an argument with him because he was the smallest man employed by the firm and, being a deaf-mute, he could not have had an argument in any case.

However, on the morning of May 10th an event took place which finally drove Kostan to action. Arriving at work, he saw Hofmann standing not in his overalls at the loading ramp, but in a neat, grey suit in the office.

'What's with Kuno?' asked Kostan of the foreman.

'He's quitting,' said the foreman. 'Guess he wants to go to Hamburg. He's got a piece of paper with that written on it.'

Helmut Kostan was finally convinced. Two minutes later, he was at the pay telephone in the café around the corner and talking to Sergeant Bohm at police headquarters.

'Maybe it ain't the fellow you're looking for,' he said apologetically, 'but he sure looks like him. You'd maybe better hurry. He's fixing to leave as soon as he gets his money.'

The sergeant did not even stop to replace the telephone in its cradle, but simply dropped it to the desk and ran out of the office. In less than two minutes, the ready car howled out of the station garage, and the sergeant and the three men on duty in the charge room piled into it. With flashing blue lights and screaming siren, the car tore through the early morning traffic and skidded into the courtyard of the Demerag Transport Company just as a little man wearing glasses stepped out of the office with his last pay envelope in his hand.

Kuno Hofmann was neither clever nor brave. He was exactly what he looked, a little, shy, mentally retarded man. He saw the police car and the detectives piling out of it with guns in their hands and he ran.

He did not run very far of course. The detectives were younger, stronger and much faster. After a very short chase, they returned, the limp ghoul dangling between two of them.

Patrolcars called in by the dispatcher at headquarters now began to arrive and Hofmann was taken in one of them to the offices of the Criminal Investigations Department while the sergeant and his party proceeded to his home address as listed in the files of the company.

Shortly after their arrival another party bearing a search warrant arrived from headquarters and the little house where Hofmann lived with an older brother and sister was searched thoroughly.

In Kuno Hofmann's room they found a Czech VZOR 7.65 mm automatic pistol which ballistics would later show to be the gun which had fired the bullets killing Marcus Adler and Ruth Lissy and wounding George Warmuth, and the now cleanly polished skull of the corpse which Hofmann had beheaded in Flensburg.

They also found an explanation of Hofmann's actions in the form of a collection of literature on witchcraft, vampirism and satanism. Sensational, paperback accounts intended for popular reading, Hofmann had apparently taken them quite literally.

At police headquarters, the forty-one-year-old Hofmann

offered very little resistance to questioning and admitted to most of the crimes with which he was charged, adding a number of which the police had known nothing. He appeared highly confused and was apparently unable to distinguish clearly between crimes actually committed and those merely thought about.

The son of a professional criminal with nineteen convictions, he and his brother had both been so savagely beaten by their father that they had become deaf-mutes and, on one occasion, both of Kuno's arms had been broken.

The beatings had also affected his mind so that his intelligence level was a low seventy, barely above that of a moron and he had had such severe sexual problems that his sister had, at one time, suggested that he buy one of the rubber dolls sold in German sex shops.

Nor was he a stranger to the police, having served a total of nine years in prison for a number of convictions on charges of theft.

Hofmann was, however, quite capable of making an adequate living and he did not lack company as he lived most of the time with his brother and sister and was always popular with the men with whom he worked.

Hofmann's problem was sex and he was not satisfied with his visits to the houses of prostitution. What he wanted was some more permanent relationship – a family, love.

The sole chance that he had had to marry a deaf-mute girl with whom he had fallen deeply in love was destroyed when the girl's parents learned of his jail record and it was not long after that when he came upon the first of the popular witchcraft books.

Kuno Hofmann had drunk the thick, gummy blood of corpses and had attempted to join his sex organs to their cold, clammy ones because he believed that this would make him big, strong and handsome, and big, strong, handsome men could marry and have loving wives and families.

Because it was his only hope, he wanted to believe this so badly that even his arrest did not shake his belief and he spent many hours in his cell writing earnest letters of appeal to the authorities that they should furnish him with a few litres of fresh, warm blood, preferably from a virgin.

He had decided that corpse blood was ineffective because the people were dead and had then switched to living victims with the Adler-Lissy murders. Since that had not worked either, he now thought that it was because Ruth Lissy had not been a virgin.

Kuno Hofmann was never brought to trial as the medical opinion was unanimous that he was not responsible for his actions. He was sent to an institution for the criminally insane where he is expected to spend the remainder of his days.

And now, of course, there really are no vampires or ghouls in Germany because the only one there was is safely tucked away in an institution. There is just one small, slightly sinister point still unexplained.

Hofmann admitted to almost everything, but not to the murder of Martha Krüger. Nor is he known ever to have had access to the twenty-two calibre weapon with which she was killed. As a matter of fact, there is considerable reason to believe that Hofmann was with witnesses at the time of the murder.

If so, then who was it who killed the young mother and drank her blood before the very eyes of her little daughter?

It couldn't have been a vampire. There are no vampires.